The Independence Movement in Quebec 1945–1980

The changes in Quebec that followed the death of Maurice Duplessis moved the province away from its traditional culture and effected a loose coalition of apparently disparate forces, all of which perceived Quebec's independence as the only way to preserve the French-Canadian nation.

This is a definitive study of the independence coalition which united organized labour, the francophone business class, and parts of the middle class in the aftermath of the so-called Quiet Revolution. Coleman examines the social, economic, cultural, and religious characteristics of the province in the late 1940s and the 1950s. He reviews the radical post-1945 rethinking of what it means to be a Québécois and presents a distinctive interpretation of the Quiet Revolution.

For him, the changes of the early 1960s merely hastened the integration of Quebec into the North American capitalist structure. The traditional view of French-Canadian culture, which saw all aspects of society centred on and shaped by Catholic social thought, was gradually replaced by a pluralist view of a Quebec of many communities sharing only the French language. Major corporations had only to speak French in order to operate effectively in the province. This was complemented by governmental desires in Quebec and in Ottawa to make Quebec's educational and social services conform to those of the other provinces, and by the declining role of the church.

The replacement of the church by the state as a focus for social institutions drew into society the rapidly growing urban working class which the church was less and less able to serve. It also spawned a new middle class of technocrats and civil servants. Coleman looks at the complex and shifting alliances among these classes as they united around the goal of Quebec sovereignty. He shows how the collapse of traditional French-Canadian culture and the process of Americanization, aided by linguistic nationalism, have produced a cultural vacuum in Quebec which even those favouring sovereignty may not be able to fill.

WILLIAM D. COLEMAN is a professor in the Department of Politics at McMaster University.

WILLIAM D. COLEMAN

The independence movement in Quebec 1945–1980

UNIVERSITY OF TORONTO PRESS

Toronto Buffalo London

© University of Toronto Press 1984
Toronto Buffalo London
Printed in Canada
Reprinted 1986, 1988, 1995
ISBN: 0-8020-2529-3 (CLOTH)
    0-8020-6542-2 (PAPER)

Canadian Cataloguing in Publication Data

Coleman, William D. (William Donald), 1950–
    The independence movement in Quebec 1945–1980

    (Studies in the structure of power: decision-making in Canada, ISSN 0081-8690; 11)

    Includes bibliographical references and index.
    ISBN 0-8020-2529-3 (bound). – ISBN 0-8020-6542-2 (pbk.)

    1. Quebec (Provincial) – History – Autonomy and independence movements.
    2. Quebec (Province) – Social conditions. 3. Quebec (Province) – Politics and
    government – 20th century.* I. Title. II Series.

    FC2925.9.S4C64 1984   971.4′04   C84-098155-4
    F1053.2.C64 1984

FOR MY MOTHER

AND IN MEMORY OF MY FATHER

STUDIES IN THE STRUCTURE OF POWER:
DECISION-MAKING IN CANADA

EDITOR: J.W. GROVE

STUDIES IN THE STRUCTURE OF POWER: DECISION-MAKING IN CANADA

This series was initially sponsored in 1958 by the Social Science Research Council of Canada to encourage and assist research concerned with the manner and setting in which important decisions are made in fields affecting the Canadian public. Its first editor was John Meisel, who continued in that capacity until 1980, by which time direct sponsorship by the SSRCC had lapsed and the series was being continued by the University of Toronto Press. The studies of decision-making are not confined to any one of the disciplines comprising the social sciences or to any one conceptual framework.

But how could Quebec surrender to the future and still remain her-self? How could she merge into the American world of machinery without also becoming American? How could she become scientific and yet save her legend?

Hugh MacLennan *Two Solitudes* (New York 1945) 70

Contents

Preface

In the course of researching this book, I made use of the facilities of a number of libraries. I would like to thank the staffs of the University of Ottawa, Carleton University, the Université de Montréal, the École des Hautes Études commerciales, the Université Laval, the University of Toronto, McMaster University, and the Bibliothèque nationale du Québec. I owe a special debt to the staff of the Department of Labour Library in Hull, Quebec, and the Bibliothèque de l'Assemblée nationale in Quebec City. Finally, the reference librarians and staff at the National Library of Canada in Ottawa were of constant assistance and played a most important role in my research.

Several organizations made materials available to me. I would like to thank the Canadian Manufacturers Association (Quebec Division), the Chambre de Commerce du District de Montréal, the Confédération des syndicats nationaux, and the Fédération des travailleurs du Québec. In this connection, I am particularly indebted to M. Gérard Turcotte of the Société Saint-Jean-Baptiste de Montréal for his help and advice during several visits to the offices of the Société.

I am grateful for the financial support provided for this project. Part of the research was completed while I was preparing my doctoral dissertation for the University of Chicago. I was supported at this time by a Doctoral Fellowship from the Canada Council. The Arts Research Board at McMaster University provided a grant for additional field work.

This book has been published with the help of a grant from the Social Science Federation of Canada using funds provided by the Social Sciences and Humanities Research Council of Canada.

A number of people helped me prepare this work. Lori Hill, Darlene Heaslip, and, particularly, Margaret Belec typed parts of the manuscript. Michael Underhill read drafts of the first chapter and provided advice and encouragement, especially in the early stages of this project. Ken McRoberts also provided some early suggestions. Michael Stein gave me an informed critique of the introduction; Peter Leslie did the same for the introduction and chapter 4; and Esther E. Enns and Richard Y. Bourhis provided me with useful advice and criticism of chapter 7, on language policy. R.I.K. Davidson of the University of Toronto Press has been supportive from the outset and always encouraging. John Parry wrestled with my prose in copy-editing the manuscript and suggested the quotation that heads the book. David Easton supervised the doctoral dissertation out of which grew the ideas and the research presented here; he has influenced me in many ways and his encouragement of my work from the very beginning has been essential to whatever progress I have made. Susan Redpath Coleman has served as a sounding board for most of what follows; her common sense and scepticism as well as her encouragement have been essential for the argument that I make below.

THE INDEPENDENCE MOVEMENT IN
QUEBEC 1945–1980

Introduction

The future of Canada as a political community is uncertain. In these rather puzzling days in the twilight of the twentieth century, supposedly Canada's century, this is one of the few facts about which Canadians agree. The hopes and dreams of this country's leaders at the turn of the century, hopes and dreams raised by the startling economic expansion that resulted from the wheat boom, now seem rather naïve and archaic. We are troubled peoples. The Maritime provinces, it now appears, were at the zenith of their strength on the eve of Confederation. The branch plant industries of southern Ontario suffer chronic whiplash from the constant stops and starts prompted by the European and Japanese challenges to American domination of the world capitalist system. The northern parts of this same province are classic victims of the 'staple trap' and hence are haunted by visions of that old Canadian phenomenon, the ghost town. The prairie provinces continue their century-long struggle to free themselves of the Ontario 'empire,' whether by seeking a fair return in the grain trade or maintaining control of natural resources. British Columbia lives on with the instability and unemployment that characterize any economy built on the extraction and export of a limited number of natural resources.

The most politically developed challenge to Canada as an entity and hence the most immediate is the movement for political sovereignty in the province of Quebec. The questions and issues raised by this movement are important not only because of their implications for the future of the Canadian political community but also because they overlap to a degree with the problems being experienced by other regions in the country. The political understanding, if any, reached with Quebec will colour the resolution of many of these other difficulties. Accordingly, the Quebec referendum of May 1980 was only a step, an indicator of relative support for and hence power of the actors involved. It resolved little. The *indépendantistes* are a political force of some importance for the immediate future. They have constructed a political voice, the Parti québécois, which is already unique in its strength and its staying power in the history of Quebec. It is more successful than the Parti national of Mercier, the Action libérale nationale, the Bloc populaire, and the Ralliement créditiste. It has a popular basis that is unlikely to be undermined in the short run.

The political question posed by the movement for political sovereignty is relatively clear. Within the boundaries of the province of Quebec is found a society that social scientists term 'ethnically pluralist.' It is composed of several cultural communities, one of which, the French, is predominant. The French-language community has lived in Quebec for close to four hundred years, and through its well-developed sensitivity to the history of those years, its religious tradition, its language, and its self-consciousness it views itself as a nation. From within that community has grown a political movement that wishes to endow Quebec and by implication this community with a sovereign state. To a degree, the shape and form of this state remain unclear but this uncertainty takes nothing away from the fundamental character of the change being envisaged.

The independence movement in Quebec has survived for over twenty years. Some might even say it has become stronger with each passing year. Despite these years and despite the continued viability of the movement, our understanding of it remains poor. When asked why there is such a strong indépendantiste movement in Quebec, the political scientist and the man in the street usually shrug and mutter something about an impatient middle class or about the French always being impatient. There have been studies of the Quiet Revolution, of the Parti québécois, and of nationalism in general, yet there have been few attempts to reflect upon the rise of the independence movement in a more comprehensive fashion. The object of this study is to try to accomplish this very task. I am presenting a wide-ranging study of political change in Quebec in the post-war period in order to suggest some reasons why there has been a thriving independence movement there since the early 1960s.

Three current explanations

A first and important step in the pursuit of this task will be the analysis of the policies, events, and thinking of the period that has come to be called the Quiet Revolution. The series of changes set in motion during this period were the catalyst to the independence movement. They sparked a reaction among a number of social groups and classes that was to grow quickly into a political movement. It therefore becomes disconcerting when one surveys the explanations for the Quiet Revolution and finds rather striking differences. The more successful explanations have focussed upon a social class or classes and seen the rise of one or more of these as critical to understanding the Quiet Revolution. Unfortunately there appear to be major differences over which class is the 'motor' or the 'spark' for change. One group argues that a 'new middle class' is the generator of change in Quebec. Another group places the emphasis on a class variously described as a bourgeoisie francophone, a bourgeoisie québécoise, or a bourgeoisie autochtone. Still another group emphasizes a rise in influence at this time of the English-Canadian bourgeoisie in Quebec.

The existence of three quite different explanations for the remarkable turn of events in Quebec between 1959 and 1965 is unsatisfactory if only because it was out of these events that the independence movement came. Eventually, I shall show that each of these three explanations captures a part of the reality and that all can be drawn upon in fashioning an interpretation of the Quiet Revolution. My analysis then will begin with a critical review of these three explanations. From this critical review I will draw conclusions concerning how my own analysis must proceed. In the remainder of this introductory chapter, therefore, the inadequacies of the existing explanations will be noted and an outline of the approach to be used in this study will be presented.

Hypothesis I: The new middle class

The more widely accepted explanation, particularly among English-Canadian social scientists, of the series of changes that have occurred in Quebec since 1945 rests on the conceptual shoulders of a mostly francophone, new middle class. This class is composed of the white-collar workers who staff the bureaucracies of ecclesiastical, political, and economic institutions. The explanation based on this class is most fully developed in the writings of Hubert Guindon, Charles Taylor, and Kenneth McRoberts and Dale Posgate.[1] These authors begin with the seemingly indisputable fact that the traditional political institutions of Quebec society – particularly those involved in the administration of education and social services – had reached a crisis by 1960. The institutions simply no longer seemed able to meet the needs of the citizens of Quebec. They were seen as corrupt, moribund, and inefficient.

Partly from within these institutions, under the guidance of progressive clerics, and partly from without, where new institutions had arisen in labour, communications, and the co-operatives, there emerged, it is argued, a new middle class. It was more modern in its thinking and more progressive in its ideas than Quebec's traditional middle class of professionals and clerics. In the critical years from 1959 to 1965, this new class challenged successfully the traditional middle class for control of the provincial state and the social and educational bureaucracies. It mounted the challenge through the agency of a revitalized Parti libéral du Québec. The Parti libéral narrowly defeated the foundering Union nationale, the supposed agent of the traditional middle class, in the 1960 election. The new premier, Jean Lesage, had gathered an équipe de tonnerre which included the former Liberal leader, Georges-Émile Lapalme, the journalist René Lévesque, Paul Gérin-Lajoie, and, later, Pierre Laporte and Eric Kierans. This team carried out the 'administrative revolution' desired by the new middle class. It moved to create a competent civil service, an expanded educational system, a publicly controlled health care system, and a series of economic institutions to give the new class a toehold in Quebec's economy.

In so moving, the Parti libéral is seen as helping to redress a lag that had developed between Quebec's political development and its social and economic development. Economically and socially Quebec was an urban, industrial society; politically it was a nineteenth-century fiefdom. The arrival of the Liberals then, it is said, ended the tenure of Duplessis's Union nationale, which had been more and more holding the province back politically during the post-war period. In breaking this hold and giving rein to the new middle class, the Liberals ushered in what has been termed the 'Quiet Revolution.' The supporters of the new-middle-class hypothesis caution, however, that this was a revolution mainly in the realm of ideology, of the mind. It was a revolution marked by the final rejection of the vision of Quebec as a society with a rural vocation, as a unanimously Catholic, defiantly spiritual entity. It meant the exuberant espousal of a philosophy of épanouissement, that is, of growth, development, and openness to industrial society. Quebec was viewed as a plural society and as a society in a hurry to make up lost time. The provincial government was hailed as the moteur principal, the leader in the movement forward.

This ideological revolution, which was conceived by the new middle class and promoted by its agent, the Parti libéral, raised expectations that were to be dashed on the shoals of the economic and political reality of Quebec. The established corporations did not open their doors to the new middle class and did not provide a francophone milieu in which their employees could work. The federal government was not ready to hand over to this class the full range of fiscal and monetary powers it desired in order to reorient Quebec along a new path of economic development and it was not eager to have francophones in its own bureaucracy. The result, so the story goes, was the fracturing of the Parti libéral into two forces, one more technocratic, more radical and dedicated to political independence, the other more economically conservative and committed to a retooling of the federal system. The struggle henceforth was between these two fractions of the new middle class and their agents, the Parti québécois and the Parti libéral.

However persuasive this explanation might appear, it merits criticism on several grounds. First, the principal agent of change in this explanation is a social class. Social classes, it must be cautioned, become agents or are mobilized to become political actors only under special circumstances. There must first be a group of individuals who occupy relatively similar positions in a particular mode of production. In addition, these individuals must be in positions where they can become conscious of their similar position and perhaps similar plight. Second, then, this consciousness develops when these individuals are opposed as a group by another class. Classes are formed into cohesive actors on the political stage through struggles with other classes. For the new-middle-class hypothesis to be valid, then, that class would need to have found itself in these special circumstances. It would have to have been in a structural position that would enable it to become a class. It would also have to have been placed in a political situation where it was likely to be mobilized as a class. Yet during the critical period for this explanation, 1959 to 1965, it is very doubtful that these circumstances existed.

1/ If one examines closely Quebec's institutions at the end of the 1950s, one finds little evidence of individuals having positions in society that would form the structural base for a new middle class. There was no côterie of francophone white-collar workers at the middle levels of large private corporations. In the established education and social service bureaucracies, there was no structural unity that would tend to create the conditions for such a class. Educational insitutions were controlled partly by the church and partly by the state.[2] Those under ecclesiastical control operated somewhat independently of each other, being organized along diocesan lines, and being controlled by various orders.[3] The church had a virtual monopoly on institutions in the social sphere, but here again the various institutions were organized separately for each diocese and were operated by a panoply of religious orders. In both educational and social organizations, the use of lay personnel was increasing rapidly, but the ranking administrative positions remained firmly in clerical hands even at this date. These latter positions would certainly have been part of the nucleus of any new middle class, but there is little evidence to suggest that the clerics involved were imbued with the ideology of épanouissement in sufficient members to have joined such a nucleus. The reaction to such modest reforms as were suggested by Frère Untel would suggest the contrary.[4]

The proponents of this hypothesis however would counter by arguing that a factor giving unity to the new middle class was its claim to power and status based on its monopoly of specialized, modern social science knowledge.[5] But where was this knowledge attained? The occupants of these bureaucracies had been educated under the traditional, classics-oriented education system in Quebec. The social sciences were hardly the important force in the universities (still controlled by the church) that they were to be a decade hence. The numbers of social science graduates during the 1950s were neither high nor growing.[6] The expansion that took place in the civil service in the 1950s drew in the main from those with twelve years of education or less.[7] Even in the education system, teachers had not been introduced to this modern social scientific knowledge. Quebec's standards for entry into the teaching profession required only a year of normal school beyond grade 11. Even then, in 1958, 48 per cent of the teachers in Quebec did not meet this minimum standard.[8] Normal schools themselves were in a deplorable state; the professors there earned less than teachers themselves, who were already poorly paid.

If one turns the spotlight on institutions outside these traditional bureaucracies, evidence of a structural base for a new middle class is more encouraging but hardly compelling. In the labour field, it was clear that some cadres in the Confédération des travailleurs catholiques du Canada (CTCC) had had a training in the social sciences.[9] Yet their involvement in the labour movement brought them closer to the working class than to the supposed new class. Further, their numbers were not large. The larger Fédération des travailleurs du Québec (FTQ) did not have cadres with a similar training. Most of its officials had worked up to leadership positions from the shop floor. There did seem to be a new breed of journalist in Quebec, particularly at Radio-Canada, but the numbers here are very small. Similarly one notes a shift to a more technical orientation in the Union catholique des cultivateurs (UCC) and the co-operatives. Still, farmers are not usually considered to be members of the new middle class. The co-operatives remained under the considerable conservative influence of the church. The latter institution still exercised significant influence over Quebec society in the late 1950s. For example, it took the somewhat renegade CTCC seven years to remove the word 'Catholic' from its name. The Corporation des instituteurs et institutrices catholiques, the teachers' union, actually became more confessional and corporatist in ideology as the decade progressed.[10]

To summarize, the existence, at a structural level, of a new middle class at the dawn of the Quiet Revolution is not as obvious as has been assumed. In some sense, it is more sensibly argued that the new middle class was a product of the reforms of the 1960s than their instigator.[11] The provincial state, in rationalizing the education and social service systems and in founding a series of public corporations during the 1960s, may have created this class in its wake.

2/ Not only is the structural position of this class in doubt, but also its existence as a conscious political agent. I have argued that individuals tend to be mobilized as a class only in opposition to other classes. The new-middle-class thesis postulates that this new class was mobilized politically in order to struggle against a traditional middle class of clerics, farmers, doctors, and lawyers that held power under Duplessis. However, little evidence of such a struggle can be adduced. Guindon himself, writing in 1960, points out that the new class was working with traditional elites.[12] Similarly, the 1960 political stance of the Parti libéral, the supposed agent of the new middle class, was not one that invited a struggle with the traditional middle class. On the contrary, the party borrowed a page from Duplessis's Union nationale and presented the electorate a platform founded on the notion of political autonomy for Quebec.[13] François-Albert Angers, a spirited representative of the traditional middle class, described that platform as 'le meilleur programme autonomiste et nationaliste dans le sens le plus positif du mot depuis les jours du Bloc Populaire; probablement, le meilleur programme du genre présenté par un des deux partis traditionnels.'[14] His words hardly sound like those of a member of a class that has just been ousted from power. Rather he actually speaks of victory. 'Dans ces conditions on peut considérer que l'option nationaliste vient d'emporter l'une de ses plus grandes, de ses plus significatives victoires depuis le début du siècle.'[15] In short, not only is the structural basis of the new middle class questionable, but also the conflict that was supposed to have forced it into the political arena was little in evidence.

3/ The first two arguments, then, against the hypothesis of a new middle class are based on observations that suggest that the conditions usually necessary for the rise of such a class as a political force were not present in Quebec in the late 1950s. A third major weakness of the hypothesis is related to the very theoretical framework from which the concept of a new middle class emerged. This concept was not an inspiration that arose simply from the patient observation of Quebec society. Rather the central role given to this class followed logically from the theoretical framework and the concepts brought to the study of Quebec by the social scientists concerned. The theoretical framework in question had been fashioned to describe a process of political development and political modernization. It was gradually elaborated, starting in the 1950s, principally by American social scientists who wished to gain some understanding and to give some direction to the many movements of national liberation occurring in the Third World at the time.[16] Using the concepts of this framework, they evaluated these movements according to the degree to which they took their societies from a traditional status to a modern one. Whether the traditional society was characterized by using the pattern variables of the sociologist Talcott Parsons or by using the more elaborated concepts of the Comparative Politics group of the American Social Sciences Research Council, it was clear that the modern status envisaged was very much akin to that of a Western liberal democracy.

Usually, within these models the catalyst to development is a native elite that has been trained by the outgoing colonial power. This élite is therefore well-schooled in the principles of liberal democracy, is familiar with Western-style administrative procedures, and as a result is sufficiently self-confident and motivated to want to rule on its own. It seeks to engineer the independence of its people by mobilizing a mass population whose expectations already have been rising with increased exposure to Western culture.

The new-middle-class hypothesis then was a logical outgrowth of the application of this framework to Quebec. Quebec was seen as a traditional society. American sociologists had already studied the French community in Quebec as an example of a 'folk culture' and hence considered it under the same light they had used to study peasant societies in Mexico and elsewhere.[17] The folk culture notions had influenced French-Canadian sociological thinking as well.[18] It was a short step to see the changes that began to manifest themselves at the end of 1950s as a movement to modernize a traditional society with a paternalistic and authoritarian political culture. The agent of these changes, the counterpart of the restless native élites of the Third World, was, of course, the new middle class, a class schooled in 'modern social science' and devoted to rationalized bureaucratic administration.

The successful application of this theoretical approach depends in part on whether Quebec should be treated as analogous to the emerging nations of the Third World. There are a number of reasons why such treatment is misleading. The people of Quebec have had a measure of self-rule for over a century that goes considerably beyond that which was possessed by the Third World colonies that achieved independence in the post-war period. It has enjoyed a parliamentary system of government that is as advanced in its development as any in the Western world. The Quebec economy, whatever its structural irregularities, shares in the advanced capitalist economy of North America in ways that most Third World countries can only dream of. The popular classes in Quebec consist in the main of an industrialized labour force that is considerably more skilled and more highly paid than the labour forces in the Third World nations in question. The rate of literacy, the degree of urbanization, the family structure, the place of religion, and any number of other indicators mark post-war Quebec as an integral part of the First and Second worlds and as no closer to the Third World than any other Western nation.

Hence an indication of how inappropriate the application of this framework is to Quebec is the treatment given by the analysts concerned to the period prior to the Liberal victory in 1960. The Quebec of the 1950s under the rule of Duplessis and the Union nationale is presented in many respects as a traditional society of the nineteenth century. The provincial state is described as committed to laissez-faire capitalism, as predisposed to avoid intervention in the economy at virtually any cost, and as unwilling to accept trade unionism. The conduct of politics is described variously as paternalistic, corrupt, authoritarian, and élitist. The education system with its clerics and its classical colleges is frowned upon as a throwback to the Ancien Régime in France. The society was considered to be largely dominated by a set of beliefs that stressed the virtues of the rural life, the advantages of the corporatism of the papal encyclicals, and the evils of the materialism of the American way of life. This tendency to view Quebec as 'traditional' and 'backward' is a logical outgrowth of the theoretical framework being used.

Such a description of Quebec in the period from 1945 to 1960 ignores many important events and changes that were taking place. Subsequent analysis in this book will show that the gap between the Quebec of Duplessis and the Quebec of Lesage and Johnson is much narrower than has been presumed. The education system, for example, was not completely church-controlled under Duplessis as is so often assumed. The provincial bureaucracy actually grew more in the 1950s than it did in the early 1960s. Jean-Louis Roy has pointed out that there was ongoing evaluation of many aspects of social policy with substantial reforms being considered and at times even implemented in the immediate post-war period.[19] He remarks on the important educational role and non-traditional character of such institutions as the CTCC, the Association professionel des industriels (API), the co-operative movement, and the universities, and one might add the Union catholique des cultivateurs (UCC) and the provincial Chambre de Commerce.[20]

It is also unsettling that this presentation of the Duplessis period as that of a grand noirceur coincided with the interpretation of history promoted by the Liberal government of Jean Lesage and such liberal intellectuals as Trudeau, Pelletier, and others involved in the Rassemblement in the 1950s.[21] Even more disconcerting, the concepts and rhetoric of national liberation often linked to theories of development were adopted freely by members of the Lesage government. The 1962 provincial election campaign, the campaign where the slogan 'Maîtres chez nous' was popularized, was fought using the language of liberation found in the Third World.[22] It is sometimes troubling when the language and thinking of social scientists are shared with the politicians of the day. The capacity of the social scientist to stand back, reflect, and if need be criticize is undercut. Furthermore, the probability increases that his or her work may come to be used by and to serve the existing authorities. In the study of Quebec, the sharing among politicians and social scientists of similar notions of development, modernization and liberation is indicative of the susceptibility of both to American concerns for development in the Third World and the intellectual debates these concerns spawned. The coincidence in perspective nonetheless is an additional factor that weakens the new-middle-class hypothesis as an explanation of events in post-war Quebec.

Hypothesis II: The 'bourgeoisie autochtone'

In recent years, a second hypothesis about change in post-war Quebec has been suggested that challenges the theory based on the new middle class. Dorval

Brunelle has argued that the central problem that gave rise to the Quiet Revolution was not the rising expectations of a new middle class but economic conditions that threatened the existence of a mainly francophone employer class owning mainly small and medium-sized enterprises.[23] He documents the rising strength of American multinational corporations in Quebec's economy in the years following the Second World War. He notes the tendency of these enterprises to penetrate further and further into the local economy of the French-speaking community. This penetration gradually eliminated many small firms and promised continuation of these processes in the years to come. The resulting concentration raised the question whether there would be a role and a place for the existing French-Canadian bourgeoisie. Brunelle writes that this question was critical because if a role and place were not found for this class, then the future of capitalist production in Quebec might itself become doubtful.

Whereas Duplessis had paid little attention to this class, the Lesage Liberals, in this view, took its concerns very much to heart. Shortly after their arrival in power, the Liberals created a body called the Conseil d'orientation économique du Québec. Such an organization had long been the dream of the French-Canadian bourgeoisie. In a short time span, the Council developed a series of proposals that were to mark the early years of the Quiet Revolution. It advanced the notion of mixed enterprises, state and private interests collaborating in major economic projects. Such major new economic agents of the 1960s based on this concept, the Société générale de financement, the Sidérurgie du Québec (Sidbec), and the Société québécoise d'exploration minière (Soquem), were all then recommended by the Council. Thus, Brunelle concludes, the ambiguous coalition of the state and a weakening, ethnically homogeneous fraction of the bourgeoisie produced a series of progressive changes (a revolution) within the capitalist system (hence quiet). He writes: 'Ce sera là le *projet* ... de la bourgeoisie canadienne-française, un projet ambigu s'il en est, puisqu'il amènera les représentants de cette bourgeoisie à être à la fois nationalistes et pro-américains, à la fois fédéralistes et autonomistes, à la fois pour l'empire qu'exerce l'entreprise privée mais aussi en faveur de la solution bureaucratique.'[24]

According to Brunelle these new public enterprises and the staff increases they and other reforms generated in the provincial civil service created the new middle class. The desire for modernization and revitalization shown by the francophone business class helped spur the drive to educational reform. The new public educational system as well sowed the seeds of a new middle class. This class thus was the product of the Quiet Revolution and not its initiator, in this view.

These arguments by Brunelle form a serious challenge to the orthodox explanation of change in post-war Quebec. To a degree, in the chapters that follow in this book, they will be expanded upon and amplified. The role of the French-speaking businessman in the changes of the early 1960s has been overlooked in the existing studies. This failing is significant, I shall show, because this particular class was active not only in directing the economic reforms of the Quiet Revolution but also in promoting important constitutional change, reforms in federal-provincial policy-making, and the idea of publicly controlled education.

Yet Brunelle's explanation is limited in scope. If one were to rely solely upon it, it would be difficult to account for the rise of the independence movement in the 1960s. What is clear is that the independence movement did not grow out of this class. The francophone business class in Quebec has been a consistent and staunch supporter of federalism. Its members from the beginning have seen independence as a threat to their access to the wider Canadian market and as a possible catalyst to economic deterioration within the province. In part, I shall argue, the independence movement has been a movement that arose in opposition to this class and its proposals. Brunelle does us the service of identifying the French-Canadian business class as being in the forefront of the Quiet Revolution. The issue that we are left with then is the consequences of the success of this class on the political plane.

Hypothesis III: Competition

A third hypothesis that has emerged quite recently appears to be opposed to both of the previous explanations. Like the theory based on the new middle class, this third hypothesis is global in scope. Gilles Bourque and Anne Legaré have proposed an explanation that focuses principally on what they call three 'fractions' of the bourgeois class.[25] 'Fraction' is a Marxist term that may be interpreted to mean a subdivision or a branch of a particular class. Bourque and Legaré suggest three bourgeois fractions are essential for understanding the political development of Quebec since the Great Depression. The first fraction is the non-monopoly, Quebec-based bourgeoisie.[26] Its members are owners of small enterprises that are highly competitive with each other and that are oriented primarily to the regional Quebec market. They have their roots in the main in the francophone community. The second fraction is the monopolistic Canadian bourgeoisie. Its members own or manage large corporations that operate mainly in oligopolistic markets that are Canada-wide in scope. It contains disproportionately many English-speaking Canadians. The third fraction is a monopoly, imperialist bourgeoisie. Its members are owners or managers of large transnational corporations that also operate under oligopoly conditions but on a global rather than a national basis. Its membership is said to be disproportionately high in Americans.

Bourque and Legaré describe the political history of Quebec by centring their analysis on the relations among these three fractions and their respective influence on the provincial government. They write that during the years 1936–60, the tenure of Duplessis's Union nationale (except for a Liberal interlude during the war), the provincial government was dominated by a power bloc comprising the non-monopoly, Quebec-based fraction and the imperialist fraction. The Union nationale, as a party, promoted and defended the interests of small francophone entrepreneurs by ensuring that they were given the business of providing the infrastructure needed by the imperialist fraction that was sweeping Quebec in search of natural resources. For example, local entrepreneurs were given the task of building the roads that were needed by the large foreign corporations to get access to resources. The Quebec-based capitalists were able to maintain this favoured position because the Union nationale had managed to add the paysans, the small Quebec farmers, as a supporting class. This coalition of social forces with their substantial financial resources assured the party electoral dominance. In promoting the interests of the indigenous small entrepreneurs, the party thus relegated the Canada-based bourgeois fraction to a position of lesser influence.

By 1960, however, the argument continues, the expansion of commercial farming had led to a substantial decline in the numbers of paysans and with it the electoral base of the Union nationale began to crumble. The ascension to power of the Liberals with their national power base turned the tables by replacing the Quebec-based fraction in the power bloc by the Canada-based fraction. The Quiet Revolution, in this view, is a series of reforms designed to bring Quebec's educational and social services in line with those available elsewhere in Canada to facilitate the expansion of English-Canadian capital in Quebec. Quebec is not seen as becoming more autonomous in this period as is usually assumed but as becoming more integrated into Canadian society as a whole. The Canada-based fraction achieved a dominant position electorally by enlisting the support of the working class. The expansion of the Canada-based fraction was seen to promise more jobs and more security for industrial workers. The Liberals promised and implemented reforms in labour relations that gave a certain security and legitimacy to organized labour. In doing so, they distinguished themselves from the Union nationale, which had confronted the labour movement at every turn.

According to Bourque and Legaré, and contrary to Brunelle then, the Quebec-based fraction of the bourgeoisie went into a period of relative decline with the onset of the Quiet Revolution. Similarly, the party that had defended its interests, the Union nationale, also began its descent into eventual oblivion. In the latter part of the 1960s, however, elements from this fraction concerned about its demise helped forge a new political vehicle, the Parti québécois.

According to these authors, the Parti québécois grew out of two movements supported by the petite bourgeoisie, the Rassemblement pour l'indépendance nationale (RIN) and the Regroupement national, and one supported by the Quebec-based capitalist class, the Mouvement Souveraineté Association (MSA). The new party was to emerge, however, as being primarily dedicated to the interests of the Quebec-based capitalist class. Using a nationalist ideology that highlighted the oppression of the French by the English, the Parti québécois added sufficient voters from the working class to its petty bourgeois support to forge an electoral coalition that was to carry it to power in 1976. Accordingly, these authors see strong parallels between the Union nationale of Duplessis and the Parti québécois of Lévesque and Parizeau. Both parties promote the interests of the Quebec-based bourgeoisie at the expense of the Canada-based bourgeoisie; both are subservient to the imperialist fraction.

This latter explanation diverges from the new-middle-class hypothesis on several key points. The Quiet Revolution was not ushered in by a new middle class but by the establishment of a dominant position on the part of a Canada-based monopoly bourgeoisie. Power was transferred in 1960 not from a traditional middle class to a new middle class, but from a Quebec-based non-monopoly bourgeoisie to this large Canada-based bourgeoisie. The independence movement was the inspiration not of a new middle class but of a coalition between the middle classes and the Quebec-based bourgeoisie. Similarly, this explanation appears to contradict that put forth by Brunelle, who argues that 1960 marked the ascension of the regional capitalist class and not its demise. In this study, it will be argued that Bourque and Legaré point to an important dimension of the Quiet Revolution, its attempt to integrate Quebec more fully into North American capitalism. However, it shall be argued also that their interpretation of the class forces behind this attempt is too simplistic and in the end inadequate.

The missing dimension

One might be tempted to play down the differences among the explanations just described by casting them as ideological. The new-middle-class hypothesis grew out of a perspective that held Western rationalized, liberal democracy up as the standard of progress. Bourque and Legaré, in contrast, begin with a Marxist problematic that sees liberal democracy as a political form fashioned to realize the interests of the capitalist class. These fundamental differences in perspective and assumptions do affect how the world is viewed and which phenomena are emphasized. However, the differences here are not just in values. Brunelle also works within the Marxist framework, and his conclusions seem to be at odds with those of Bourque and Legaré. Further, Bourque and

Legaré were well aware of the new-middle-class hypothesis and examined it using their categories and found it empirically wanting. The proponents of the theory of the new middle class were certainly well aware of what they would call the English-Canadian business élite in Quebec, but they did not see this élite as a key factor in accounting for the Quiet Revolution.

In short, it will be my view that each of these explanations points to important lacunae in the other, and aspects of each are complementary to the other. One of the tasks of this book will be to show the nature of this interdependence. To do so, however, it will be necessary to add a second dimension to the analysis found in each of these three competing explanations, that of ideology. All of them take as their starting point a social class. They assume that this social class exists and is reasonably conscious of its interests as a class. I prefer to begin more ambiguously and to treat the existence of classes as an empirical question. Social classes, in the sense of conscious social actors, are formed through conflict and mobilization that take place not only in the economy but also in the political arena and the realm of ideas. The full analysis of a society that takes social class as a central starting point must leave open the possibility that classes do not exist but may be formed in the context of struggle. Each of the three explanations examined above has explored the dimension of struggle in the economy and in the political sphere. None has paid enough attention to the world of ideas and of ideologies and how these help form social classes. This gap is quite surprising, because most social scientists agree that many of the most critical changes in post-war Quebec were changes in ideology, in views of the world. The examination of the realm of ideology will be central to understanding fully the rise of the independence movement.

The ideological dimension

During the Duplessis years, a series of important developments altered the ideology of opinion-makers in French-speaking society. In several institutions of Quebec's francophone community that had been established relatively recently and were not under complete ecclesiastical control, the individuals involved embarked upon an interesting process of self-reflection. I speak here first of the various Catholic Action organizations such as the Jeunesse étudiante catholique (JEC), the Ligue ouvrière catholique (LOC), and the Jeunesse ouvrière catholique (JOC). These organizations, which had first developed in Europe as part of the church's response to industrialization and which were supported by Pius XI in the encyclical *Quadragesimo Anno* published in 1931, brought an important change to the Catholic church in Quebec. They were the first institutions concerned with the temporal social problems of the lay Christian to be led by laymen. The clergy played only an advisory role. I refer also to the Confédération des travailleurs catholiques du Canada (CTCC) under the leadership of Gérard Picard, who became its president in 1946, and Jean Marchand, who became its general secretary in 1947, and to the co-operative movement, which was strongly influenced by Père Georges-Henri Lévesque, founder of the Social Sciences faculty at Université Laval. Another more informal organization was the group of literati who formed around the *Refus global* manifesto published in 1948. Working in these milieux, individuals were better able to view the church from an external perspective. They came to realize that a monolithic ideology dominated the thinking and orientation of the French-speaking community's economic, political, social, and religious institutions. Such a realization allowed them to see the dominant ideology in relation to others. Once this process of reflection was begun new vistas of thought and new perspectives on society began to emerge. A reading of journals in Quebec in the late 1940s and the 1950s shows this prospect generated immense excitement in many intellectual circles.

In most studies of Quebec during this period, this shift in consciousness is well-documented. The later rise to prominence of Pierre Trudeau, Jean Marchand, and Gérard Pelletier has led social scientists to pore back over the pages of *Cité libre,* the struggles of the CTCC, and the movement against Duplessis.[27] What is less often remarked upon, however, is that these changes occurred simultaneously with some intense reflection upon the traditional values and culture of French Canadians.

Throughout his tenure as premier, Duplessis engaged in a series of battles with the federal government in order to defend the autonomy of Quebec. In one of the more important of these battles, as part of his political game, he commissioned a study into Quebec's constitutional problems. The report of the fabled Tremblay Commission was a remarkable intellectual achievement. Its four volumes are an exemplar of powerful prose, cogency, and brilliant logic. It was written by some of the most capable intellectuals of the traditional élites of the French-speaking community. These commissioners defined explicitly what in their view was unique and valuable in the culture of French-speaking society in Quebec. In particular, they singled out the community's dedication to spiritual values, its unique classical education system, its private, church-controlled and -inspired social welfare institutions, and its rural, agricultural heritage. They were committed to preserving these institutions and practices which they saw to be the product of centuries of development. They sketched out a political program complete with detailed political demands that in their view had to be followed if this unique culture were to survive.

That these particular commissioners should follow such a course is not surprising, and knowledge of it is hardly new to the scholarly community. Nevertheless, what is not remarked upon often is that the political program of the Tremblay Commission became the basis, the cornerstone, of political strategy by the government of Quebec throughout the 1960s and into the 1970s. It may be argued that the various movements for independence and for renewed federalism that have emerged since are all variations on the Tremblay theme.

This conclusion is important because the dynamic of social change outside the political arena during the 1960s was not in a direction that would have been welcomed by the Tremblay Commission. The questioning of the dominant ideology in the French-speaking society and with it the growing criticism of the extensive penetration of the church into the social fabric of the community that I mentioned above led to the promotion of an idea that was heresy to the commission, that of pluralism. Increasingly intellectuals and opinion leaders argued that the French-speaking community was not homogeneous, that it supported a variety of ideologies, and that its institutions should be more adapted to this situation. As consciousness of division within the community increased, there was a tendency to examine more closely institutions in English Canada and the United States as possible models for use in a plural society. What is essential to note here is that the very social and educational structures and the very penetration of the church into the community's life that were being scrutinized with a critical eye had been defined by the Tremblay Commission as the hallmarks, the foundations, of the unique culture of Quebec's French-speaking society. Furthermore, these structures had been championed because they represented a shield against the North American society that now was being examined with interest. It was on the assumption that these structures needed to be protected and preserved that the Tremblay commissioners had constructed their political program.

Throughout the 1960s and 1970s, there was an interesting contradiction between the political reforms being implemented and the program or strategy being used for their implementation. The political program elaborated with painstaking care by the Tremblay commission was being used to alter fundamentally the very institutions the program had been designed to protect. The commission was correct in defining a strategy designed to affect fundamentally traditional institutions but in doing so it also opened the possibility that its strategy could be used to affect these institutions in ways it never intended. The rapid attack on traditional institutions that came at this time led directly to the growth of the independence movement when largely foreign borrowings were put in their place.

The independence movement has arisen because the political changes in the early 1960s undermined several basic institutions and practices of traditional French-Canadian civilization. The institutions and practices that replaced the old did not renew French-Canadian civilization but contributed to its further demise. Perhaps no factor illustrates this process better than the place of language in political struggles and ideological debate. By the late 1960s, with the 'reform' of educational and social welfare institutions and the withdrawal of the church into more strictly spiritual realms, the most evident distinguishing characteristic of the French-speaking community became its language. The struggle to preserve a distinctive culture became in many instances a struggle to preserve the use of French. Whereas language had earlier been one of several foundations of French-Canadian civilization, by the late 1960s it often appeared to be the only visible foundation left.

I will show, that the policies on language pursued by governments beginning in the mid-1960s had the effect of undermining the French language as a cultural foundation. The policies developed have transformed French from an informal language not used in several key spheres of economic life into a standard language helping to integrate the French-Canadian community into the dominant culture of North America. French, which had been one of several barriers restricting contact between les Canadiens français and les autres has become the policy instrument for breaking barriers among the several cultural communities in Quebec. The struggle for autonomy outlined by the Tremblay Commission had been a struggle to preserve the culture of a single community. The struggle for autonomy in the 1970s was a struggle to integrate several cultures through the use of a common language, French. If language is being increasingly lost as a tool for cultural preservation, should we be surprised to find individuals saying a break has to be made, new powers must be garnered, a society has to be rethought if it is to continue at all?

Aim of this study

This study will outline and weave together this series of cultural and ideological changes with the development of social classes. I have only indicated the blueprint for the analysis to follow. In giving this emphasis to the ideological dimension, I am indicating that it has a significant autonomy from the mode of economic production and the organization of social classes. The degree of autonomy will vary over the period being studied. What will become clear is that after the period of the supposed Quiet Revolution, that is after 1965, social classes increasingly become the dominant actors on the political stage. The political confrontation and disputes in the period leading up to 1965 have the effect of creating social classes and hence of fostering class struggle. After 1965, the discussion of cultural and ideological change can have meaning only if it focuses upon social classes.

This study will demonstrate that Quebec society has redefined itself in fundamental ways in the post-war period. In embarking upon this process of reflection and redefinition, the members of this society have become increasingly divided. They have divided along class lines, with the capitalist class on one side, the working class on the other, and the various sections of the petty bourgeoisie shifting constantly between the two. They have also divided along lines of language and of ethnicity. It is a matter not simply of the English versus the French, but also of tensions among vocal smaller groups such as the Jewish, Italian, Greek, Inuit, Cree, and Haitian communities. The members of the French-speaking community themselves are divided along religious lines. The movement toward secularization and toward a plural Quebec society is strongly opposed by many who see Catholicism as still an integral part of any French community in Quebec and by others who wish to use Catholicism to preserve some mythic ideal of a unique people living in Quebec.

The movement toward political independence is a phenomenon of too much complexity to be treated as the vehicle of a particular class pursuing its own particular interests. The movement is a coalition of various classes and groups who agree that the first step to a better future society is the achievement of political sovereignty. They agree on this first step for different reasons. In the interests of the political success of the movement, these differences are quite deliberately played down. The means have gradually been elevated to the status of an end in itself. Keeping the coalition together has been a remarkable political achievement in the face of these differences. The fact that the coalition has not broken up is an indicator of the depth of the grievances of the various partners. They strongly desire political independence. A promising future is not possible without it. The ultimate contribution of this study then will be to move from a discussion of the increasing divisions within Quebec society to provide some suggestions why many of these divisions have been overcome in a single political movement advocating radical change. The understanding of both these divisions and this unity is necessary before a satisfactory understanding of the independence movement can be attained.

This book will be divided into two parts in order to carry out the proposed analysis. Part I will consist of three chapters that will provide the historical background and a foundation for the analysis of the processes of class formation and ideological change that have been noted above. Chapter 1 will describe the post-war Quebec economy and will demonstrate the extent to which Quebec's economy was and is underdeveloped. Chapter 2 will describe the cultural institutions and the dominant ideology that have traditionally distinguished French-speaking society in Quebec, with special attention to education, social welfare, and the philosophy of the Catholic church on the relations between the spiritual and temporal realms. Chapter 3 will move into the political arena by describing the struggle over the control of taxation and of culture that arose between the federal government and the government of Quebec in the late

1940s and early 1950s. Out of this struggle emerged two remarkable reports, that of the federal government's Royal Commission on National Development in the Arts, Letters and Sciences (the Massey Commission), and that of the Tremblay Commission. The conflicting visions of Canada contained in these reports provide an invaluable introduction to the events of the late 1950s and thereafter. In addition, the analysis carried out by the Tremblay Commission provided a blueprint for action that should have been followed if the traditional culture were to be preserved. A sustained contrast between this blueprint and the policies that eventually emerged will be central to the development of my interpretation of the independence movement.

Part II will include the examination of four sets of changes that have occurred in Quebec since the late 1950s. Each set has had an impact upon the growth of the independence movement. Chapter 4 will study the political response of the Quebec government to demands to reverse the underdevelopment of the economy. It will show that this response served only to integrate the French-speaking community more fully into the continental economy, to expand the size of the francophone capitalist class, and to radicalize portions of the working class. The next three chapters show the effect of this economic program on areas of social life crucial to cultural development. Chapter 5 will examine the several attempts of the government of Quebec to develop a policy on culture. Included here will be studies of the Department of Cultural Affairs, international relations, communications, immigration, and changes in institutions administering social welfare. Chapter 6 will study the changes in Quebec's educational system from its old élitist classical traditions to its present pragmatic and instrumental focus. This analysis will of necessity include an examination of the change in the role of the church in Quebec society and the impact of that change on French-Canadian culture. Chapter 7 will focus explicitly upon language policy. It will be shown that the tendency over the past fifteen years has been to change the function of the French language from that of being an informal language to that of being a standard language as defined in sociolinguistics. This change in function, it will be argued, complements the economic program of the provincial government and is a threat to the survival of a distinctive culture in Quebec, and not its saviour as is commonly argued. Chapter 8 will trace the growth of the independence movement in Quebec and analyse the coalition of class forces that comprises the movement. Conclusions from chapters 4–7 will be used to develop an explanation of why the movement has come to exist, and the chapter will end with some thoughts on the future of the independence movement.

PART ONE
Post–1945 Quebec:
Dependency or survival?

1

Underdevelopment in a dependent economy

Flashes from the nickel-plated microphone played on his spectacles, and above his head waved the tricolour, the Carillon flag with its four fleurs-de-lys, and the white-and-gold flag of the Vatican. The Cardinal folded his hands and in a strong, sweet voice he began to speak of the Sacred Heart with a dignity which the purity of his language transformed into an artistic act of faith. His words, carried by the loudspeakers, floated serenely above the motionless heads. Then slowly his voice swelled out, vibrating with a profound steadfastness of purpose. The supreme moment had come. The crowd held its breath ...

'The Church does not bless war, but she blesses the sword of those who know how to use it for good. Those who are allied to us, by treaty, by blood, by language or by political solidarity, have the right to count on our good wishes, our prayers and EVEN OUR SACRIFICES TO ASSURE THEIR VICTORY.'

The terrible blow had fallen. The numberless crowd wavered and let out an astounded sigh of despair.

Roger Lemelin *The Plouffe Family* trans Mary Finch (Toronto 1975) 360–1

The transfer of the colony of New France from the French to the British in 1763 had profound economic consequences for French Canadians. Processes were set in motion that eventually stripped them of any important role in the economy of British North America. Whether this situation resulted from the severing of the French mercantile bourgeoisie from the colony, as Michel Brunet has argued, or from the sheer dynamics of a colony being shifted from one metropole to another is less important here.[1] The point is that by 1810 French Canadians had lost their dominant position in the fur trade, were virtually excluded from the rising trade in timber, had no position of importance in the colonial bureaucracy, and had turned to the land and the growing of wheat and were faring poorly there. They found themselves in an economic position that we shall call dependent, which they resented, and which has stayed with them throughout their history.

In the years immediately following the Second World War, quite remarkably, the positions occupied by French Canadians in the North American economy were as minor as they had been in 1810. Virtually all the important industries in the province and all the senior positions in management were owned by or held by English Canadians or Americans. For close to 150 years, the French Canadians had been absent from the centres of economic power in their own land. This position of weakness had led élites typified by Lemelin's cardinal to adopt humiliating political positions, to bargain for second-class places in government, and to countenance feelings of inferiority on the one hand and hallucinating messianism on the other. This seeming inability of French Canadians to assert themselves economically over the years had helped foster myths among English Canadians that cast the French as lacking business sense, as lazy, simple, priest-ridden peasants.

A satisfactory explanation of this continued economic subjugation can be based neither upon myths such as these nor upon the easily invoked spectres of discrimination and racism. One must look beyond feelings and beliefs to more basic structures of social and economic activity. The great movements of reform in French-Canadian history, whether they be that of the patriotes of 1837, the Action libérale nationale during the Great Depression, or the Parti québécois of today, have certainly focused their attention on these kinds of structures. In my view, the economic activity of Quebec is integrated in a particular fashion with all the economic activity in North America. The manner in which this integration has taken place has fostered an economic structure in Quebec that is dependent, to be even more specific, underdeveloped, to a certain degree. This structure of underdevelopment has had the effect in the twentieth century of keeping French Canadians under-represented in the ranks of the industrial proletariat and the traditional professions. The continued inferior position of French-speakers is a product of the relationship between Quebec's economy and the major economic centres of North America.

Accordingly, this chapter is devoted to an examination of the structure of Quebec's economy immediately following the Second World War. In seeking to understand this economy and its position in the North American capitalist system, I shall rely on the social science concept of dependency. I shall explore in the abstract what is meant by the concept and what the characteristics of a dependent economy are. Using this theory, it will be demonstrated specifically how Quebec's economy was underdeveloped and how this state of underdevelopment has contributed to maintaining French-Canadian society in a position of remarkable economic weakness.

Further, it will be argued that by the late 1940s the pattern of underdevelopment in Quebec had created an important class division within this society. An industrial proletariat had gradually evolved and come to live largely outside the traditional institutions of French-Canadian society. The traditional middle class, the liberal professions, and the clergy lived to a significant extent on the fringes of the industrial economy and had a culture quite different from the working class. This division it will be argued in chapter 2, placed great pressure on traditional French-Canadian culture and brought its survival into question.

The concept of dependency

The concept of dependency has been used extensively in the study of political economy in Canada in recent years. It was originally fashioned to explain the underdevelopment of many Central and South American economies. It provided an alternative theory of development to the one found in functionalist theories, an example of the latter being the new-middle-class hypothesis discussed in the Introduction. Rather than viewing the various Central and South American societies as moving inexorably along the path from primitive traditionalism to industrial modernization, the theorists of *dependencia* described the traditional-modern bipolarity of these societies as a product of the manner in which they have been integrated into the imperialist capitalist system. In recent years, theories of dependency have been refined and have been increasingly used in the study of Third World countries outside the Americas.

Usually, these theorists do not include Canada or Quebec in their lists of dependent societies. Canada is treated as a member in good standing of the advanced capitalist countries at the centre of the world capitalist system, or, along with Australia and New Zealand, it is put in a separate category of 'White Settler Dominions,' which are seen as closely tied to the capitalist centre.[2] Several Canadian theorists have noted the difficulty in classifying Canada as 'dependent' in the usual sense. Glen Williams has remarked upon the immense gaps that exist between Canada and most countries in the Americas, Africa, and Asia.[3] He argues that heavy foreign investment and a reliance on the export of raw materials, factors often used to justify classifying Canada and Quebec as dependent, are not sufficient conditions for the use of the concept. Similarly, Wallace Clement, using his extensive study of economic élites in Canada and the United States, has concluded that Canada should not be referred to as dependent in the usual sense of the word.[4] While Canada and for that matter Quebec do rely on a resource hinterland for exports, both also possess a fairly large industrial manufacturing sector. Further, in the financial field particularly, Canada has its own transnational corporations with branches in many of the underdeveloped areas of the old British Empire.

Finally, Leo Panitch, in a review of the use of dependency theory by Canadian analysts, has pointed out that Canada is distinguished fundamentally from classically dependent societies because of the presence of free-wage labour since its early beginnings.[5] He describes how the proletariat that developed in Canada was a high-wage proletariat and how this created particular problems for the expansion of an indigenous industrial capitalist class and thereby opened up the possibility for dependent industrialization. He therefore resists the Latin American models and distinguishes Canadian underdevelopment by referring to three factors: 'a significant level of production of the means of production in the imperial country, low domestic technological development and research expenditure by the branch plants of multinational corporations, and relatively low exports of finished products.'[6]

Thus Canada, including Quebec, appears to share some characteristics with dependent societies – it relies extensively on the export of raw materials and its economy is largely foreign-controlled. But when one examines its industrial sector, its financial institutions, its level of services, and its standard of living, it could hardly be more different from Third World countries. These peculiarities of the Canadian and Quebec situations suggest that the concept will need to be used relatively. That is, it will be a kind of ideal type we can use to size up the position of Quebec, all the while knowing that the gaps we find existing between Quebec and developed countries may be small compared to those that would be found in a comparison of Third World countries with these same developed countries.

In a situation of dependency, the state of one society is conditioned or necessitated by the state of another. The relationship implies that the dependent society makes its choices in a situation where it does not usually set the terms or parameters of the choices.[7] At the level of individuals, mobility occurs under conditions strictly defined by the dominant society.[8] Economic growth occurs as a kind of reflex of the growth of the economy of the dominant society.[9]

This definition, however, remains somewhat ambiguous, in that no society is absolutely free of constraints on its choices. Given the interdependence of the countries of today's world, one could label virtually any country dependent. In order to restrict the definition to a limited number of cases, the concept of development must be introduced. Dependency refers to a relationship between two societies where the capacity of one society to develop is restricted or conditioned by another. The key to the understanding of dependency is therefore the concept of development.

Development refers to changes initiated by the society itself designed to realize its own social, economic, and cultural goals and to employ its own natural resources as much as possible toward those ends. The society adapts itself to its environment on its own initiative.[10] It makes the major choices on how to deploy and use its resources. For a dependent society, such major choices are usually made in a dominant society. It is geared to realizing not its own goals but those of another society. Dependency will be a matter of degree, with some societies having a weaker capacity than others to set and act upon their own goals. Some societies will have less control over the use of their resources than others.

This definition implies therefore that development be distinguished from the concept of growth. Simple growth, whether an expansion of per capita GNP or the differentiation of a political bureaucracy, is as often the result of changes in the dominant society as it is of development. Development is in many respects likely to be discontinuous and not a process of simple quantitative growth along a particular index.

In short, dependency refers to a relationship wherein one society's development is restricted by its functioning as a more or less connected part of another. The dependent society will thus be limited in its ability to choose how to use its own human and natural resources and thus in its ability to create a communal way of life best suited to its values and needs.

If in the Canadian case we cannot seize upon a heavy reliance on the export of raw materials as an indicator of dependency, and if dependency is compatible with a somewhat advanced industrial sector, how do we identify dependent development? Samir Amin, who has extensively investigated the problem of dependency and underdevelopment, suggests that there are three structural features that characterize dependent underdevelopment.[11] First, in an underdeveloped economy the level of productivity varies extensively among the various sectors of the economy. Often the agricultural sector is significantly less productive than the manufacturing sector, for example. Amin adds that this unevenness in productivity creates large inequities in the distribution of income and wealth in the population. In contrast, a developed economy is marked by more balanced productivity and hence less unevenness in the distribution of wealth.

Second, an underdeveloped economy does not form a coherent whole; it does not work as a single economic system. Rather, to use Amin's terms, it is 'disarticulated.' The various sectors of the economy do not build up exchanges among themselves but develop independently through exchanges with outside economies. The resource sector may be highly developed and the industrial sector less so, or vice versa, simply because each has developed in conjunction not with the other but with a dominant external economy. This kind of situation leads to anomalies such as a country being rich in iron ore and coal and yet being a heavy importer of steel.

Third, trade in an underdeveloped country is almost exclusively with countries at the centre of the capitalist mode of production. This commercial dependence on the centre is complemented by an increased financial dependence. The underdeveloped economy comes to experience balance-of-payments problems as profits generated internally leave the country, making it more difficult to invest sufficiently to integrate the sectors of the economy.

While the analysis of dependency in Quebec will rely largely upon the definition above and the structural characteristics outlined by Amin, one complicating factor will also be considered. Some scholars argue that Amin's analysis fails to take sufficient account of the actions of transnational corporations and state agencies in both central and peripheral nations.[12] The degree of underdevelopment and its specific character will depend upon how extensively transnational corporations specifically have come to dominate the market. In some cases, the market for a product may be closed, in others it may be oligopolistic, and in still others quite free. The actual institutions active in respective economic sectors will affect significantly the intensity of underdevelopment.

The question of dependency in Quebec

Unevenness in productivity

Let us begin by picturing the ideal type of the developed, independent economy. Presumably, the members of this society will have experienced economic expansion throughout their territory. Land will be used efficiently for agriculture. Some of the agricultural produce will be sold on the domestic market, and the rest will be exported. Agricultural producers will use the profits they make to expand and to make even more efficient their operations. Their demands for equipment to accomplish these goals will help generate an indigenous industry in farm machinery. This industry will draw on a steel industry that in turn will use whatever resources in iron, coal, and energy are possessed by the society. If these kinds of linkages are developed, each sector in the economy will tend to be quite profitable, workers in each sector will tend to be rewarded more or less equally, and productivity in the sense of wealth created will be relatively equal throughout the society.

For many countries in the world, of course, such a balanced economy is not possible, and this ideal type is utopian. However, for Quebec, such an ideal is not so improbable or remote. The St Lawrence River Valley, the plains around Lac St-Jean, and parts of the Outaouais have prime agricultural land. The province possesses large deposits of iron ore and other minerals and an abundance of hydro-electricity. It has been endowed with many other natural resources, its forests in particular, that are suitable for trade, which would help to create the wealth needed to invest in industrial development. There is no deficiency in the province's material position sufficiently serious that would lead virtually automatically to underdevelopment.

TABLE 1
Gross productivity per capita in Ontario and Quebec

	Quebec		Ontario	
	1935	1955	1935	1955
Agriculture	351.81	2 334.52	590.47	3 276.53
Mineral extraction	2 637.85	14 693.79	5 051.53	9 591.72
Forestry	n.a.	4 009.96	n.a.	4 010.00
Manufacturing	4 202.98	13 786.58	5 039.54	15 667.17
Average	1 903.80	9 897.01	2 633.31	11 668.90

SOURCE: Figures adapted from Appendice B₁ of André Raynauld *Croissance et structures économiques de la Province de Québec* (Quebec 1961).

In the developed economy, according to Amin, the wealth created per capita in the various sectors of the economy is more or less equivalent.[13] The agricultural producer is close to being as productive as the worker in industry. The degree of skill and knowledge required by labour in one sector is close to that required in another. One does not find a centuries-wide gap between the agricultural producer, the roller in a steel mill, and the faller in the logging industry. The amount of capital invested per worker in one sector is not significantly more or less than that found in other areas of the economy. In short, the developed, independent economy has an even quality; one does not find glaring inequalities in the distribution of income or in the wealth of individuals as one moves from agriculture to the primary extraction of resources to manufacturing and services.

One approach suggested by Amin for gauging the degree of evenness in the economy is to examine the distribution of gross product per occupied person in the various economic sectors.[14] He finds that in 1960, there were significant differences between the United States and Britain on the one hand and Latin America on the other. In Latin America, the ratio of agricultural productivity to that of other activities was 1:3; in Britain it was practically 1:1 and in the United States 1:2. Similarly, if one takes the major sectors of the economy and examines the productivity in each, the degree of unevenness is also shown. For Latin America, the extreme ratio observed is 1:11 (between agriculture and extraction industry) whereas it is 1:1.4 in Britain and 1:3 in the United States.

Table 1 presents similar data for Quebec and for Ontario. In 1955, when the Quebec economy had stabilized after wartime expansion, one finds that the ratio of agriculture to that of all activities is 1:4.24, a figure higher even than that reported by Amin for Latin America. If the ratio between agriculture and mineral extraction, the most extreme possibility, is calculated, we find the figure to be 1:6.29. This ratio is somewhat below that found in Latin America. These figures are marked improvements over the same ratios in 1935; the former was 1:5.41 and the latter 1:11.95 in that year.

These ratios for Quebec can also be compared to those of Ontario, Canada's wealthiest and most developed province at that time. For Ontario, the ratio of agriculture to the average in 1955 was 1:3.56, and the most extreme ratio (agriculture to manufacturing) was 1:4.78. Both ratios are lower than those found in Quebec but still somewhat higher than those calculated by Amin for the United States.

In making these comparisons between Quebec and Latin America, despite the apparent similarities, one must not conclude that Quebec's economy is sadly underdeveloped. The important factor differentiating the two cases is the relative importance of agriculture in the economy. A relatively small proportion of the labour force in Quebec earns its living on the farm, whereas in many Latin American countries agriculture is the activity that occupies the greatest proportion of citizens. However, the relatively low productivity of the combined agricultural and forest sectors in Quebec, the latter sector being an important part of the economy, is suggestive of some unevenness in the generation of wealth. As late as 1955, working a subsistence farm supplemented by winter work in the forest was still quite common. While Quebec was perhaps not as seriously underdeveloped in the early 1950s as the classic Latin American cases, it was, on the basis of this first indicator, quite clearly at a level of development well below that found in the United States and Britain.

The degree of integration of economic activity

A second important characteristic of the developed economy, according to Amin, is that it is autocentric:[15] the economy functions as an integrated whole, the primary exchanges of each sector are with other branches of the same economy. Such a system is to be contrasted with an underdeveloped economy, where the various sectors develop in relation to a dominant external economy; exchanges here take place mainly between the respective sectors and an external economy. The economy of the one society develops almost as a distorted reflection of the dominant one. The various sectors grow in relation to each other not in an ordered fashion but in response to the needs of the dominant economy. The stage of development reached by one sector of the economy will be virtually unrelated to the stage reached by another. If and when the dominant economy no longer has a need for the products of a sector of the satellite economy, that sector is likely to fall into a depressed state, with no prospect of a resuscitation spurred by assistance from within.

In the cases of Canada and Quebec, such a process of disarticulation takes a particular form because of the initial dependence on staples. The concept of a staple has been prominent in the study of Canadian political economy.[16] It refers to a natural resource to be sure, but a resource that plays a particular role in the economy. A resource is termed a staple when its place in the economy is so central that it largely determines the pattern of social organization and communication in the society. Thus, if production of the staple is threatened in some way, the probability of serious disruption in the society is high.

Economic historians generally agree that in the case of Quebec, first fur and then timber were staples during the nineteenth century. Economists are in some disagreement over whether one might characterize pulpwood and such minerals as iron and asbestos as staples in the twentieth century. The issue is complex, because often the production of the resource may account for a minor part of the overall gross national product.[17] Yet the theory says not that it should account directly for a large proportion of the GNP but that it be sufficiently central to the economy that it is in the interest of the society to organize itself around its production. As this study proceeds, it will become increasingly evident that the Quebec economy is built around production of such resources as pulpwood, iron ore, asbestos, and hydro-electricity. For this reason, it will be helpful to speak of that economy as a staple economy. Using the theory of a staple economy, we can trace how ideally such an economy might become on one hand autocentric or on the other hand underdeveloped.

The staple approach is not a general theory of economic growth, but was developed specifically for the atypical case of the newly colonized country.[18] At the outset, such a country is distinctive in that, given a native population that is small and easily repressed, there is usually a very favourable man-land ratio and a certain absence of inhibiting traditions. None the less the migrant brings with him certain values and traditions as well as expectations about a standard of living. Further, he is particularly reliant upon the mother country for goods. He thus begins a search for goods that are in demand in the mother country and that will yield the largest profit so that the expected standard of living might be achieved. Generally such goods have been those required for the manufacture of luxuries or those only slightly available in the mother country.

If indeed such goods or staples are found, they quickly become the leading sector of the economy and set the pace for economic growth. The staples are invariably resource-intensive at the start because of the small domestic market and population. A society is gradually organized on a basis that provides the most efficient production of the staple. Continued viability and growth of the economy will depend on what Melville Watkins calls the 'spread effects' of the staple sector.[19] The distinctive spread effects that occur will draw their character from the particular properties of the staple and from its structure of production.

The particularities of the staple and its products, which are relied upon by the society, are paramount in determining the organization of society as well as the possibilities for future development. For example, the development of wheat as a staple export to Europe dictated an east-west communication and transportation system in Canada that would send the grain out and take the immigrants in to settle the prairies. In contrast, the exploitation of pulpwood in Ontario and Quebec led to the development of hydro-electric power and a north-south transportation grid to reach American markets.

The particularities of the staple and its production are important because they determine what production factors will be needed, what intermediate inputs will be required, and the possibilities for future processing and the distribution of income.[20] A staple economy is basically insecure – its dependence on one or two raw exports leaves it vulnerable to other areas for markets and for manufactured goods and to any technological change that may ease the demand for the staple or open up new sources. To sustain itself, it has to be able either to drift from one staple to another, which requires a certain abundance of resources, or to be able to generate enough income from the staples it produces to broaden its economic base.[21] In the latter case, not only must sufficient income be generated, but also it must be distributed more or less equally.

A successful staple implies that sufficient capital is produced for further investment. Watkins outlines three investment roads carved out by an expanding export sector. (If these roads are followed, then the economy will become autocentric in Amin's sense). First, capital can go 'backward' into the production of inputs for the export sector. Whether this route can be fruitfully followed depends upon the particularities of the staple and the infrastructure it requires. When it occurs, such investment may, in turn, have its own spread effects. For example, the investment in a transportation system such as railways or in extraction equipment for mines may lead to technological advances sufficiently distinctive to generate an independent, thriving export sector.

Second, one can take a 'forward' route and invest in industries that use the staple export as an input. Innis notes that the creation of such industry often prolongs the life of a given staple for the producing country.[22] Its creation gives the society in question some control over the future of the resource by making it possible to create a demand for manufactured goods that use that resource as a base.

Third, an expanding export sector may be used to develop domestic industry and thus to satisfy the consumer demands of the population that have accumulated around the export industry. Clearly, primary determinants will be the size of the domestic market and the amount of aggregate income generated by the staple sector. Assuming that the income is retained domestically (an assumption not always tenable, as will be shown when we examine how a staple economy becomes dependent), a second determinant for investment along this third route is the distribution of income. If the production of the staple creates a highly skewed income distribution, two separate markets will ensue. One will be oriented to subsistence goods and the other toward luxuries, neither of which induces indigenous development. However, a more equalized distribution of income tends to create a broadly based market for mass-produced consumer goods.

In summary, in this model, the successful production of a staple is central to the development of an autocentric economy. The entire social organization, including transportation, trade, financing, and governmental activities, is geared to the production of the staple. Thus the particular qualities of the staple affect the kind of transportation system built, the orientation of the country in trade, its need for technology, and so on. Further, the means of production coupled with the peculiarities of the staple determine the size of the domestic market as well as the distribution of income. The staple may nor may not create the capital required for the sustenance and development of the population it supports. The importance of the particular qualities of the staple underlines the role of chance in determining the success or failure of newly colonized countries. The resources they can produce will depend on the level of technology available and the external demand for those resources.

The dependent staple economy

Dependency has been defined as a relationship between two societies wherein the development of one is restricted by the development of the other. Such an economy is particularly susceptible to a condition of dependency and thus to a lack of integration. Assuming, first, that the economy has 'taken off,' its future viability and hence development still remain hinged on international demand for its staple or staples. It is unlikely to be able to marshal the resources, both human and natural, necessary for adaptation and growth, without such reliable markets. Nevertheless, assuming, second, that the economy has the markets for a reasonable period, a staple-based society remains somewhat unprotected against a dependent relationship.

In order to take off and, once established, be able to shift from one resource to another, a staple economy invariably requires a large amount of outside investment. Further, the shift from one staple to another invariably involves if not a totally new at least a substantially revised infrastructure and a resulting need for more capital. For example, as Canada shifted from fur and timber, which used water as their transportation means, to wheat, which relied on the transcontinental railway, massive amounts of backward investment were required. The bulk of these funds had to be obtained from abroad. Because the staple economy sometimes is forced to shift from reliance on one staple to reliance on another, the need for such backward investment remains somewhat constant. In brief, this need to finance the supporting structure for the staple, when coupled with a need for capital in order to produce the staple, leaves the staple economy particularly open to foreign influence.

The critical point for the study of dependency in a staple society is, therefore, investment in and hence ownership and control of the resource sector. If control of this sector does not remain with the society, its defences against dependency are reduced to virtually nil. Further, if the resource sector passes out of the control of the society, the likelihood that dependency in the resource sector will have its own spread effects on forward and consumer investment is high. In Canada in general and in Quebec specifically, control of the resource sector has generally been lost through foreign direct investment in the resources.

Direct investment is made to create some permanent facility abroad to process goods for either the export market or the domestic market of the staple country. Such investment invariably involves the importation of personnel, technology, and equipment, as well as funds. The direct investor is acting to secure control of these markets. To this end, he needs a permanent facility in the foreign economy. It thus becomes clear that if the resource sector of the staple economy is supported by direct investment, effective control of that sector is far more easily lost. This becomes evident when one examines the institution that usually works through direct investment – the transnational corporation (TNC),

The TNC is distinguished by its tendency to view the world as a single economic unit:

Because its primary purpose is to organize and integrate economic activity around the world in such a way as to maximize global profit, the global corporation is an organic structure in which each part is expected to serve the whole. Thus in the end it measures its successes and its failures not by the balance sheet of an individual subsidiary, or the suitability of particular products, or its social impact in a particular country, but by the growth in global profits and global market shares.[23]

As Levitt argues, for Canada the subsidiaries of the TNC replaced the operations of earlier Europe-based mercantile companies in extracting the staple and organizing the supply of market goods.[24] Transnational corporations are profoundly national in character, reflecting a contemporary form of national economic expansion.[25] They seek to maintain for their home countries a share of foreign markets, a position in foreign economies, and access to foreign raw materials. The imperatives of technology and the large amounts of time and capital they commit dictate a highly centralized organization that engages actively in planning. Planning serves to reduce risks and to introduce rigidities into the international economy. The ultimate effect is to push risk onto less integrated producers and manufacturers in the hinterland economies and, as Harold Innis remarks, to squeeze unorganized labour.[26]

The global corporation establishes its predominance through control of three factors – technology of production, finance capital, and marketing.[27] A branch plant invariably receives its technology from its parent firm and is prevented from using that technology for other than the firm's ends. The result is that the executives of branch plants tend to become managers and administrators and not entrepreneurs. Similarly, research and development are done in the home country, with the obvious effect of leaving research development in the host country lagging. The multinationals have also worked toward the international-ization of finance capital through consortiums such as the Orion Bank.[28] They are able to borrow money virtually anywhere in the world. This ability, when joined with their power and prestige, means that they are able to attract local financing at the expense of local entrepreneurs. Finally, their control over marketing companies allows them to mount global advertising compaigns designed to define needs for the world consumer. This creation of wants is part of and hence vital to the success of the planning operations of the firm.

In this brief survey it is evident that direct investment implemented through the transnational corporation can become a harbinger of dependency. It implies not only that enterpreneurial decisions in the areas controlled will come from the parent firms, but also that the consumers of the host country will find themselves adopting needs based on a foreign tradition. In the case of Quebec, then, the entry of transnational corporations onto the scene has especially serious consequences. To the extent that they become concerned with producing for the Quebec market they might alter the structures of needs inherited from the traditional culture.

Dependency is introduced into the staple economy through foreign direct investment in the production of the staple itself. Such investment is usually welcomed by both societies involved. The investor, usually a foreign manufacturer who processes the staple, is able to ensure a supply of inputs to his manufacturing concerns as well as to tie up convenient sources of the resource and thereby enhance his market position. The host country, in turn, secures stable markets for its resources and hence steady job opportunities and income.

However, the costs of such direct investment in the resource sector may very well include a loss of autocentrism, as a Canadian government study of foreign direct investment has shown.[29] First, these investors, because of their economic power and low-risk status, often gain privileged access to domestic capital and real resources, thereby restricting the capital supply for indigenous forward or consumer-demand investment. Second, the economic priorities and structure of economic expansion come to reflect the priorities of foreign firms and their governments rather than indigenous needs. The staple sector of the host society becomes truncated and separated from other economic sectors. Third, the backward vertical integration of foreign resource producers creates strong barriers against significant resource production by domestic operators. Either they are forced to buy from the foreign operators or, if they extract the staples themselves, they find themselves with higher costs and prices because foreign branch plants can charge costs back to their parent firms, thus effectively squeezing the domestic producers. These domestic producers are unlikely to construct significant linkages between the resource sector and other branches of economic activity. Fourth, the integrated nature of the staple-extracting companies means that the raw resources are often exported directly to manufacturing plants owned by the companies in their own country. This practice truncates the staple economy by denying it the further opportunity to expand through forward investment, that is, to develop a secondary manufacturing sector.

In summary, foreign control through direct investment in the resource sector reduces the capacity of a society to use its own resources to satisfy indigenously defined priorities and needs. Domestic entrepreneurs are squeezed not only by their foreign competitors but also by the meagre amounts of capital that are left to them. The lack of control over staple production, the leading sector of the economy, restricts its spread effects and frustrates indigenous entrepreneurship in forward and consumer-demand manufacturing. The profits, dividends, and royalties from this sector will tend to flow out of the country. Weakened capacity for development and increasing dependence in the resource sector are likely to spill over into the secondary manufacturing sector.

A full examination of whether the Quebec economy is autocentric would require a detailed examination of the province's economic history, a task outside the scope of this study. Nevertheless, an indication of the degree to which the economy of the province functions as an integrated system may be obtained by reviewing several sets of data. These data are principally for the year 1960, not for the immediate post-war years. They are acceptable, however, because they pertain to the economy before the Quiet Revolution was under way.

First, then, we have agreed that control of the major staples in the economy is virtually a necessary condition for autocentric development. Table 2 indicates that this condition is hardly met. In the mining industry, over 50 per cent of production is controlled by enterprises that are not Canadian. Further, the French-speaking community, which accounts for over 80 per cent of the province's population, lays claim to only 2.2 per cent of mining production.

TABLE 2
Locus of control of major economic sectors in Quebec based on value added (1961)

	French Canadian	English Canadian	Foreign
Agriculture	88.3	11.7	0
Mining industry	2.2	46.0	51.8
Manufacturing	10.2	43.7	46.1
Construction	36.5	42.5	21.0
Transportation and communications (private)	37.5	49.4	13.1
Wholesale trade	28.7	42.8	28.5
Retail trade	36.9	48.5	14.6

SOURCE: André Raynauld *La Propriété des entreprises au Québec* (Montreal 1974) 44 ff

Outside the mining industry, another important staple is pulpwood. Yet here as well, 41.9 per cent of the pulp and paper industry is controlled by foreign enterprises and only 4.8 per cent by French Canadians. In the primary metals industry, where ore is processed so that it may be used in secondary production, 86.5 per cent of the industry is owned by foreign corporations.[30] In short, this examination of the sectors where Quebec's staples are prominent indicates that control over their production is largely in foreign hands. Further, French Canadians are almost totally excluded from the staple sectors.

On the basis of this analysis one might expect further that Quebec's economy will possess some of the traits of an underdeveloped economy. This is indeed the case. Iron ore is a central resource to any industrial economy; around such a resource, a society can erect a steel industry. A steel industry can provide the foundation for many important heavy industries, such as the manufacture of machinery and transportation materials. By the end of the Second World War, Quebec had moved to extract the ore from its vast northern iron reserves which contained about 90 per cent of Canada's iron. By 1960, these mines were in full operation. In that year, 90.3 per cent of the ore mined was shipped for export in raw form, primarily to American steel mills.[31] A second mineral important to Quebec's post-war economy is asbestos. Quebec is not only the largest producer of asbestos in Canada, but, in 1960, was the second largest producer in the world. In 1955, of the more than 1,000,000 tons of asbestos mined, 94.3 per cent was shipped for export in raw form.[32] In 1960, 95.5 per cent of the total mined found its way out of the Eastern Townships to export markets in raw form. These two minerals, which had the potential to generate significant development in other sectors of the economy, were used strictly to satisfy the needs of the American economy. Their production is virtually incidental to the other sectors of Quebec's economy. The examples of iron and asbestos are by no means exceptional. Raynauld has demonstrated that in 1949 92.8 per cent of all minerals extracted in Quebec were exported in brute form.[33]

Not all Quebec's staples, however, are divorced from forward linkages. A useful counter-example is pulpwood. Mainly because of the intervention of the federal and provincial governments in the early days of the industry, much of the wood cut is manufactured in Quebec into pulp, which has been used mainly to make newsprint for American newspapers. Yet even this example of a successful forward linkage being generated from a staple is not as developed as it might be. Because many of the major companies in the pulp industry have been owned by American interests, production has been aimed at American papers. Other production has been devoted simply to the manufacture of wood pulp, a relatively crude product that is then exported for further manufacture. In 1950, Canada's leading export was newsprint, and the third-ranking export was wood pulp.[34] In short, part of the production of the pulpwood resource is also being exported in rather brute form, and this fact probably helps explain why Quebec has never developed a fine-paper industry. However, the performance of the pulpwood industry is definitely superior to that of the metal-mining industry. Amin suggests that in a developed economy only 6 per cent of a primary resource is shipped abroad in brute form.[35] If one assumes that wood pulp is a manufactured product, only 7.2 per cent of the timber cut in Quebec is exported unprocessed.[36]

Other aspects of the structure of Quebec's economy indicate that the economy is only weakly autocentric. Amin writes that in a disarticulated system light industry and crafts will be much more significant in terms of value of production than heavy industry. Table 3 shows that light industry in Quebec generates more than twice as much value added as heavy industry. This difference suggests that the various manufacturing industries in Quebec are not well articulated. Data collected by Raynauld for 1949 provide evidence for this point. In primary iron and steel, over 50 per cent of the output is exported.[37] Yet in the sector that uses primary iron and steel to manufacture more specialized products over 50 per cent of the input factor is imported. Similarly, over 65 per cent of the non-ferrous metal products manufactured in Quebec are exported rather than being used by other more specialized industries. In the manufacture of textiles, close to 50 per cent of the product is exported, and yet in the manufacture of clothing, which uses the products of the textile industry, enterprises import textiles worth more than they buy on the Quebec market. If an economy was autocentric, would it be exporting $153.6 million worth of textile products on the one hand and importing textiles worth $124.94 million for its clothing industry on the other?

TABLE 3
Amount of value added in each economic sector in Quebec
in 1961 (in millions of dollars)

	Amount	Percentage
Agriculture	231.0	2.56
Forestry	110.0	1.22
Fishing, hunting, trapping	4.0	.04
Mining	218.0	2.41
Light manufacturing	1 965.6	21.76
Heavy manufacturing	814.5	9.02
Construction	593.0	6.56
Transportation and communications	950.0	10.51
Electricity, gas, water	250	2.77
Trade	1 123	12.43
Finance	1 057	11.70
Services	1 265	14.0
Public administration	454	5.02
Total	9 035.1	100

SOURCE: Adapted from Office de planification et de développement du Québec (OPDQ) *Analyse structurelle à moyen terme de
l'économie du Québec* (Quebec 1977) 238

In reviewing the evidence on the degree of integration of the economy,
Amin's second indicator of underdevelopment, the results are mixed. It has
been argued that the key to autocentric development in a staple-based economy
is the retention of control over the production of staples. If a society loses
control here, it becomes highly probable that the staples will be exploited to
satisfy foreign needs. The likelihood of their having spread effects, particularly
to secondary industry, is low. After 1945 Quebec did not have control over its
staples, and its economy accordingly shows some disarticulation. The mineral
industry in particular was divorced from production in other sectors. Even
within the manufacturing industries, production in one sector often seems
unrelated to production in the other sectors. The one exception to this pattern,
an important one, is the use of forest resources. Only 7 per cent of forest
production is exported in raw form, the rest of the timber cut being used by
industries in the province. In short, the Quebec economy appears in some
instances to be underdeveloped when measured by Amin's criteria for
autocentrism. Yet the degree of underdevelopment is not as universal in Third
World countries.

Trade patterns

The final characteristic of a dependent economy outlined by Amin is closely related to the previous two. In the underdeveloped economy, trade is overwhelmingly with the dominant, advanced capitalist countries. The usual objects of trade are raw materials. This fact, however, does not automatically signal underdevelopment. Rather, such a trading pattern must occur in conjunction with the first two properties of underdevelopment: the production of raw materials is not integrated with an autocentric economic system, and the productivity of labour varies widely from one branch of the economy to another. When such a trading pattern occurs under these conditions the economy will be said to be commercially dependent. What primary or secondary industry does grow will be poorly interconnected, creating a need to import capital and intermediate goods. Terms of trade are likely to worsen gradually, leading to problems with balance of payments.

In looking back over the discussion of the previous two characteristics of underdevelopment – unevenness in productivity and poorly integrated economic activity – it is evident that Quebec's economy was partially underdeveloped. Accordingly, one would expect that a review of its trading patterns in the immediate post-war period would show further developmental weaknesses. Although the data are not as plentiful as one might hope, they do remain consistent with the earlier findings. Table 4 presents Quebec's leading exports and imports in the year 1949. That minerals in raw form are second on the list of exports is not surprising. It has already been noted that minerals are a key staple of Quebec's economy and that their production is relatively divorced from the secondary sectors of the province's economy.

Similarly, the overall importance of the forest resource in the economy is underlined by the fact that paper products are the leading articles for export. It has been demonstrated above that unlike the minerals industry, the forest industry has been developed in an effective fashion in turns of integrating primary and secondary production of the resource. However, the category of paper products defined by Raynauld and used in Table 4 is rather comprehensive. It includes wood pulp, a relatively crude product; newsprint, a roughly fabricated product; and fine papers and boxes, more carefully manufactured products. Unfortunately, the data are not broken down into these categories, preventing us from assessing directly the relative importance of each of these components. Data for Canada as a whole in 1949 do exist and may be used as a rough guide for assessing the relative importance of the components of the paper products category. In Canada, in 1949, the total value of paper products exported was $623,596,000. Of the total, $170,675,000 or 27 per cent was derived from wood pulp, $433,882,000 or 70 per cent from newsprint, and

TABLE 4
Leading exports and imports of Quebec in 1949 in terms of value (in millions of dollars)

Exports		Imports	
Paper products	352.0	Textiles	130.44
Minerals (brute form)	167.6	Clothing	124.94
Clothing	158.6	Petroleum and coal	94.07
Textile products	153.6	Transportation	
Chemical products	84.5	equipment	60.79
Tobacco products	82	Paper products	58.38
Iron and steel products	73.9	Iron and steel products	56.43
Electrical apparatuses	72.7	Chemical products	46.08
Transportation equipment	62.0	Confectionery, sugar	39.28
Petroleum and coal	61.1		

SOURCE: Figures adapted from André Raynauld *Croissance et structures économiques de la Province de Québec* (Quebec 1961) Table 40

$19,039,000 or 3 per cent from papers other than newsprint.[38] By this breakdown, and given Quebec's dominant position in the Canadian pulp and paper industry, a reasonable revision of the list of exports in Table 4 would show newsprint still leading the list but closer in value to minerals, and wood pulp probably in fifth place.

Such a revision emphasizes again that Quebce had a foot in both the developed and underdeveloped camps. On the negative side, it was exporting its mineral resources and over a quarter of its pulpwood resource in relatively raw form. It had either no secondary capacity (minerals) or inadequate facilities (pulpwood) to be characterized as autocentric. On the positive side, a brief review of other leading exports indicates the presence of secondary industry on a scale not likely to be found in most Third World societies. Capital goods and intermediate products do not dominate the province's leading imports. In the textiles, clothing, transportation equipment, chemical products, and paper products industries, the province maintains a healthy balance of trade. Similarly, there is no evidence that in 1949 the province was in any serious financial difficulty. Its debt was not especially heavy or growing particularly quickly. In summary, the terms of trade enjoyed by Quebec were not as poor as one might expect in an underdeveloped economy.

Conclusion

Given that Quebec's economy in the immediate post-war period manifested certain characteristics of dependent capitalist development, these characteristics in turn had consequences for Quebec society and specifically the

French-Canadian community. The large differences in productivity between the agricultural and forest sectors on the one hand and the mining and manufacturing sectors on the other hand correspond to a growing division within the French-Canadian community. There remained a sector in the francophone community that was rural in character, generated its income from a mixed agriculture-forest economy, and had only limited ties to urban centres. A survey of farms in Nicolet County in 1947–8 showed farms of a semi-subsistence kind, generating 43 per cent of their total living expenses on their own.[39] Only 58 per cent of the homes were electrified; in 59 per cent the kitchen stove was the only form of heat. Every family member over the age of 16 had attended church at least twenty times a year. Even as late as 1956, in a survey of farms carried out by the UCC, of the 60,621 farms studied, only 46.1 per cent lived entirely from the income of their farm operations.[40] Another 32.3 per cent added to their incomes by working as *bûcherons,* and 21.6 per cent had jobs in industry. Throughout the 1950s, this agricultural-forest nexus gradually broke down, as Fortin has shown in a series of remarkable studies.[41]

Nevertheless, between 1945 and 1955 there remained a significant group of individuals earning their living from the soil and the forest whose lives were influenced by a series of traditional institutions, largely controlled and operated by the church. The church linked this economic group to a traditional intelligentsia of clerics, lawyers, and doctors, who had ties to both urban industrial society and this rural society. These élites were mainly anti-capitalist in ideology and devoted to the institutions still operating in the rural communities.

The split economy of the francophone community separated these two groups from several others tied to the resource-extracting and manufacturing sectors. First, these industries had created a proletariat increasingly concentrated in large urban centres. This latter class lived largely outside the traditional institutions of French-Canadian society and had adopted many aspects of the materialist, consumption culture of urban North America.[42] The disarticulated relationships among the various industries discussed tended to produce high unemployment and with it a general sense of insecurity and malaise among many workers.[43] Second, in isolated pockets of the economy there had grown successful entrepreneurs in the francophone community. Although largely shut out of primary and secondary industries, they had some strength in retail and wholesale trade, transportation, and food processing. Members of this class were fiercely pro-capitalist and yet insecure. Their small numbers and their lack of capital left them constantly threatened by large corporations from English Canada and the United States. Third, and in a haphazard way, a service class for the industrial economy was beginning to appear in the area of technical and vocational education and trade union and credit union management. All three groups – the working class, the small entrepreneurs, and the service class – had a stake in industrial capitalism. They also were less directly touched by the church and by the traditional institutions of French Canada. They were increasingly distinct culturally from the rural class and the traditional intelligentsia.

The fractured and variable dependent economy was reflected in a degree of division within the French-Canadian community on the social and cultural plane. This disunity posed certain fundamental questions for French Canadians as a nation. The gradual isolation of the traditional cultural practices of the community and their decline in importance among large portions of the community threw into question the very survival of the once distinctive cultural group. There were increasing clashes and contradictions between the practices of the industrialized sector and those of the rural sector. Further, the federal government, which supported increased industrialization, was beginning to create institutions and policies in education and social services to facilitate the progress of industry. These came to compete with the traditional counterparts long established in the French-Canadian community. Thus an important political dimension came to overlay the division within the francophone community.

In the next two chapters, these divisions in the socio-cultural and political planes will be studied in depth. I will trace the development of these divisions after 1945. It will be shown that by the end of the 1950s, the path of increased integration into the capitalist system supported by the second urban group of classes became established as the dominant route. This decision, I shall eventually show, planted the seeds of the independence movement, which arose out of frustration at the inability of the francophone community to define and maintain a distinctive culture while advancing further along this path.

2

Catholic social thought and traditional French-Canadian culture

Visitors to Quebec cannot help but be struck by the magisterial architectural presence of the Roman Catholic church in the province's cities and towns. The churches are often magnificent buildings; the old classical colleges are usually found in commanding settings on hills or large tracts of land; and abbeys rest in tranquil landscapes spotted throughout the countryside. These buildings are witnesses to the former influence of the church in Quebec. Their majesty and even the wealth of which they silently speak are a testimony to an institution the tentacles of which once reached deep into the social life of the French-Canadian community. Until recently, the Catholic religion and the culture of French Canada were strongly intertwined. The institutions traditional to French Canada were Catholic institutions. Being a French Canadian and a Catholic amounted to much the same thing. This particular religion-based culture had arisen largely out of the institutions of rural French Canada and had been intellectualized by the traditional middle class of clerics and liberal professionals. The culture had the most meaning for these groups and classes and had less meaning for the social groups that had grown up in Quebec with the expansion of industrial capitalist production. As a consequence of this division, a second set of institutions and a different culture gradually began to grow in Quebec during the first half of the twentieth century. This second group of cultural practices did not directly challenge the traditional culture; it simply supplanted it more and more. In doing so, it created a potential crisis because the resulting division in French-Canadian society posed a problem for its continued survival.

In order to understand the social, political, and cultural changes that occurred in Quebec beginning in the late 1950s – the changes out of which the independence movement was to grow – one must be familiar with how traditional French-Canadian culture and its institutions were defined. Knowledge of these traditional components will facilitate the explanation of why they could not embrace the newer social groups in the francophone community. Further, it will be possible to understand the links between the economic structure described in the previous chapter and the cultural institutions found in the French-Canadian community. This chapter will begin by examining how traditional intellectuals in French Canada defined their own culture and related it to the Catholic religion and Catholic social thought. Once we have defined some basic premises of the long dominant ideology, ecclesiastical, educational, and social welfare structures will be studied as the exemplars of the traditional culture. By supplementing this discussion with a survey of the second set of institutions that gradually grew up in the shadow of the traditional culture, our understanding of the divisions described at the end of chapter 1 becomes more complete.

Culture and Catholic social thought

The French-Canadian intellectual community was, of course, not completely homogeneous. There were divisions within it over many issues, particularly those related to the national question and the strategy of the nationalist movement. However, in some areas of the community's concerns, acknowledged leaders can be identified.

In Catholic social thought, the leading exponents belonged to the Jesuit order and spoke from platforms specifically created and manned by that order. In 1912, the Jesuits, following an interdiocesan congress organized by the Fédération générale des Ligues du Sacré Coeur, created the École sociale populaire (ESP). The congress had concluded that workers in French Canada needed to be organized into Catholic unions or 'professional associations' and that Catholic social doctrine needed to be popularized. The ESP was organized in order to work toward these objectives. It was run single-handedly for many years by Père Joseph-Papin Archambault, SJ. In 1921 the work of the ESP began to be supplemented by yearly workshops – Semaines sociales – on issues related to Catholic social thought. In 1936, the Jesuits began publishing the journal *L'Ordre nouveau* as an additional vehicle for popularizing their thinking. It was succeeded by *Relations,* which began publishing in 1941. Père Archambault was the leading force behind both the semaines sociales and the journals.[1] As Archambault became older, Père Richard Arès, SJ, gradually assumed many of his responsibilities, becoming successively director of the ESP (which changed its name to the Institut social populaire [ISP] in 1950), editor of *Relations,* and chairman of the semaines sociales.[2]

Accordingly, in presenting aspects of Catholic social thought developed in Quebec, I will use primarily articles and papers drawn from these three institutions.[3] In addition, the work of Esdras Minville on the concept of culture will be used. Minville wrote a number of works on this topic which were warmly embraced by intellectuals.[4] His influence on such matters was sufficiently high that he was given the task of writing the section on culture in the report of the Royal Commission of Inquiry on Constitutional Problems (Tremblay Commission), a section that has been acclaimed by many, both supporters and opponents, since its publication.

The concept of culture used by French-Canadian intellectuals was broad. It was defined to be an 'organic collection' of three elements – knowledge, means of expression, and values.[5] Knowledge was meant to include a range of phenomena from the elementary rules of practical life to the sciences and to philosophy and theology. Means of expression referred primarily to language. Values were understood to be the 'criteria of appreciation' men used in judging how knowledge should be brought to bear when acting in the world. These three elements have evolved from the centuries-long experience of a people living on a particular territory under somewhat autonomous political structures and have produced a deep sense of community and, with it, an identity, a feeling of being a nation.

According to the traditional intellectuals of French Canada, the guiding force behind the development of this culture and its stock of knowledge and values was the Catholic religion. Religion gave a culture its shape; religion was the inspiration behind its rules of everyday life, its philosophy, its theology. Religion anchored the values upon which decisions were eventually made. The report of the Tremblay Commission described the relationship this way: 'Religion and culture thus meet in humanism, with culture receiving from religion, more or less directly and completely, its general inspiration and directive thought; while religion borrows from culture such and such means of integration within the diverse manifestations of daily life, such as morals, customs, traditions etc.'[6]

For these intellectual élites, the distinctive characteristics of French-Canadian society arose out of the teachings and practices of the Catholic church. It is useful to examine how the teachings of the church in Quebec described the role of the church itself in society. What kinds of lines are drawn between those aspects of social life that might be described as spiritual and those that are temporal? The answer will of necessity draw upon Catholic social thought in Quebec – a corpus of teachings that arose on the basis of two papal encyclicals, Leo xiii's *De Rerum Novarum* (About New Matters) (1891) and Pius xi's *Quadragesimo Anno* (1931) on the fortieth anniversary of the first. These were supplemented by a series of statements on social issues by the popes, particularly by Pius xii, whose energetic speech-making provided continual elaborations and refinements to his predecessors' teachings. The encyclicals and other papal teachings were carefully studied in Quebec, with interpretations and popularizations being published by the ESP, by the semaines sociales, and by *Relations*.

The new social philosophy that gradually emerged was seen to be spiritualist, in contrast to the materialism of the two philosophies the church found unacceptable, liberalism and socialism. It sought to propose solutions that would curb the alienation of the working classes in industrial capitalism and provide the institutional framework needed to retain that class among the faithful. Accordingly, the thought of the popes was seen as directly relevant to French-Canadian society, where the working class was gradually slipping beyond the influence of the church and the established institutions of French Canada.

The Catholic church in Quebec was, of course, actively behind many of these established institutions. It interpreted its role broadly, seeing a spiritual dimension to much of social activity. Its extensive penetration into French-Canadian society was challenged for the first time in decades by several articles that appeared in the first few issues of *Cité libre*. This journal, which began to publish in 1950, has a somewhat celebrated status because Pierre Elliott Trudeau and Gérard Pelletier were its first editors. The challenge to the church's position led to the writing of a series of articles by Père Arès in *Relations,* which state cogently the teachings of the church in Quebec on these matters.[7]

Arès rejected the idea that the world could be divided into spiritual and temporal orders. Both orders were part of what he called the natural realm, and all aspects of this realm needed the grace of God. If the natural realm was not so blessed, those acting in it could never realize their full potential and hence could never be reintegrated into the supernatural order of God. Arès posited that the church had received from Christ several powers that were to be used to bring the grace of God to the natural realm. First, it had the power of order, that is, the power to introduce every person to the supernatural realm and to help maintain for each a place in that realm. The church accomplished this task by making God's grace available to the individual through the sacraments. However, it recognized also that if individuals were to follow such practices, they would need first to have certain basic physical needs such as food and shelter satisfied. The recognition of this fact meant that the church had to take an interest in man's material well-being if it were to carry out fully the mission implicit in this power of order. Hence it might be within the church's purview to help workers to organize in order to obtain a just wage, or to promote the use of housing co-operatives if the price of shelter was dear, or even to promote economic development of a region where times were hard. All of these activities were engaged in by the Catholic church in Quebec.

Second, the church had the power of a master, the charge to educate the faithful. As interpreted by Arès, this too was a power with an extensive scope. The church had the power and obligation to teach any or all truths necessary for men and women to obtain salvation. These truths were not only those that were strictly religious, because the religious was understood to colour all. Hence Christian men and women were to be educated in Christian schools, schools where all subjects, be they history, philosophy, or mathematics, were presented from a Christian point of view. This power was thereby interpreted to mean that the church should have ultimate control over the education system in society. The extensive powers over education held by the church in Quebec were seen to be entirely consistent with this magisterial power.

Third, Arès wrote that the church had a juridical or governing power in the sense that it was the final arbiter over what was good and what was evil in society. Again, therefore, this power was not restricted to spiritual matters. The questions of good and evil cut squarely across the whole plane of social life – politics, labour relations, appropriate recreational activity, literature, the arts, the curriculum in the schools, the content of the news media, and so on. The church in Quebec had reserved for itself the right to intervene in all these areas and did so often, when it perceived a need to decide on what was right and what was wrong.

Fourth, the church was seen to have a special mission of charity. When established institutions were inadequate or normal avenues to change were blocked, resulting in the creation of particularly disadvantaged situations or unwarranted suffering, the church was to provide aid and service to the needy and the sick. On the basis of this mission of charity, the church in Quebec erected institutions for the delivery of social services, ranging from hospitals to orphanages, from mental asylums to welfare agencies. The justification for this mission was once again that unless these services were provided the individuals involved would be incapable of giving proper attention to their spiritual needs.

The extensive intervention into social life that the church practised and that it defended on philosophical grounds pointed by implication to certain forms of social organization and to a restricted role for the state. In order to understand these forms, one must begin with the church's conception of the individual. Catholic intellectuals in Quebec described their philosophy as 'personalist,' that is, it was centred on the individual person. The central goal of human existence was the achievement of salvation for the individual person. This objective is achieved in two ways. The individual seeks and obtains the grace of God which is necessary for salvation, and the individual receives the material and spiritual support from society that he or she needs in this quest. Social institutions are subsidiary to the individual in the sense that they exist to provide the individual person what is needed in order for that person to receive the grace of God. Society is thus not organized to achieve individual material goods, as in the case of liberalism, or collective material goods, as in socialism, but to facilitate the achievement of an individual spiritual good, salvation. Those social organizations that arise to support this individual quest – the family and professional associations in particular – are deemed the most acceptable and the most important.

The organizations particular to a capitalist economy were expected to conform to this personalist principle as well. They thus were to function so as to distribute material goods in such a way that material deprivation could never force an individual off the path to salvation. While the church's thinkers generally supported capitalist organization in principle because it worked on the basis of individual initiative and private property, they were also critical of the materialist orientation it often assumed.[8] Thinkers such as Arès and Marcel Clément saw the system as too much concerned with the promotion of individual material interests, particularly those of capitalists themselves. The consequence of this orientation was the class struggle, as workers strived to obtain a more just material return. The system became diverted from its real purpose and appeared distorted; in reality the interests of workers and capital were the same, and neither class could exist without the other. Following the teachings of Pius XI, Clément and Arès proposed a corporatist reorganization of capitalism in Quebec as a solution to this problem.[9] Professional associations would be set up for each class. These would co-operate, first, in managing the individual enterprise, second, in managing the affairs of their respective industry or economic sector in a 'corporation,' and third, in a 'Chamber of Corporations' that would direct the economic life of the whole society. Through such an organization, it was hoped, the orientation of the economic system to facilitate individual salvation could be achieved. These ideas always remained rather vague, and there were prolonged debates over how such a system might be erected and particularly over how much employees should share in the management of firms with their employers.[10]

The state was part of society, and the principe de subsidiarité was to apply to it as well. It was to act or intervene only to support the individual person in his or her spiritual quest or to ensure that the common good was realized. The common good implied that the interests of all in salvation were at stake. If the economic well-being of families could be maintained only through a common or unified action, the state could intervene. If the prospect loomed that family heads could not earn a just wage, the state had a duty to intervene to right the situation. When the state acted on such matters, it had to be obeyed because its authority came from God: 'C'est Dieu, non le peuple, qui donne aux gouvernants l'autorité qu'ils ont. Le peuple, lui, désigne celui ou ceux en qui l'autorité reposera. Cela fait, le peuple ne peut pas, selon son caprice, sous prétexte qu'il est souverain, désobéir aux lois, ni aux ordres de ceux qui commandent.'[11] It is also clear from the writings on the state that intervention was sanctioned with some reluctance. Strong contrasts were drawn between the supporting activity that was acceptable and the state activity that marked a socialist system. There was deep concern that the state be as absent from social life. as possible and an implicit hope that in a corporatist society the role of the state would be minimized even further.

In concluding this brief discussion of Catholic thought, several points should now be clear. First, at an ideological level, a wide avenue was left open to the church to influence and even control major social institutions. Philosophically, virtually any intervention of the church into temporal affairs could be justified. Second, to be consistent with the spiritualist individualism of the ideology, private institutions, particularly those with ecclesiastical links, were preferable to public institutions. No institution was acceptable if the individual or family could deal with the problems of concern on their own. All institutions and public policies were to support individual initiative and not to displace or render unnecessary such initiative. The definition of a religion-based culture for French Canada coupled with the extensive penetration of the church into social affairs meant that the distinctiveness of French-Canadian culture was rooted in the Catholic religion. Take away that religious influence and one would be taking away much of what was distinctive and integral to that culture.

The Catholic church and French-Canadian culture

The organizations of the church

The extensive role of the church envisioned in the social thought of the period corresponded rather well to the role played by the church in French-Canadian society. The church had a say in a considerable range of activity through a network of organizations over which it had varying degrees of control. It also controlled large areas of the educational system and ran most of the social service institutions that operated in the francophone community. In these institutions, it operated largely free of state interference on the basis of an unwritten concordat with the Duplessis government. In the late 1940s it could still be said that the clergy occupied 'une place de choix, un statut spécial qui est à la fois au dessus et en dehors des autres groupes sociaux.'[12] Among young French Canadians, the clergy enjoyed a 'suprématie incontestée' in terms of prestige, a further indicator of the importance of the church.

The church reached the French-Canadian population through three different kinds of organizations: Catholic social action, Catholic Action, and parishes. The organizations varied in the secularism of their concerns and in the degree to which they were controlled by the clergy. Those in the first group have been described by Abbé Gérard Dion as organizations of 'Catholic social action.'

These organizations were usually founded jointly by clerics and laypersons, were run largely by laypersons, and were mainly dedicated to the pursuit of secular goals. Yet they were to operate on the basis of Catholic social principles and were to be concerned with applying the teachings of the church to their particular concerns. The strongest organizations in this category were the Confédération des travailleurs catholiques du Canada (CTCC)[13] and the Union catholique des cultivateurs (UCC).[14] Other examples were the Association professionnelle des industriels (API), the Corporation générale des instituteurs et institutrices du Quebec (CIC), and many co-operative associations.[15]

The CTCC was founded in 1921 in order to provide a central organization for the growing numbers of Catholic trade unions in the province. These organizations had first taken root in the Chicoutimi area shortly before the First World War and had spread rapidly with the support of the clergy in the ensuing years. The church strongly favoured such indigenous unions over the foreign American unions because it disliked the neutralism and the politics of the latter organizations. The CTCC pledged, in its Declaration of Principles to respect and promote the social doctrine of the church. Most locals had an aumônier or chaplain who was supposed to give advice on such matters but who often in the early days ran the local single handedly. The church was at least brought into contact with some members of the working class through the CTCC. The CTCC organized less of the labour force than the international unions and only a small proportion of the working class was even organized, and so the number of workers being contacted was still quite small. In contrast the UCC, which was founded in 1924, grouped most of French Canada's farmers. It sought simultaneously to educate farmers in the arts of agronomy and to instruct them through cours à domicile in the church's principles of social life. The local curés in rural areas took an interest in and promoted the UCC, but it remained essentially a farmers' organization, with a Catholic orientation.

The second set of organizations was referred to simply as 'Catholic Action' groups. They were usually founded by the clergy, were run primarily by laypersons, and had both secular and spiritual objectives. Unlike the Catholic social action groups, they were formally part of the institutional church and were generally co-ordinated at the diocesan level. Catholic Action groups had been formed with the goal of bringing the church into contact with various economic groups and particularly workers. They were organized along class lines and thus sought to acquaint the church with the economic situation of its members in a more intensive way than was possible in a parish. The most prominent groups of this kind were the Ligue ouvrière catholique (LOC), the Ligue indépendante catholique (middle classes and professionals), the Jeunesse ouvrière catholique (JOC), the Jeunesse agricole catholique (JAC) and the Jeunesse étudiante catholique (JEC).

The activities and fate of the LOC were perhaps typical of the second type of group. On its tenth anniversary in 1949, the LOC listed among others the following accomplishments: creation of vacation camps for workers' families, a family budget service, a housing service, a social circle for women, and courses in household arts.[16] It published a newspaper, *Le Front ouvrier*, between 1944 and 1950, and is chaplains, along with the chaplains of the JOC, published a monthly journal, *L'Action catholique ouvrière*.[17] These activities suggest that the LOC sought to bring the church into closer touch with the problems of the working class. Yet its success was quite limited; it remained a rather small organization. Its membership declined gradually after 1950 as did the numbers of militants in its companion organizations.[18]

The third type of organization, the parish, remained the primary focus of church activity. The parish was a community of believers living in a defined territory of limited size. It was headed by a parish priest or curé who may have had one or more assistant, depending on the size of the community. These priests administered the sacraments, said Mass, and serviced the various spiritual needs of the faithful. The organizational form of the parish in the French-Canadian church had been developed in rural areas. In this setting, the spiritual community defined as the parish coincided with the economic and social community. Economic activity was largely contained within the territory, either on farms or in the village. Social ties also tended to be primarily between local community members and not with those outside. Accordingly, the parish church and its tributary organizations and leagues were at the centre of the community's life. Religious ritual was integrated fully into economic activities and into major social events. The curé often enjoyed a position of considerable power and authority in the community. The clergy was very much of the people, being heavily recruited from rural areas which thereby strengthened further the sense among the people that the church was of them.[19]

This particular organizational form was not carried over to urban industrial settings successfully.[20] In these settings, the spiritual community defined by the parish boundaries no longer coincided with the economic and social communities. The members of the parish often worked outside its boundaries in a variety of factories and offices. They did not interact as a community on the economic plane as they did in the rural areas. Similarly social activity was no longer confined to the parish. Cinemas, dance halls, the races, radio, and television all involved recreational activity beyond the control of the parish priest and were no longer social activities involving only parish members. Even schools in the urban areas need not necessarily draw exclusively from one parish. The parish thus became more exclusively a religious community only. The curé no longer knew his parishioners well and could not monitor their social and economic activities closely. The weakness of the parish unit was gradually forcing the state to assume many traditional parish functions, such as ministering to the needy. Those Catholic Action organizations that might have been expected to strengthen the parish in the face of these difficulties often compounded the problem. They tended to be administered by a central office at the diocesan level, and cells were often organized at the workplace rather than within a parish. Gérard Pelletier drew the following conclusion in 1952: 'La paroisse n'existe plus comme centre de vie, elle n'encadre plus rien qu'une pratique de moins en moins vivante; elle devient un lieu, un territoire et cesse graduellement d'être une communauté.'[21]

In summary, the three types of organizations related to the church were not working effectively to allow it to exercise two of the powers defined by Arès. The church could not follow through upon the power of order because it increasingly lacked contact with important groups whose members thus could not be shown the way to salvation. Similarly, in urban settings, the church had more and more difficulty in exercising a juridical power. It was unable to control such new recreational activities as the cinema and dance halls. It lacked contact with many and hence was unable to persuade and cajole through appeals to spiritual principles. The organizations of Catholic social action tended more and more to be religious in name only and secular in orientation and practice. The Catholic Action movement was ambitious, and its chaplains were most dedicated, but it had little success in bringing the urban proletariat more effectively under the influence of the church. The parish was no longer the strong community it once had been but more and more peripheral to the lives of urban residents, particularly workers. Attendance figures at Mass tended to be lowest in working-class districts.[22] The picture was, however, not quite as dark when it came to the exercise of the magisterial power and to the pursuit of the mission of charity. In the next two sections, Quebec's educational system and social services in the post-war period will be examined.

The educational system

If one asked most intellectuals or politicians or even liberal professionals in French Quebce in the 1940s which institition was the most developed and finest representation of their culture, invariably they would point to their educational system. They would comment upon its religious character, its long history, and its uniqueness in North America. They would describe the exceptional role schools had played in socializing the youth of the nation into the virtues of piety and patriotism. Premier Duplessis summarized this view when he said: 'Nos écoles sont des forteresses, des bastions indispensables, essentiels à la conservation de nos traditions religieuses et nationales auxquelles nous tenons, que nous avons le droit de conserver et que nous entendons conserver.'[23] On what basis were such claims made? How unique was the system of education in French Quebec?

Prior to 1964, the educational system was not unified but was comprised of three quite distinct subsystems – English Protestant, English Catholic, and French Catholic. The English Protestant system was similar to those found elsewhere in English Canada. The English Catholic system occupied a kind of middle ground between the other two, with its roots in the Irish and later the Italian communities.[24] Finally the Catholic system for the French-speaking community was unique in North America, tracing its roots to the first efforts to educate in New France. It was distinguished first by being largely controlled by the Catholic church and not by the provincial government and hence the state. Second, the programs available upon completion of primary school, the first six years, included that of the collèges classiques which formed a route to higher education quite particular in North America to French Canada.

That the church should have assumed a large role in the administration of education in French Quebec should not be surprising in light of our earlier discussion of Catholic social thought. Under the terms of this ideology, the parents of a child had the primary responsibility for his or her education. The church retained as well an exclusive right to give a religious education to all those baptized in the faith. It also reserved the right to control and watch over all educational systems in all aspects that concerned specifically the Christian education of its members. Based on this latter right, the church saw itself as having an indirect right to found and operate schools.[25] The state was to be subsidiary to both the parents and the church. It could protect children by supplementing parental deficiencies such as a lack of wealth or a lack of capacity. The state might define a certain number of conditions for the education system necessary for the temporal common good or even create schools that had a direct link to such a good.[26] Still, it was expected to tread softly and conservatively in taking any such action.

If the first function of the school was to be a religious one, viz contributing to the salvation of the individual, the school was also assigned a second role by the ecclesiastical or political powers. The school was to serve as a means for conserving the national culture and for cultivating patriotism. Patriotism, in the view of leading intellectuals, was a virtue, a form of Christian charity, an expression of piety.[27] Arès, in his study of the national question, writes: 'Le patriotisme est la vertu morale qui nous incline à aimer notre patrie et à lui rendre tous les devoirs que la piété nous prescrit envers tous ceux qu'à un titre quelconque nous tenons pour auteurs de notre existence.'[28] Because such a love for the *patrie* involved not only those who surrounded the individual, but also those who had preceded him or her in the past, the study of history was mandatory in the quest for this virtue. In the view of many, the need to preserve the national culture could best be satisfied by having a school system dedicated to forming a true élite whose members were aware of national problems and were dedicated to public service.[29]

In a fashion, the educational system for the French Canadians of Quebec followed both these religious and national principles. Beginning in 1875, the direction of education in the province had been vested in a body called the Conseil de l'instruction publique. This council, in turn, was divided into two confessional committees, the Catholic Committee and the Protestant Committee. These operated independently of each other and directed the educational systems. The Catholic Committee was composed of all the bishops in Quebec and an equal number of laypersons appointed by the Lieutenant-Governor-in-Council after consultation with the bishops. It had responsibility for drawing up all regulations, defining programs of study, publishing guidelines for the selection of textbooks, elaborating regulations for the training of teachers, administering normal schools, and setting official examinations.[30] There was no minister of education as was found in other provinces, but a superintendent of public instruction who was in charge of administering the decisions of the respective committees. The Catholic Committee remained very much under the bishops' control and included only rarely a teacher among its members.[31]

The range of instruction controlled by the bishops through the Catholic Committee was extensive. First, the committee administered primary school, which covered six grades. All pupils were initially under its jurisdiction. Upon completion of the primary grades, four options were available in theory to the pupils: entering the labour force, a classical college, an école primaire supérieure, or a vocational school. First, they could terminate their formal education if they had reached a specified minimum age.[32] Second, they could go on to attend a classical college. The classical college had been an important institution of learning in Quebec since before the conquest. Its eight-year program traced its roots to the classical education given by similar institutions in pre-revolutionary France.[33] At the end of the eight years, successful students were awarded a baccalauréat ès arts, a degree that marked a level of education somewhere between senior matriculation and a bachelor of arts in English-Canadian universities. True to its name, the curriculum of the colleges emphasized the classics and included the study of Latin and Greek as well as ancient history. Students were also instructed in French, the history of Canada and Quebec, geography, and mathematics. Relatively little attention was paid to the natural sciences until 1949, when Université Laval created a new philosophy-science program.[34]

The colleges were private institutions requiring the payment of tuition fees. They tended to draw disproportionately highly from the children of administrators and professionals. In 1954, nearly half (46.5 per cent) of the boys in the classical colleges had fathers in this group.[35] Similarly, they catered mainly to a male population, with the first college for girls being founded only in 1908. In general, they were founded and run by priests, although in later years more and more lay teachers were hired. Only two were founded by laypersons, and both of these arose after 1945. The primary function of the colleges, in the eyes of their founders, was preparation for the priesthood. The main exceptions to this pattern were several colleges, such as Jean-de-Brébeuf in Montreal, which were founded by the Jesuits to educate the ruling élite of the community.[36] The combination of clerical leadership, and emphasis on the classics, the cultivation of religion, the importance given to history and culture, and the sense of community that arose from being part of a historical tradition came together to form an educational institution unique in Canada. The classical colleges were very much a component of French-Canadian culture and were looked upon with pride by the élite of the nation.

Until the beginning of the twentieth century, these two options after elementary school – entering the labour force or attending a classical college – were the only ones available. Shortly after the First World War, the Commission d'écoles catholiques de Montréal (CECM) responded to increasing demands and began to open a new system of schools called écoles primaires supérieures, which became the third option. These schools were public, with no tuition fees required (unlike the colleges), and were designed to provide a more advanced education for young people entering the labour force. The Catholic Committee recognized these schools officially and reluctantly in 1929. The reluctance can be interpreted as recognition that a new institution of a different sort was being created in order to compensate for inadequacies of the old system. After the Second World War, demands that these schools offer their students the option of taking the classical colleges' program increased rapidly. The issue gave rise to immense conflict within the church. The écoles primaires supérieures for example, were often administered by brothers. Under their own constitution, brothers were forbidden to teach Latin (a sacerdotal privilege) and thus to give the classical course. The colleges themselves fought vehemently against such a change. They argued that public schools would never promote the traditional values of French Canada in the manner of the colleges. They feared that the colleges would lose students and financial support. The strain on the college system would threaten the existence of a vital foyer culturel of the community.[37] The efforts by the colleges failed, and in 1955 public schools were finally given permission to offer the classical program.

The importance of this struggle can be understood only if the relationship between the classical colleges and the two principal universities of French Canada – the Université de Montréal and Université Laval – is understood. Like the colleges, these universities were private and controlled by the church. The chancellor was invariably the local archbishop and the rector a cleric. All classical colleges were affiliated directly to one of these two universities through an institution called the Faculté des arts (which is to be distinguished from a Faculté des lettres or an arts faculty in English-Canadian universities). The colleges were subject to the universities particularly on matters of curriculum. In addition, admission to the prestigious faculties of medicine and law was restricted by the universities to college graduates. As late as 1953, 100 per cent of law students, 100 per cent of dental students, and 99.9 per cent of medical students at the universities had graduated from a college.[38] The struggle to introduce the classical program into the public sector was thus also a struggle to open up access to the traditional élite professions of French Canada.

Until this time, the écoles primaires supérieures could hope only to have their graduates enrol at university in the commerce and science faculties, which were rather poorly developed. In 1952–3, 74 per cent of the students enrolled at the École polytechnique and 56 per cent of those at the École des hautes études commerciales did not have a baccalauréat ès arts.[39] The clergy viewed them with some suspicion, fearing that they would siphon off potential clerics. The success of the écoles in the commerce and science faculties must not be given undue weight, however. The colleges remained to the end the pride of the political and ecclesiastical leaders; they enjoyed a privileged relationship with the universities. The écoles remained, in the apt words of Frère Untel, an 'afterthought.'[40]

From the early twentieth century on, a fourth option for young people leaving elementary school was gradually developed, also as a result of inadequacies in the established system. Various departments of the provincial government began to set up vocational schools in order to train a more skilled labour force. The Department of Labour created apprenticeship centres; the Department of Agriculture, a dairy school and middle-level agricultural schools; the Hunting and Fishing Department, fishery schools; and Lands and Forests, forestry schools and schools to train wardens. A veritable panoply of schools enjoying state support appeared – for example, in furniture making, textiles, and electrical work. In addition, beginning in 1923 with the écoles primaires supérieures particularly, schools began to be divided into sections – industrial, commercial, agricultural, and home-making. Over the years, students graduating from these secondary-level schools were presented with the opportunity to attend a wider number of advanced technical schools or 'institutes' corresponding to each of these four fields. These technical institutes were also public but in the hands of the state, not the church. The latter institution paid relatively scant attention to this evolving system of technical education growing under the wings of the state. It saw the new state-run institutions as being necessary for the temporal common good and accepted that they could be run only by laypersons.

I have argued that the Catholic church in Quebec had difficulty in keeping the predominantly urban proletariat in the flock. Its social ideology had not anticipated its growth and hence was developed only as a reaction to other ideologies. Its institutions, particularly suited to the small-commodity production of the nineteenth century, had difficulty accommodating the new classes spawned by the capitalist mode of production in the twentieth century. What is more, the system of education, which had been developed to encourage professional vocations or to return boys to the farm at the age of puberty, had little room for the growing working class. As this class became more settled in urban areas it demanded, through its leaders, greater access to wealth and position.

Operating within its existing structures, the church sought to expand the number of classical colleges, the prescribed route to such wealth and position. From 1635 to 1939, 68 colleges had been founded in Quebec; from 1940 to 1965, 135 new institutions were created.[41] This perhaps valiant attempt to incorporate the new within the old was unlikely to succeed. With each new college that opened, the church spread its priests out more thinly at a time when vocations were beginning to fall. In 1951, only 8.8 per cent of the teachers in the colleges were laypersons. A decade later 35.1 per cent of the teaching staff were lay.[42] The entry of each layperson into the system weakened the church's control and hence its capacity to maintain the cultural tradition of the college. What is also evident, however, is that the scramble to open up new institutions did not keep up with the demand. Classical sections began to be set up in new public secondary schools, the status given to the écoles primaires supérieures after 1956.

More and more persons eluded the church's grasp completely after elementary school by entering vocational and technical schools wholly controlled by the state. These schools were guided in their programs not by the prevailing ideology and religious culture but by the dictates of the labour market. Such dictates were the same in French Canada as in other capitalist economies. At the end of the Second World War, Quebec still possessed a unique educational system derived from or related to its special religious-based culture. But it was clearly reaching a crisis: it was increasingly being supplemented by another system that was expanding in size and founded on different principles. The future of the traditional system, in short, was becoming increasingly uncertain.

The social welfare system

The system of social welfare that had developed in Quebec's French community was also an object of pride and a hallmark of the traditional culture. Like the system of education, it traced its roots to New France and was largely inspired by Catholic philosophy. It too was mainly administered through the offices of the church.

Ideally, in a society that was true to Catholic principles, there would be only a minimal need for social assistance. Workers would receive a just wage and producers a just price, enabling them to have a family, to feed and clothe that family, to provide dignified housing, to procure sufficient education for the young, and to compensate for sickness and old age.[43] The family would be the source of assistance to its own aged, infirm, and handicapped. Such an ideal state does not often occur, and society is usually called upon to aid in the care of those in need, whether they be physically or mentally handicapped, orphans, or paupers. In such instances, the local communities, particularly the parishes, are asked to come to the aid of these individuals. The initiative is to be mainly private, based on the practice of the virtue of charity. The state is assigned what is now a familiar role. It seeks to encourage and support where necessary private initiatives to provide social security. In the words of Pius XII, 'La mission de l'État est de contrôler, aider et régler les activités privées et individuelles pour les faire converger harmonieusement au bien commun.'[44] The state must take care not to substitute its own actions for such initiatives.

In 1945 Quebec's French community still possessed a system of social assistance inspired by that of seventeenth-century France.[45] The latter had · emphasized the natural solidarity of the family and the parish. Where these groups could no longer handle problems, general institutions of social assistance were set up, using donations from the wealthy who wished to practice the Christian virtue of charity. Institutions such as the Hôtel Dieu in Montreal were originally created under these circumstances. The re-establishment of the civil code in 1774 permitted the continuation of this system after the conquest. During the nineteenth century more and more institutions were founded on the diocesan level as the problems became too large for the parish. The French influence was continued with the introduction of the Saint-Vincent-de-Paul societies, which quickly came to play an important role in the province. The various institutions – hospitals, orphanages, and homes for the aged or invalids – were all run privately, usually by religious orders and with only irregular support from the state.

Similar to the situation in education, however, the rapid growth in the urban working class between 1891 and 1930 and the concomitant weakening of the family structure increased the need for institutional assistance. In 1921, the provincial government created a statutory basis for the funding of various institutions of social welfare. While they remained in private hands, they now could count on regular state funding to support their activity. The church remained the dominant force in the system. Hospitals were still run mainly by religious orders. Agencies for other social services were organized by the diocese and usually included institutions that ministered to needy children, orphans, and the physically and mentally handicapped. Crèches, maternity hospitals, and assistance to illegitimate children were also in private, ecclesiastical hands.

The capacity of the church to continue to administer social assistance declined as the urban proletariat grew. The province began to enter the field more actively: it set up professional agencies of social workers in 1929, increased its support to municipalities, which assumed responsibility for hygiene, contagious diseases, and the like, and created the Department of Welfare in 1946 to oversee its growing involvement. By war's end the traditional institutions remained largely in place but other, more public facilities were beginning to arise. It was uncertain whether the two systems could co-exist or whether one would absorb the other.

Conclusion

The division in French-Canadian society that existed on the economic plane, described in chapter 1, was reinforced in part by divisions or cracks on the cultural plane. French-Canadian culture had traditionally drawn its inspiration from the Catholic religion. It had developed institutions for a society where religion could be fully integrated into economic and social life. With the continued development of the capitalist mode of production, new social groups were created. Their members lived in communities not easily within the reach of the church's institutions and worked in jobs which the church had difficulty integrating into its life of ritual. Wage labour by definition was not as free to bring the church into the factory as the farmer was to bring it into his fields.

In order to satisfy both the needs of labour for skills and the needs of capital for skilled labour, new educational institutions, public secondary and technical, were created under the auspices of the state. They were not controlled by the church or inspired by it. They were apparently part of a new, materialist culture. Similar developments took place in the delivery of social services. New institutions of a public rather than a religious kind were developed to serve the needs of an urban society. Accordingly, the economic groups growing in the more advanced capitalist sector of the economy were least likely to view traditional French-Canadian culture as something that had to be preserved. For them, it was already becoming a hindrance and hence something to be rejected. Understanding this point is critical to understanding the character of the Quiet Revolution.

It should also be noted that the traditional cultural practices of French-Canadian society were complementary to its economic underdevelopment. First, the social ideology described in this chapter does not necessarily lead to a critique of the capitalist state, particularly the non-interventionist capitalist state. The ideology defines a facilitative or supplementary role for the state, a role that was consistent with the laissez-faire approach of the Duplessis government. Both the church and Duplessis saw a move to create a more interventionist state as a move toward socialism. Hence the policy of Duplessis, which favoured a kind of buccaneer resource capitalism unfettered by state regulation, was one that the church found acceptable on principle. However, this ideological commitment carried with it the seeds of crisis. As the capitalist mode of production became more centralized and concentrated in the province, it was likely to generate increased state intervention and a more rationalized system of social welfare. If there was to be an increased demand for education and for social services, the church would need to expand its own personnel or to increase lay involvement in its institutions. The former seemed scarcely likely, because the church had little success in recruiting from the working class and its traditional areas of recruitment – farmers and independent professionals – were declining in number; the latter promised an ever-weakening hold on these institutions for the church.

Aside, however, from the shared view on the role of the state found among ecclesiastics and politicians, the educational system facilitated underdevelopment. Its goal was to educate an élite that would hardly be in a position to or wish to challenge the economic order. It was designed to produce traditional professionals, priests, and perhaps politicians. Little status was given to training in economics, management, engineering, or the sciences. Further, the whole emphasis in the colleges on the classics, on religion, and on intellectual and spiritual matters fostered an antipathy toward the material and corrupting world of business. The educational system was not likely to orient its graduates toward challenging directly the economically subordinate position held by French Canadians.

Within itself the educational system carried additional seeds of crisis. As the working class grew and as it continued to be only weakly affected by the church's institutions, it demanded additional education of a kind that the church was unwilling and probably unable to provide. Similarly, as capitalism entered a more and more advanced phase, employers began to demand labour with more skills and more training. Questions about why French Canadians should remain economically subordinate in their own land had always been present and were bound to redound eventually on the educational system. The state in setting up its technical institutes and its vocational schools was responding somewhat to these demands. As its efforts became more intense, it created a more and more elaborate series of institutions and thus assumed more of the role traditionally reserved for the church.

The efforts of the church to establish its own system of institutions did, however, produce a coterie of organizations indigenous to Quebec and relatively autonomous from similar institutions operating elsewhere on the continent. The suspicion cultivated in these institutions toward the institutional imperialism of these others further cemented this independence. The more these institutions – the CTCC, the UCC, and the teachers' corporation – followed a separate path of development, the more likely they were to become staging points for a critique of underdevelopment. It was uncertain in the early 1950s, however, what would happen to these organizations once the church receded in influence. Would they gradually be integrated into North American networks or would they find sufficient resources to build a new and separate path?

In addition, Catholic social philosophy, with its emphasis on individual responsibility and localized communal solutions to problems, provided some values that could be of use in any struggle against underdevelopment. French Canadians were accustomed to building institutions communally from the base up and were oriented in a direction from which a more autocentric economy might be built. They had erected an impressive series of financial institutions – the caisses populaires of the Mouvement Desjardins for example – which gave them an independent, albeit small, economic basis for future growth. The emphasis on communal activity which was part of the traditional culture is surely a basic prerequisite for autocentric economic development.

In the early 1950s the 'writing on the wall' was beginning to appear for the church's ideology and its organization of French Canadian social life, but it was not indelible. The defenders were to seize upon the Tremblay Commission in the mid-1950s as a means of elaborating a strategy to ensure their continuance. The political suggestions that emerged from this study were to colour political behaviour for the next two decades and to hide partially the continued decline of the traditional culture. Having seen what preserving the traditional culture entailed, we shall now examine the political means proposed to achieve that goal.

3

The Tremblay Commission and the defence of French-Canadian culture

In the 1950s, many intellectuals in Quebec, both inside and outside religious life, came to realize that the systems for educating French Canadians and for meeting basic social and health needs were in a state of crisis. It was increasingly unclear whether they could survive as they were. Such realizations raised questions of the highest order because the institutions under fire were considered to be some of the most splendid examples of French-Canadian culture and to be integral to its transmission. The developing crisis could be traced to a growing contradiction between the structure of an economy being increasingly harnessed to serve the needs of American capitalism and cultural institutions and practices that had developed to complement a more rural economy based on independent commodity production. This crisis was also beginning to strike hard at the French-Canadian nationality in Quebec; it had implications even wider than those for education and social services.

With Quebec's economy becoming more and more integrated into the continental economy, with the increasing pre-eminence of large corporations that dominated and shaped continental markets, there came pressure for homogenization of social conditions and social relations in the societies tied to these markets. If the needs of consumers could become more similar, if the commodities produced could satisfy larger and larger populations, if educational systems everywhere could be relied upon to graduate competent men and women, if the hospitals and social services could be comfortably used by anyone from anywhere in the continent, productivity and efficiency could be enhanced and profits increased. Quebec's francophone community was more and more party to these markets; advertisers sought to convince its people that their needs were like those of other North Americans; the same goods were marketed in Quebec as elsewhere; workers there were feeling a need to demand more education, particularly of a technical nature; and health care specialists felt pressures to meet continental norms and standards. The questions being raised about the educational and social systems were indicative of a larger series of questions that implied that the traditional culture might be breaking down.

Matters might have been simpler if it had been up to the government of Quebec alone to respond to these pressures, but this, of course, was not the case. Quebec was a province of Canada, and the central government was conscious as well of pressures being placed on Canadian culture as a result of American economic expansion. Whether the growing concern of the federal government over the fate of Canadian culture reflected a need to legitimate the dominating presence of American capital in Canada or was a genuine attempt to stem the Americanization of culture in Canada is not the issue here. From the point of view of much of Quebec's élite, the possibility of positive intervention by the federal government into cultural domains was cause for considerable alarm. In their perspective, any intervention by the federal government would by definition be an intervention inspired by the culture and values of English Canada and thus a threat to the survival of French Canada.

Accordingly, the appointment of the Royal Commission on National Development in the Arts, Letters and Sciences (Massey Commission) in 1949 was greeted with considerable anxiety. A commission that was to investigate Canadian culture in light of the following goals could potentially attack the heart of the cultural institutions of French Canada: 'That it is desirable that the Canadian people should know as much as possible about their country, its history and traditions; and about their national life and common achievements. That it is in the national interest to give encouragement to institutions which express national feeling, promote common understanding and add to the variety and richness of Canadian life, rural as well as urban.'[1] This action was viewed with suspicion even more because the commission also had the charge to investigate the advisability of federal support for university education. For French Canadians, federal involvement here was not only unconstitutional, but also was likely to put additional pressure on their educational system to change its structures and curricula in order to be more compatible with English-Canadian educational practice.

If these direct challenges to the persistence of a unique French-Canadian culture were not enough, the government of Quebec also found itself in the midst of a dispute that raised fundamental questions about the degree of autonomy it had for acting to protect the interests of the French-Canadian nationality. Toward the end of the Great Depression and during the Second World War, taking its inspiration from the theories of John Maynard Keynes, the federal government had moved to centralize fiscal and monetary powers. Provinces entered into tax rental agreements with the federal government whereby they yielded their power to tax in return for grants from the federal government. Throughout this period, the federal government increased its use of direct taxation, the primary mode of taxation left to the provinces under the terms of the British North America (BNA) Act, aside from natural-resource royalties and sales taxes. In times of emergency such as war, even the government of Quebec had been willing to yield some of its normal taxation powers. Such concessions were seen as temporary, because they were an aberration of federalism as Quebec's ruling élites saw it. Canada, in their view, was a compact of provinces, each sovereign in its own domain and having agreed to grant certain powers to a central government. Sovereignty meant further that each provincial government should have access to the financial resources it needed to tend to its jurisdiction. The provincial governments should not in any way be dependent financially on the federal government.

After the end of the Second World War, the federal government pushed to continue the system of tax rental agreements. Such a policy meant for Quebec the continuation of its loss of control over direct taxation, a method of taxation that could vary in its incidence, depending on cultural practices. It meant a continued dependence on a federal government which was viewed as foreign and biased toward English Canada. It certainly meant a loss in sovereignty for a government that had traditionally defended its autonomy with considerable intensity. It was, in short, another in the series of challenges perceived by French-Canadian élites to their capacity to maintain their culture.

These perceived obstacles to the continued épanouissement of French-Canadian civilization – the growing weakness of traditional institutions, the increased involvement of the federal government in cultural policy, the desire of the federal government for increased fiscal powers – were all fused into a single series of events in the early 1950s. The confrontation that ensued between Ottawa and Quebec was to lead finally to a solution, albeit temporary, of several of these problems.

Even more important for our purposes here, the struggle led to the creation by the government of Quebec of the Royal Commission of Inquiry into Constitutional Problems (the Tremblay Commission.) Drawing upon the intellectual resources of Quebec's traditional and nationalist élite, it analysed systematically the challenges to Quebec posed by American capitalism, by federal intervention into cultural policy and education, and by federal desires for more fiscal powers. In a well-argued presentation, it sketched out a series of proposals designed to ensure that French-Canadian civilization could survive and flourish. The suggested political program served as a guide for Quebec's political leaders for the next twenty years. The socio-cultural proposals languished, soon to be labelled retrograde. That the latter could be dropped and the former retained is a crucial point for explaining the relative successes and failures of the independence movement in subsequent years. The rejection of the commission's social, cultural, and economic recommendations will be seen to be a clear indicator of the character of the changes that overtook Quebec in the years following the report of the Tremblay Commission.

This chapter will begin by examining the crisis that led to the creation of the commission. Next, the commission, its charge, and its composition will be presented, and its report will be studied in order to outline the political program it proposed. Once outlined, this program will be used as a point of reference for the study of events related to Quebec's dependency in the post-war period, a study that will begin in part II of the book.

Development of the crisis

The Massey Commission was formed at a time when political leaders and other élites in Canada conveyed in their speeches and writings a sense of optimism. Canada had emerged from the Second World War with a solid international reputation and an image of strength. There was a sense that the country would continue to grow in political stature and that its economy would expand to new heights. It was felt that the country was beginning to establish its own traditions, its own cultural institutions, and its own networks of communication. Authors, musicians, artists, actors, publishers, and others were beginning to assume a greater place in the nation's life and to have a larger influence on their countrymen. The time had come for a pause to reflect on these matters.

The commissioners saw the juncture as critical: 'The innumerable institutions, movements and individuals interested in the arts, letters and sciences throughout our country are now forming the national tradition of the future. Through all the complexities and diversities of race, religion, language and geography, the forces which have made Canada a nation and which alone can keep her one are being shaped.'[2] The Liberal government in Ottawa chose Vincent Massey, son of one of Ontario's great industrial families and chancellor of the University of Toronto, to head the commission. Joining him were four people of different but solidly intellectual backgrounds: Arthur Surveyor, a civil engineer from Montreal; Norman A.M. MacKenzie, scientist and president of the University of British Columbia; Père Georges-Henri Lévesque, founder and dean of the influential Faculty of Social Sciences at Université Laval; and Hilda Neatby, a historian from the University of Saskatchewan.

The intellectual orientation of the commission, however, did not dispel the fears of many in Quebec over federal intervention into the sphere of culture. Many nationalists supported Duplessis, who pronounced the commission an unwarranted intrusion into areas of provincial jurisdiction and called for a boycott of its proceedings. Experience had taught the traditional élites in Quebec that the federal government in Ottawa was not binational but staffed and controlled by English Canadians. Accordingly, federal government expansionism posed little danger of a cultural kind to English Canadians, in the view of French Canadians. The Chambre de Commerce du District de Montréal (CCM) articulated this traditional perception in its brief to the Massey Commission. Speaking of English Canadians, it wrote: 'Ils risquent en somme peu de choses, car, formant la majorité dans l'ensemble du pays, ils ont la certitude que toute intervention du gouvernement fédéral dans leur vie nationale s'inspirerait de leur conception à eux et irait par le fait même dans le sens de la consolidation et de l'épanouissement de leur culture.'[3] This view of the federal government had been central to the writings of Groulx and the Action française and had led nationalists to preach a falling back on a strengthened provincial government in order to counter the federal presence.

The commission completed its work in 1951 and submitted a report consistent with both the expectations of intellectual excellence and the fears for federal intrusion. The influential and usually nationalist Jesuit journal *Relations* in an editorial lauded the commission on three counts.[4] It praised the high intellectual and moral value of its report, its emphasis on things of the spirit. It noted with satisfaction its sympathetic attitude toward French Canada – its respect for bilingualism, its openness to French-Canadian intellectual values, its call for a second French broadcasting network in Canada, and its espousal of a French radio station to serve the Maritime provinces. And it welcomed the commission's frank and open Canadian nationalism.

The same editorial, however, singled out several troubling aspects of the report. In particular, it worried about what it called l'étatisme culturel, the tendency of the commission to promote more and stronger national cultural institutions – the Canadian Broadcasting Corporation, the National Film Board, a National Library, and national museums and galleries. The recommendations that the federal government centralize all its cultural activities and create a granting council to promote the arts, letters, and sciences were also noted with concern. In short, the report raised the prospect of the imposition of cultural institutions and practices from above by a government taking its inspiration from a community whose values differed from those of French Canada. The opposition subsequently expressed in Quebec to the creation of the Canada Council, the establishment of the National Library of Canada, and to the centralization of cultural affairs in the 1960s under the secretary of state may be traced back to this view of the Massey Commission.

These points of concern about the Massey Report would probably not have created a political crisis in Quebec. However, joined to these recommendations was another suggesting federal involvement in the funding of higher education in Canada. If acted upon, such a recommendation would result in a serious blow to one of the institutional pillars of French-Canadian civilization and would represent a rejection of the spirit that lay behind the division of powers contained in the BNA Act. The commission, however, saw matters somewhat differently.

The end of the Second World War brought a period of rapid growth to Canadian universities. Large numbers of returning veterans took advantage of government programs enabling them to obtain a university education. The depressed economy that had existed before the war had been conquered, and post-war prosperity gave further impetus to the growth of the universities. The federal government sought to aid the universities in their attempts to absorb the new students by setting up grants that gave the institutions $150 for each veteran registered. A survey of major Canadian universities showed that such grants constituted on the average between 10 and 15 per cent of the universities' income by 1949.[5] These grants were supposed to end in 1951. However, with provincial governments unwilling or unable to maintain certain levels of support, the universities, all of which had added new programs and expanded their physical plants since the war, found themselves faced with the unhappy prospect of raising student tuition to very high levels in order to avoid a serious financial crisis.

The question was accordingly raised by several universities whether the federal government might ease the situation somewhat by prolonging its aid to the universities. Such a policy, however, was acknowledged as problematic because section 93 of the BNA Act defined education to be under the exclusive domain of the provinces. Within Quebec, the prospect of the extension of the grants was even more alarming because it would mean federal intervention into a sphere of society that was jealously guarded as a jewel of French-Canadian culture. It would raise questions particularly about the status of the classical colleges and, if implemented, might force these institutions to conform more to the English-Canadian model of higher education.

Briefed by all sides on this issue, the Massey Commission sought to pick a path through this minefield. It began by defining education broadly to be the 'progressive development of the individual in all his faculties, physical and intellectual, aesthetic and moral.'[6] It noted two means for achieving this goal: 'formal education in schools and universities and general non-academic education through books, periodicals, radio, films, museums, art galleries, lectures and study groups.'[7] The constitution, it was argued, had given the provinces responsibility for the former means in particular. The commission also suggested that education was primarily a personal responsibility. Further, any group could presumably help the individual to assume that responsibility. There was no general prohibition in Canadian law that said that only the provinces could furnish assistance. What is more, in the commission's view, the federal government had a responsibility to promote particularly the general education of all Canadians: 'If the Federal Government is to renounce its right to associate itself with other social groups, public and private, in the general education of Canadian citizens, it denies its intellectual and moral purpose, the complete conception of the common good is lost, and Canada, as such, becomes a materialistic entity.'[8]

The commissioners argued for universities having a function beyond formal education, that of providing more general education and of supporting the arts,[9] and thus of being much more than provincial institutions. They noted that in the areas of Canada outside Ontario and Quebec, universities were local patrons of the arts and also served remote communities through extension programs. The universities played important parts on the national stage as well – many had developed special areas of study that drew students from all provinces and from other countries. Many served as a preparatory ground for careers in the public service and the armed forces. Finally, universities in Canada were the primary centres for scientific research, thus contributing to the strength of the national economy. In light of these functions, which made universities institutions of national importance and dispensers of general education, and in light of the financial difficulties they were facing, the commissioners concluded that the federal government had a responsibility to fulfil. They recommended that the federal government provide annual contributions to support the work of the universities. The Liberal government acted expeditiously on the commission's request, putting a plan of aid into effect in the summer of that year.

Reaction in Quebec was mainly negative.[10] The traditional intelligentsia was particularly vehement. Representative journals such as *Relations* and *L'Action nationale* argued that the BNA Act made no distinction between formal and general education. All aspects of education were to be covered, accordingly, by section 93 and thus controlled by the provinces. Richard Arès recalled the position of Catholic philosophy.[11] A Christian society should seek to avoid state involvement and instead promote measures that would ensure universities could be self-supporting and self-financing. He argued that although the federal government may see itself having a responsibility for university education, it had a prior responsibility to respect the legal order; and the legal order, of course, gave the provinces responsibility for education. The Montreal Chambre de Commerce sent a brief to the federal cabinet and to the provincial premier. It asked Duplessis to accept the federal government's aid for one year only and to press it to change its course. The chamber justified its reluctance to support the federal policy in the classical fashion: 'Accepter l'aide fédérale à nos universités, c'est accepter de céder ce droit de diriger nos institutions de culture et d'enseignement, c'est un refus d'accepter de prendre nos responsabilités et à la fois c'est de se mettre à la merci d'autorité fédérale qui, à date, est loin de s'être manifeste impartiale et juste envers l'élément canadien-français.'[12]

The federal government did not change its policy. After a year, following the advice of the CCM, Duplessis forbade Quebec's universities to collect the federal funds. Such a decision, however, was hardly welcomed by the province's universities, which needed additional financial support. Within a year, Duplessis moved to satisfy this need. His means, however, were not the usual. They were devised to bring funds to the universities but also to precipitate a crisis in another sphere of federal-provincial relations, taxation.

Early in 1954, Duplessis levied a tax on the personal incomes of residents of Quebec that amounted to 15 per cent of the federal tax on personal incomes. Anyone examining the Canadian constitution and its allotment of taxing powers from afar would hardly raise an eyebrow at such a measure. Yet in the context of post-war Canadian federalism, Duplessis's legislation was seen to be radical.

The tax and the justification behind it represented a view of federalism rather opposed to the view popular in Ottawa and had been pressed on Duplessis by an interesting coalition of the French-Canadian small business class and the traditional conservative intelligentsia.

The meeting ground for this coalition was the Chambre de Commerce du District de Montréal. In the period following the depression, there had been increased interaction between faculty at the École des hautes études commerciales (HEC) and the Montreal chamber. In particular, economists Esdras Minville and François-Albert Angers, who were on the faculty of the HEC, became involved in the activities of the chamber. Minville and Angers were both strong nationalists and close supporters of Abbé Lionel Groulx. Both as well had ties to the church hierarchy. Minville served on the prestigious commission générale of the semaines sociales during this period.[13] Minville was elected president of the CCM in 1947, which signalled his and Angers's influence on the chamber.

In April 1947, the CCM sent a brief to the federal government devoted to an analysis of the crisis in federal-provincial relations on fiscal matters referred to in the introduction to this chapter. The chamber reiterated the basic principle that the federal government and the provinces were sovereign in their respective areas of jurisdiction. Each government had to have access to the taxing powers it needed to fulfil its responsibilities. The chamber was strongly opposed to continuation of the wartime practice whereby provinces entered into tax rental agreements with the federal government to facilitate the latter's pursuit of Keynesian policy. Yet it endorsed the principle of equalization as central to any federal system.

In 1947, both Ontario and Quebec refused to enter into tax rental agreements for reasons similar to those articulated by the chamber.[14] Positions on both sides remained relatively firm in the ensuing five years. Angers, always the radical, began to push for recognizing that the provinces have primary initiative in direct-taxation.[15] The CCM carried its lobbying effort to the provincial body, the Chambre de Commerce de la Province de Québec (CCPQ). In a letter to Prime Minister Louis St-Laurent in June 1951 it floated the idea that the provinces be able to deduct provincial income taxes from the federal tax. Such a policy would have involved a change to article 32 of the federal tax law, which allowed individuals to deduct provincial taxes only to a level of 5 per cent of the federal tax. By 1952, the CCM had met with success in its approaches to the provincial chamber. The CCPQ issued an official opinion identical to the position of the CCM and later accepted the idea of Angers that the provinces have primacy in direct taxation.

Duplessis held firm and refused to enter into a tax rental agreement with the federal government in 1952. Ontario changed its mind after being offered a new arrangement and signed. Quebec thus found itself isolated on a matter that its leaders felt was essential to the working of Canadian federalism and indeed it often has been. The mood was sombre. Angers wrote in *L'Action nationale:* 'L'heure est grave, car comme aux années 1837 et 1838, c'est l'Union qui se prépare dans le même esprit que Lord Durham a cristallisé dans son rapport: britanniser le Canada par l'anglicisation des Canadiens-français, par la destruction de leurs institutions, de leur langue et de leur foi.'[16] The CCPQ, which was meeting at the time, sent a delegation of 600 persons to see Duplessis. It called upon the premier to set up a royal commission to inquire into the organization and functioning of the fiscal system as it affected the provincial government, the municipalities, and the school boards fulfilling their functions. They asked that the commission consider how the financial and fiscal system of the province fit into that of the whole country.[17] Duplessis was reluctant but later changed his mind, and the Royal Commission of Inquiry on Constitutional Problems (Tremblay Commission) was born in February 1953.[18] It began its hearings in November, and all the while the fiscal crisis continued. Further, the universities in their briefs to the commission made strong pleas for additional support, especially in light of their inability to collect federal grants. Under strong pressure from the commissioners, early in 1954 Duplessis levied a personal income tax equal to 15 per cent of the federal tax.[19] This went beyond 5 per cent of the federal tax, the amount deductible under the agreements, and meant double taxation for Québécois. The monies collected through the new tax were to be given to the universities in lieu of the federal grants. Duplessis and the chambers immediately began a campaign for full deductibility of the tax. The problem was eventually to be resolved in an innovative way with the development of the tax abatement system, a topic to which we shall return in part II. At this point, however, I shall pause to examine the thinking on Canada and its régime that was precipitated and that shaped political action for years to come.

The Tremblay Commission

Its purpose and members

The act creating the commission was assented to on 12 February 1953.[20] In a long preamble, it set out the framework within which the commission was to act. It began by reiterating Henri Bourassa's notion of a cultural compact, that is, the idea that Confederation was a 'pact of honour' between the 'two great races' which founded it, the French and the English. This notion, the predecessor of such concepts as biculturalism, duality, and d'égal à égal, will be central to the commission's report.[21] The commissioners will identify the French community with the government of Quebec and the English community with that of the federal government, an ideological position that will be shown to have awesome political consequences. The preamble noted that the rights and responsibilities of the government of Quebec could not be exercised and discharged without its having the fiscal resources it needed to preserve its 'financial independence.' Arguing that the encroachments of the federal government had made the exercise of those rights and the discharge of those responsibilities more and more difficult, the commission was asked to investigate the distribution of taxes among the three levels of government, the invasion of the federal government into other governments' tax fields, and the consequences of such an invasion.

Existing evidence suggests that Duplessis had expected the commission to conclude its investigation quickly and to supply him with a brief report that could be used in his war with the St-Laurent government.[22] He believed that the question of the division of powers as they pertained to taxation was a narrow, well-circumscribed topic that could be studied in a short time. The commission, somewhat to his puzzlement and disappointment, saw things much differently. Its members saw the issue of fiscal responsibility and federal encroachment to be at the heart of the Canadian system of government and hence requiring extensive research and analysis. The commissioners were sworn in on 2 March 1953 and immediately began mapping out the plans for their investigation. They were to draw upon their own considerable expertise and a large program of research in producing their report. In November 1953, they also began an ambitious schedule of public hearings, holding 97 sessions between then and 23 June 1954 and receiving 217 briefs. Their final report had four volumes, with the third being composed of two book-length parts.[23] They attached to the report eleven research appendices which it had drawn upon in many parts of the final report.

The commissioners were drawn from the coalition of traditional middle-class intelligentsia and the French-Canadian small business class. For members of the former group, the commission was an opportunity to reflect systematically on the means of preserving the culture and way of life they cherished and saw slipping away. For members of the latter, it was an additional vehicle in its struggle to ensure a strong government in Quebec which could protect its interests, increasingly threatened by the process of concentration in corporate capitalism. Three members were chosen after strong representations by the CCM.[24] Esdras Minville, Groulx's student and former president of the CCM, was director of the École des hautes études commerciales and dean of the Faculty of Social, Economic and Political Sciences at the Université de Montréal. He had contributed to the Rowell-Sirois Commission's research program and had published a series of essays on economics and another series on French-Canadian culture.[25] He had been president of the Ligue d'Action nationale from 1934 to 1944 and a director of the Société Saint-Jean-Baptiste de Montréal (SSJBM). He wrote the important section on culture in the commission's report.[26] Père Richard Arès, SJ, was assistant director of the Institut social populaire and associate editor of *Relations*. He was a specialist in Catholic social thought, writing long works on corporatism and nationalism, and on constitutional matters and federalism.[27] A strong nationalist, he was later editor of *Relations,* successor to Père Archambault as head of the semaines sociales, and moral counsellor to the SSJBM. He wrote the historical section and the federalism section in the report. Honoré Parent, a lawyer, was also recommended by the CCM. He, like Minville, was a former president of the CCM and a former director of municipal services of the city of Montreal.

Also on the commission was Paul-Henri Guimont, an investment dealer, secretary of the Faculty of Social Sciences at Laval, where he was an opponent of Père Georges-Henri Lévesque, and a graduate of HEC. Representing the English-speaking community was John P. Rowat, chairman of the Protestant Committee of the Conseil de l'instruction publique and chairman of the Protestant School Board of Montreal. Rowat apparently played a minor role on the commission and was described by other members of it as not being 'un homme à problèmes.'[28] Chosen to chair the commission was Judge Thomas Tremblay, a friend and confidant of Duplessis with views compatible with the Montreal group. In short, the commissioners formed what Durocher and Jean have called a consciously structured group, which saw itself as having a mission to preserve French Canada.[29]

The commission's central assumption

The basic assumption underlying the recommendations advanced by the Tremblay Commission was hardly startling, given the ideologies that had existed in French Canada. The assumption can probably be traced as far back as nationalism itself. None the less, it comes to occupy a central place in the thinking of the nationalist intelligentsia only after the successive defeats experienced by French Canadians: the illegal amendment of the Manitoba Act in 1890 and the redrafting of the Autonomy Acts in 1904–5, which together deprived them of their rights in western Canada; Regulation 17 in 1912, which removed French as a language of instruction in Ontario schools; and conscription in 1917. The nationalism that resulted from these defeats, the nationalism of the Ligue d'Action francaise and Lionel Groulx, was centred on Quebec. Consideration of Canada, of Bourassa's vision of an Anglo-French confederacy, was relegated to the oblivion that the vision's sponsor chose for himself at the end of the First World War. For the Tremblay Commission, as for Groulx, the province of Quebec embraced on its territory a community that was unique in its origins, history, religion, and culture. It could not be assimilated to or made compatible with any community existing in any other Canadian province. Accordingly, the government of the province of Quebec itself had a unique responsibility. It was to be the guardian of the French-Canadian nation, which had been born and raised on its lands and waters. No other provincial government was a national government in this sense. The only government on the same level as that of Quebec was the federal government, which in the commission's view was the national government of the English-Canadian nation. The commission developed this argument by examining successively the concept of culture and the spirit of Canadian federalism.

In the commission's view, the degree of responsibility that would be assumed by a national government was immense. Culture, it will be recalled, included the collection of knowledge possessed by the community, the means of expression, including language, used by the community, and basic values. A national culture is the particularization of these components based on a distinctive national genius (French, English, and so on) and philosophy of life (Christian, materialist, pagan, and so on).[30] This particularization yields a diverse set of institutions and customs. In the commission's view, the critical factor that contributed to the uniqueness of a culture was the national genius. It was composed of native qualities of temperament that 'are themselves the fruits of a long-elaborated biological and psychological heredity.'[31] Culture was not chosen but something into which one was born. French-Canadian culture was lived and expressed by individuals who had their biological roots in French Canada and who thus had access to the French genius. Culture, by implication, did not constantly change with circumstances but was fixed and rooted in human nature. A national culture, one might conclude, will only survive and flourish if it is separated from other cultures by clear boundaries.

This conclusion is supported by other arguments of the commission. The survival of a national culture depended upon the existence of a homogeneous ethnic environment, which included homogeneous systems of institutions, customs and beliefs, linguistic unity, and consistency in organizational practice. The consequences of not maintaining such an environment were grave: 'If the data of an outside culture become of current utility or, for one reason or another, are imposed; if one of the functions of collective life proceeds from an inspiration foreign to the culture or is, in fact, dominated by foreign elements, the relations of cultural exchange between Man and his social environment are mixed up; the homogeneity of the ethnic environment is weakened and the nation's renewal organism and then, sooner or later, its survival are threatened.'[32]

Ensuring a homogeneous environment was a task that fell in part upon the state. The state, to be sure, does not confer upon the environment its cultural character. This comes from the nation and the particularization of values forged by the national genius. The state rather guarantees certain liberties to the nation, the conditions that the nation needs to express itself freely. At the same time, the state is to follow the subsidiary principle discussed in chapter 2. Its policies and actions must conform to the spirit and character of the institutions, customs, and other practices generated by the nation. Specifically, the state had to ensure that its own organizational principles, such as efficiency and bureaucratic rationality, did not restrict the spirit of the institutions in the ethnic environment.

To summarize, culture as conceived by the commission was seen to be supported by a broad range of institutions, customs, and practices of the national community. The culture of the French-Canadian nation was the product of the historical, psychological, and biological characteristics that had developed among the descendants of the pioneers of New France. Presumably, the members of the nation could be identified using a combination of genealogical, linguistic, and religious criteria. The nation, to survive, had to strive to prevent the entry of foreign elements into its environment. This could be accomplished in part by cultivating attachment to their culture among members of the community. It also would be facilitated by a state that was willing to respect the national culture and to tailor its policies to conform to that culture. The state had to be prepared to intervene, if necessary, to ensure the continued homogeneity of the ethnic environment. What is the referent here for the concept of the state? In a federal system, it could in theory be the central and provincial governments or one but not the other of these two levels. The commission, however, was quite clear: based on its understanding of Canadian federalism, it referred to the provincial government of Quebec as the state.

The commission devoted considerable thought to the meaning of Canadian federalism. It rejected the common notion that the Fathers of Confederation had assigned powers of a general interest to the federal government and those of a local interest to the provinces. Rather, it suggested that the division of powers found in sections 91 and 92 of the BNA Act was a codification of the informal practices that had developed in the province of Canada between 1840 and 1867.[33] These had reflected a tacit decision to entrust to the general government only matters of common interest to the French and English, thereby leaving the task of settling all matters particular to the way of life of a region to the respective leaders of Canada East and Canada West. On this basis, the BNA Act assigned to Ottawa areas common to French and English – general services such as defence and the post office, technical services such as coinage and weights and measures, and the public debt. It gave the provinces responsibility for 'everything which touched the human side most nearly and which most influenced the Canadian citizen's manner of living.'[34] In short, 'social and cultural activity forms the very essence of that autonomy which was juridically guaranteed to the provinces by the Act of 1867 and for whose maintenance the Fathers of Confederation entrusted economic and fiscal powers to the provincial legislatures.'[35]

Given that the commission felt that the BNA Act gave the government of Quebec authority over all matters arising from its historical, cultural, and religious character and granted powers over civil rights and aspects of language to the provinces, the government of Quebec had a special mission. The Canadian constitution had made it the 'accredited guardian of French-Canadian civilization.'[36] The commissioners did not consider seriously the proposition that the federal government could also be a guarantor of French-Canadian culture.[37] They considered it to be thoroughly infused with the values and institutions of English-Canadian culture. The English-Canadian nation enjoyed the protection of the nine other provincial governments as well as that of the federal government. The history of Canada had shown that French Canada had to go it alone with Quebec.

The political program developed in great detail by the commission was based on the assumption that French-Canadian culture could survive and develop only if the provincial government of Quebec had primary responsibility for the organization of life in Quebec. If the government were to accomplish this crucial mission, two conditions had to be satisfied. First, it had to have the

liberty to promote unhindered the development of French-Canadian civilization. This meant that it should be left all initiatives for providing the province
with suitable cultural and educational institutions and all other initiatives that,
without being specifically cultural, gave life to the culture and to the milieu in
which culture took root. The commission was amazingly broad in its definition
of such initiatives. They included economic projects for developing the territory
of Quebec, industrial use of resources, and all social projects touching upon the
family, work, mutual aid, and charities.[38] Second, the government had to have,
as a complement to liberty, security: its liberty had to be respected under the
existing constitution. Security meant also that French-Canadian civilization
had to be accepted as integral to Canada by English Canadians.

These two conditions were further translated into specific demands and
proposals which were to influence so much the political strategies and debates
of the 1960s. Of the commission's many demands and proposals, several are of
particular importance for understanding the Quiet Revolution and its after-
shocks. These are related to taxation powers and control of the ethnic
environment, including education and social welfare.

The division of taxation powers

Taxation is at the heart of the capitalist state. It, along with borrowing on the
capital markets, is the primary mechanism used by the state to obtain the
material resources it needs to function. For the Tremblay Commission, it was
perhaps even more important because the conservatism of its members led them
to lay little stress on borrowing. If the province of Quebec were to be the
guardian of the French-Canadian nation, and if further 'it cannot envisage the
possibility of sharing the burden' because 'its character of principal political
centre of French Canada obliges it to keep the initiative and the full
responsibility for the policies to be employed to satisfy them,' then it had to be
financially independent.[39] Such a conclusion complemented well the commission's view of federalism (and was resurrected in the constitutional discussions
of 1979–81). The commissioners believed that federalism involved an
association of equal authorities, each sovereign in its respective jurisdiction.
Concomitantly, each of these sovereign authorities had to have the capacity to
procure on its own initiative through taxation the financial resources it needed
to fulfil its responsibilities. One sovereign authority should never be dependent
on another for its financial resources.

The modalities of the taxation system in a federal régime were crucial,
because they determined whether the various autonomous units of the régime
were financially independent and because they reflected culture and had an
impact upon culture. The system of taxation, like that of education or social

welfare, had to take its inspiration from the basic values of the national culture. It had to be an integral part of the homogeneous ethnic environment. For the Tremblay Commission, this meant, first, that the taxation system had to be personalist in the sense described in chapter 2. Following from Christian philosophy, the taxation system should afford maximum freedom to the individual in his or her pursuit of salvation. It should be inspired by the principle that institutions of society should only supplement or support the individual but never take the initiative away from him or her. The commissioners contrasted such a taxation system with a socialist-Marxist-totalitarian system, where presumably the state has primacy over the individual. Second, the taxation system had to respect the spirit of the BNA Act. As we have seen, the commission argued that the constitution gave control over culture and the way of life of groups to the provincial governments and control over general matters common to all groups to the federal government. Similarly, those modes of taxation that most directly affected the way of life of citizens should be made available to the provinces, and those modes that affected individuals in a more general way should be given to the federal government.

Based on these principles, the commission proposed a rather radical change in the Canadian fiscal system. Beginning with the dominion-provincial conference of 1960, these proposals were to form the basis of Quebec's position until the late 1970s. The commissioners recommended that the provinces have the primary initiative in the field of direct taxation because of its greater impact on the way of life of citizens.[40] Indirect taxes would be left to the federal government.

First, personal income tax should be collected only by the provinces: the various exemptions and modalities of personal income tax could affect significantly family life and the socio-cultural milieu. F.-A. Angers wrote two important works on these issues for the commission, and it relied heavily on these studies.[41] He had been arguing for several years that Quebec should adopt this position.[42] In 1962, he again made the case in the no-nonsense terms that had swayed the commission:

Par l'impôt direct, le gouvernement change le statut de la famille, impose aux cultivateurs de payer des salaires à leurs enfants, oblige les gens à prendre des allocations familiales dont ils se passeraient si on leur donnait des exemptions suffisantes. En somme, il se sert de l'impôt pour forcer les individus à entrer dans un plan, décide de la façon dont nous devons faire nos charités etc. Ça touche à tout, l'impôt direct; à nos personnes, à la famille, à nos biens. Les provinces doivent en prendre le contrôle absolu.[43]

Using the same kind of logic, the commission recommended that the provinces collect succession taxes: 'The system of transmitting property conditions the ways of life of individuals and of families as well as the amassing and development of property. Therefore it is most important that no outside influence should prevent this system's operation.'[44] The commission suggested also that corporation income taxes be primarily reserved to the provinces. Here the arguments are less compelling. It suggested that such taxes could be used to finance policies to develop natural resources ('the economic basis of the province's economy') and welfare policies. The commissioners added that provincial retention of this tax was an additional safeguard against the spread of socialism in Canada. Why this should be so is not clear. At various points, the commission suggests that the federal government is socialist in orientation, and so perhaps any attempt to deny that government resources could be seen as a blow against socialism.

In exchange, it would seem, for the personal and corporation income taxes, the federal government was to be assigned what the commission called 'direct taxes on consumption.' The general retail sales tax, gasoline tax, fuel oil tax, tobacco tax, and taxes on alcoholic liquors, meals, transfers of real estate, transfers of personal securities, and so on would be transferred from the provinces to the federal government. These taxes were perceived to be more consistent with the general functions assigned to the federal government. Left in the hands of the provinces, such taxes could be used to erect economic barriers throughout the country. The commission felt, it would appear, that the federal government had the responsibility to ensure the proper functioning of a nation-wide market.

One might question the commission's reasoning here. Might not the levying of indirect taxes have as significant an impact on culture as an income tax? Arguments could be made that indirect taxation could have an immediate impact on culture. For our purposes, however, it is less important to question the commission's reasoning than it is to understand it. The commission proposed that the whole field of direct taxation, including personal and corporation income taxes, be reserved to the provinces. Such a change would, in its view, guarantee the provinces financial independence, which it felt was critical to the successful working of Canadian federalism. It would also guarantee that the provinces could legislate on matters closest to the life of individuals and hence be consistent with the spirit of the constitution. And it would enhance the probability that political institutions would be created that were in harmony with the national culture and ethnic environment of French Canada.

Control of the ethnic environment
In chapter 2, I described how the institutions forming Quebec's social welfare and educational systems were cherished and protected because of their specifically French-Canadian character. I noted that these two systems were

under stress because of the inability of the clergy to expand as quickly as the demand for services and because of the increased consciousness of the industrial working class and its demands for more education and better health care. Many of the submissions made to the Tremblay Commission spoke of these problems. The commissioners were aware of these problems and commanded several research projects to investigate them further. In the end, based on its public meetings, its research, and its members' thinking, the commission recommended some political reforms and a social revolution.

Since 1945, the federal government had moved toward creation of a national system of social security. Constitutional amendments, agreed to by the federal government and the provincial governments, had given the federal authorities responsibility (in 1941) for unemployment insurance and (in 1952) for old-age pensions. Such actions, as one might expect, were greeted with hositlity by the nationalist intelligentsia. Ottawa was the government of English Canada, and its programs drew their inspiration from its culture. Speaking to the semaines sociales in 1959, Claude Morin, for the next twenty years adviser to governments on federal-provincial relations, but then a young graduate in social service administration from Columbia University, described the ensemble of Canadian social security programs as profoundly marked by the individualism of the Anglo-Saxon spirit.[45] Established in light of the Anglo-Saxon and Protestant conception of life, they gave little consideration to the communal and familial values at the heart of French-Canadian society.

The commission argued that if its fiscal reform was implemented, Quebec would have the financial independence it needed to direct its own social welfare services. Such a system, if it were in harmony with the indigenous culture, would help preserve and enrich that culture. Accordingly, the commission recommended that responsibility for all social security policy be given to the provinces. It asked further that the constitutional amendments on unemployment insurance and old-age pensions be rescinded. The provinces were closer to the regional problems that generated unemployment and thus were better placed to treat them. The provinces, accordingly, should also be given a larger role in the development of manpower policy.

The commission reasserted Quebec's determination to control all facets of its educational system. It rejected firmly any form of federal intervention, including grants to the universities. It noted that its proposed changes in taxation would ensure that provinces would have the financial resources they needed to support completely the universities. The commissioners took pains to refute on an ideological plane the arguments mounted by the Massey Commission favouring federal support to the universities.[46] In particular, they noted that the latter's distinction between formal education and general education or culture had no legal basis. The constitution simply assigned 'education' to the provinces and this general term embraced both of the Massey commissioners' categories. The Tremblay Commission added that to proceed otherwise would be to oppose again the spirit of the constitution, which left matters closest to the way of life of citizens in provincial hands. It gave little credence to the argument that all governments had the right to contribute to the education of the individual. This proposal simply belied the raison d'être of the federal system, which for good reasons assigned particular responsibilities to particular levels of government. Relying extensively upon a brief submitted by the Université de Montréal, the commission countered the argument that universities filled a national role and hence merited the support of the 'national government.' It cautioned that the universities were integral components of educational systems defined and organized by the provinces. The universities made their contribution to the country through their functioning as parts of these systems. Thus they had to be supported by provincial governments which were best attuned to the philosophy and culture of that educational system.

These restatements of fairly traditional demands for autonomy in the social and educational spheres were remarkable for two reasons. First, the ideological justification for these traditional demands was made explicit, and the commissioners' perception of what was at stake was very clear. Second, these demands were part of a larger set designed to secure for the province sufficient autonomy to carry out a virtual social revolution. The revolution that the commissioners had in mind was the opposite of the revolution, however quiet, that was soon to take place. When obtained, the powers demanded by the commission were used primarily in ways it feared most; its political program and restructuring of federalism, once partially implemented were used to destroy the culture it cherished.

In reviewing the overall state of the French-Canadian community, the Tremblay Commission concluded that a serious gap had developed between the character of the traditional institutions of French-Canadian society and the way of life of many members of that society. The way of life of the industrial working class was a matter of special concern.[47] Quebec had become industrialized. With industrial capitalism had come economic and political practices and institutions of British or American origin which had created among French-Canadian workers a movement toward individualism, liberalism, and materialism. These goals were contrary to the communalism and spiritualism characteristic of French-Canadian culture. People began to think and act according to the orientation of the places where they worked rather than the places were they prayed, played, and were educated. The commission saw tension between the increasingly dominant values of the workplace and those of the nation and its institutions. The pressures on the educational system and the health care system discussed in chapter 2 were gradually and surreptitiously changing them to conform to the values of the industrial capitalist world.

The Tremblay Report did not shy away from what it saw. A major reordering was necessary: 'The whole institutional system which, up to now, has been the broadest and most synthetic expression of French Canada's special culture, must be completely remade along new lines.'[48] The commissioners argued that the traditional culture had to be broadened in order that it might embrace fully the activities in the workplace. They called for a systematic change in all of the society's institutions in order to make them reflect the communal and Catholic values of French Canada, of what they called the 'old spirit.' Science and technology should not be shunned; rather they should be used judiciously and selectively to further the progress of the nation and its values as they had been. The new technical and vocational areas of education and the new social services designed to serve the urban proletariat could no longer be allowed to develop outside traditional structures. Even the character of economic activity itself had to be changed to conform to traditional cultural principles. The workplace had to be brought back within the boundaries of the French-Canadian cultural community. Liberal capitalism was recognized as a threat to French-Canadian civilization, and the society had to be revolutionized.

The large measure of political autonomy called for by the commission was deemed necessary to permit this reordering of Quebec's French-Canadian community with a minimum of interference from outside. A homogeneous ethnic environment had to be reconstructed. The commissioners believed that French Canada had a unique history, values, and way of life; they never questioned this assumption and accepted it as an article of faith. They thought that given a measure of autonomy and the opportunity to live according to their own devices with minimal commitments to the outside, these values and this way of life would work themselves back into all facets of the daily lives of members of the nation and would generate institutions true to tradition and adequate to the technological age. The political program that was to inspire political action in Quebec for years to come was thus conceived originally in the hope that institutions could be moved away from the spirit of capitalism to embrace the spirit of New France.

The commissioners' plans were never realized. The gap between culture and ideology on the one hand and major institutional practices on the other left open an alternative route of change, which had consequences quite different from those hoped for by the Tremblay Commission. Instead of revolutionizing the institutional order, a society might reorder its culture and ideology to be more compatible with that order. The gap might be closed by facilitating the development being taken by the economy, by the educational system, and so on and at the same time reflecting critically on the past, on the thinkers of the past, and on the values they prized. Many social scientists in Quebec think that this is precisely what occurred during the Quiet Revolution. Guy Rocher, a sociologist active in the reform movement of the 1960s, describes the changes of the early 1960s as follows:

C'est précisément parce que la révolution tranquille a été préparé par une lente et laborieuse remise en question d'idées, d'idéologies, d'attitudes et de mentalités qu'elle a été d'abord et surtout une mutation culturelle. La révolution tranquille n'a pas entraîné de changements très importants dans la structure économique du Québec, ni dans les institutions principales de la société; elle n'a pas été une révolution sociale, mais une certaine révolution culturelle. Elle a provoqué des changements d'esprit, mais peu de transformations structurelles.[49]

In short, the revolution called for by the Tremblay Commission never took place because the values it cherished were jettisoned. Without accepting Rocher's view, we can note that consequences the commission foresaw if events took such a turn. 'If, under pretext of economic stability, social security, uniformity of material living conditions from one end of the country to the other or of administrative simplification, French Canadians instal in their midst any organizational forms whatever, without making sure these are in harmony with their general concept of life, they condemn themselves, sooner or later, to anemia and cultural sterility.'[50]

Conclusion

The Tremblay Commission recognized clearly the crisis in French-Canadian society and its institutions, the dimensions of which were described in chapters 1 and 2, and proposed a solution: restructure the institutions serving French-Canadian society so that they all reflect the traditional values of French-Canadian culture. These changes were to involve not only education and social welfare but also the organization of economic activity. Members of the commission desired the establishment of many small enterprises because they saw these as compatible with a strong family life and as facilitating co-operative, Christian relationships between the *patron* and his workers. These kinds of changes were seen by the commission as a means to reintegrate the industrial working class and the new service classes of industrialized Quebec into the traditional order.

This solution to the crisis was indirectly political because significant political changes had to occur if it were to be realized. The government of Quebec had to receive sufficient powers to enable it to act as the national government of the French-Canadian nation. These powers included sole responsibility for education, for the delivery of social services, for the support of culture, and even for the deployment of natural resources. The commission accordingly recommended that only the government of Quebec be allowed to collect direct taxes – personal and corporate – in the province. The federal government would be left with the field of indirect taxation to finance its programs.

Two characteristics of this schema are important to the analysis that follows in this study. First, the definition of the government of Quebec as the national government of French Canada tended to place it on a level equal to that of the federal government, which it saw as the government of English Canada. All the arguments that could be mustered by the federal government in support of policies to preserve Canadian culture could then be used by the government of Quebec in support of parallel policies to preserve French-Canadian culture. Frank R. Scott, writing in the *McGill Law Journal* in 1955, discussed further the implications of these assumptions.[51] Instead of Canada being composed of one central government and ten provincial governments, it is defined to be composed of 'two races, equal in status,' one speaking through the government of Quebec and the other through the 'central' government in Ottawa. In his words, Canada becomes a 'dyarchy.' Once accepted, this assumption is the logical antecedent of such later concepts as 'associated states,' 'sovereignty-association,' and political independence. The Tremblay Commission laid the logical groundwork for the development of these ideologies and hence the movements that supported them.

Second, the Tremblay Commission's analysis emphasized a change of values and institutional adaptation in spheres outside the economy. While certainly conscious of the economic position of French-Canadians, the commissioners did not centre their analysis on economic questions. While regretting the dependent position of French Canadians in Quebec, they saw this as a consequence of a weakening in the national resolve and a rejection of traditional values. They did not speak seriously of the reverse causal sequence, as we can see in several rather unrealistic and conservative economic proposals. They did not apparently understand the consequences of urbanization and industrialization and believed that the ninteenth-century dilemma of demographic expansion was still present.[52] The economy in Quebec had to expand in order to accommodate this overflow. They spoke of the traditional concern for the stabilization of rural areas because 'country areas are the permanent reservoir of a people's living forces.'[53] They referred to the rural areas as a 'sociological laboratory' where the pure French-Canadian cultural response to industrialization could be nurtured and developed.[54] The membership of the commission's Père Arès in the Société canadienne d'établissement rural (SCER) and the Société d'études rurales, groups dedicated to increasing the numbers of French Canadians living in rural areas, illustrates the close ties between the commission and the myth of agriculturalism.[55]

Therefore, this report and its program singularly ignored economic dependency and the impact of economic structures on society. Its adoption by whatever party or movement carried with it this bias. It fostered concern with issues of political jurisdiction and created room for the belief that political change was the key to all other change. It was more easily accepted by those groups and classes unwilling to undertake critical reflection on the structure of the economy and on economic dependency. It was written by individuals who saw expanded industrial capitalism as a cultural intrusion and thus something that could be either ignored or changed by shifts in cultural behaviour. Yet these same people were reluctant to reject capitalism completely because of its emphasis on individual resourcefulness and its tendency to promote freedom of the individual.

The task of the chapters that follow will be to trace in detail the interaction between the program for power outlined by the Tremblay Commission and the various groups and classes struggling for power in Quebec society. This analysis will clarify the structure of the movement for political independence and help us to understand its successes and failures to this day.

PART TWO
The Quiet Revolution and after:
Integration or independence?

4

Economic policy:
A road to independence?

On a tout essayé pour rendre le système économique supportable. Fallait apprendre l'anglais pour travailler: on l'a appris mais ça n'a pas marché. Fallait s'instruire pour s'enricher: on s'est instruit mais on est toujours aussi pauvre. On a nationalisé l'éléctricité, mais la Baie James nous glisse entre les mains. On a fondé la SGF, mais elle ferme les usines de Sogefor dans lesquelles nous avions mis beaucoup d'espoir. On a fondé la caisse des dépôts et placements, mais la plus grande partie de nos épargnes est toujours entre les mains des trusts financiers. On a tout essayé. Mais aucun contrôle gouvernemental n'a réussi à civiliser le système économique.

> Confédération des syndicats nationaux *Il n'y a pas d'avenir pour le Québec dans le système actuel: La CSN propose un changement radical* (Montreal 1971) 3

The journal *L'Action nationale,* founded in the 1930s, was the successor to Abbé Lionel Groulx's earlier review, *L'Action française.* Like its predecessor, *L'Action nationale* espoused a philosophy that combined radical nationalism with a conservative interpretation of Catholic social and economic thought. In light of this philosophical approach, one could not fail to be struck by a short and intense debate over the orientation of nationalist groups that occurred in the journal's pages in the early 1950s. Through the pen of Jean-Marc Léger, a young recruit to the journal, a series of articles emerged that joined a certain radicalism in economic and social thinking to traditional nationalism.[1] In the brief he wrote on behalf of the Ligue d'Action nationale for the Tremblay Commission, Léger spoke seriously about the possible recourse to nationalization and socialization of the production of natural resources in Quebec. The old guard of the nationalist movement reacted to such an approach with barely restrained virulence, and Léger's position in the journal was less prominent thereafter.[2] These events indicate that during the 1950s some individuals in traditional nationalist circles were beginning to question the received wisdom on economic and social factors. Such questioning, combined with changes in thinking in the French-Canadian business community and in the ranks of organized labour, eventually laid the basis for the Quiet Revolution.

In writing about post-war Quebec, it is conventional to refer to the period between the death of Duplessis in September 1959 and the beginning of 1965 as the Quiet Revolution. I shall not depart from established usage, although the term is sufficiently ambiguous to refer to practically any kind of change. The objective of this chapter is to begin formulating an interpretation of what occurred in Quebec during these years and to show the consequences of these happenings. For reasons that will become apparent, such a beginning must entail an examination of economic policy.

The proposals for economic change that served as the basis for policy during the Quiet Revolution did not emerge from a new middle class. They cannot be said to have emerged solely from the ranks of the francophone business class. Rather, the resultant economic policies were the joint product of the political activity of three social groups: the organized working class, the francophone business class, and elements from the traditional middle-class intelligentsia. While these three groups never joined formally under one banner, their political demands in the economic field were sufficiently complementary that we can refer to the groups as a Quiet Revolution coalition. These groups were given some unity through the actions of the Parti libéral, which adopted their proposals, put them into a single platform, and called upon each of the groups to support the party and its program.

The overall aim of the economic policy that emerged after the Parti libéral victory in June 1960 was to create viable and competitive capitalist enterprises controlled by members of the francophone community. These enterprises, would be sufficiently strong to allow the francophone community to become a full participant in the advanced industrial economy of North America. The means envisaged was the establishment of institutions that would compete with the dominant enterprises controlled by non-francophones and that would eventually wrest some markets from them. Bourque and Frenette are thus incorrect in suggesting that the Quiet Revolution marked an increase in influence of the English-Canadian bourgeoisie.[3] However, much of their analysis of changes in social and educational policy is still valid, because the period saw a stronger push to integrate the francophone community into an advanced industrial capitalist economy, a point important to their analysis.

The objective of full participation in the North American economy appealed also to our three groups. For the small business class, it appeared a prerequisite if any viable capitalist class were to exist in the francophone community. The pressures of concentration and centralization of capital and the absence of francophones from key sectors of an industrial economy brought the continued existence of this social group into question. Organized labour was experiencing again a period of high unemployment, which it had come to expect would accompany underdevelopment. It saw the strengthening of enterprises controlled by the francophone community, particularly if based upon exploitation of the province's natural resources, as a means of regularizing the business cycle and stabilizing employment. The traditional middle class, as we have seen in part 1, was more and more concerned that the institutions and cultural practices it supported were being undermined by economic changes. A part of this group followed the Tremblay Commission and felt that these institutions and practices could be protected and reaffirmed only by reorienting the economy away from expanded capitalist development. However, another part drew a different conclusion and suggested that if control of economic activity by the francophone community could be expanded significantly, the new capitalist order could be directed so as to be compatible with the established culture of the French-Canadian community.

The policies that were developed on the basis of this goal did not satisfy all three groups in the coalition. While they did perhaps lay the basis for a stronger capitalist class in the francophone community, they did not bring greater control over resource production or more stable employment as desired by organized labour. The degree of economic control desired by the traditional middle class was not achieved, and it continued to experience the breakdown of traditional French-Canadian culture. In the early 1970s, the nature of economic policy was changed in order to de-emphasize competition between a nascent francophone capitalist class and other fractions of the capitalist class in North America. The new policy stressed co-operative economic development and gave a further boost to the growth of the capitalist class in the francophone community. The new policy, however, sealed the fate of the Quiet Revolution coalition, and its final break-up coincided with a rise in support for political independence. The movement for political independence that gradually coalesced contained organized labour, the traditional middle class, and a new middle class spawned by the expansion of the provincial government into social and educational policy and by an expansion in the communications industries during the 1960s.

This chapter is devoted to the presentation of the evidence and arguments that support this interpretation of the economic policies of the Quiet Revolution and their consequences. It will begin by examining how the Quiet Revolution coalition on economic policy came to be formed during the 1950s. This analysis will be followed by a study of the pursuit of a new economic order through the consolidation of sources of capital, the attempt to modernize the enterprises of the francophone community, and the pursuit of greater control and more indigenous processing of natural resources. These policies will be studied over the twenty-year period 1960–80. Later in the chapter I shall examine the debate over public vs private control of the economy and the process of class formation that led to the break-up in the coalition, and I shall consider specifically the hydro-electrical power and the forestry industries.

The emerging consensus on economic policy

The Quiet Revolution coalition is composed of three social groups: members of the traditional middle class, who were nationalist in the French-Canadian tradition and begrudgingly acquiescent in the face of expanded capitalist development; the francophone business class; and organized labour (primarily francophone). In this section, the economic views of each group will be reviewed. I will show that these views tended to be complementary and that they were woven into a common position by the Parti libéral. This party sought the support of each of these groups in the 1960 provincial election.

The analysis of the traditional middle class is based on my reading of documents and publications of the old nationalist societies, particularly the Société Saint-Jean-Baptiste de Montréal (ssjbm). The business-class perspective is developed from a study of the Chambre de Commerce de la Province de Québec (ccpq) and the Chambre de Commerce du District de Montréal (ccm), the leading business groups of the day. The analysis of the labour position arises from the study of the major labour organizations: the Confédération des travailleurs catholiques du Canada (ctcc), the Fédération provinciale du travail du Québec (fptq), the Fédération des unions industrielles du Québec (fuiq), and the Fédération des travailleurs du Québec (ftq), formed in 1957 following the merger of the fptq and fuiq.

First, in the mid-1950s we find the nationalist traditional middle class beginning to criticize the way French Canadians did business. In the early twentieth century, French-Canadian business practices had been assailed by writers such as Errol Bouchette, Édouard Montpetit, and Victor Barbeau. The data from early studies by Hughes and MacDonald and Vèzina and later analyses by Raynauld leave little doubt that French-Canadian enterprises were small, usually family owned, and concentrated in areas on the fringes of Quebec's resource-based economy.[4] The French-Canadian business firm was attacked as being too much based on family. Individual businessmen were using the firm as a means to support the family. Once the firm had grown to a size that facilitated this objective, entrepreneurs became complacent, conservative, and uninterested in further expansion.[5] The ssjbm criticized French-Canadian businessmen for being concerned too much with saving rather than with investing in expansion, too individualistic and unwilling to seek out partners, and afraid of expanding the firm to that point where authority would need to be delegated to others. French Canadians, it was felt, had to develop large enterprises, capable of competing effectively with those owned by non-francophones.[6]

With the demand for restructuring the French-Canadian firm came also a campaign for increased control of Quebec's economy by French Canadians. Politically, this campaign followed a tradition in French-Canadian nationalism that emphasized the importance of economic control. The precursor to the campaign in the 1950s was the Action libérale nationale and its efforts in the 1930s. The nationalist societies reorganized the old 1930s program of Ligues d'achat chez nous under the direction of a new body, the Conseil d'expansion économique (CEE). Rather than using the old approach of campaigning against purchases from non-francophone enterprises, the CEE was expected to promote the advancement of French-Canadian enterprise. The nationalists hoped to use it to stimulate greater francophone participation in commercial, industrial, and financial affairs and to draw attention to the existing accomplishments of French Canadians in the world of business.[7] The CEE campaigns were supplemented with calls upon large non-francophone firms to absorb more francophones into their operations.[8] In rejecting the family firm as a base for economic development, these nationalists moved away from more traditional positions on the place of business in the French-Canadian community and thus from the Tremblay Commission as well.

This rejection of traditional positions is also exemplified by the adoption of a more positive attitude toward the state. For example, in 1954 the SSJBM called upon the Quebec government to create a department with wide responsibilities for directing the development of the province's ample natural resources.[9] It suggested also that Hydro-Québec be given wider jurisdiction over hydraulic resources. Hydro-Québec had been created by the Liberal government of Adélard Godbout through the purchase of Montreal Light, Heat and Power Ltd in 1943. It was hoped that an expanded Hydro-Québec would give the government increased leverage in directing resource development and thereby indirectly increase the influence of French Canadians. The SSJBM proposal for a new resources department was picked up by the Liberals and put in their 1956 and 1960 electoral programs.[10]

Second, representatives of French-Canadian business also stepped up demands for a change in the structure of French-Canadian firms. Recognizing a need for pooling large sums of capital in order to bring this about, the Chambre de Commerce de la Province de Québec (CCPQ) called for the creation of a banque d'affaires. Such an investment bank would develop the sources of capital needed for the expansion of French-Canadian firms. The notion was picked up and promoted by the SSJBM, and after 1955 a number of attempts were made to create such an institution. The most notable, a well publicized attempt, was the Corporation d'expansion financière.[11]

The CCPQ began also to favour a more positive role for the provincial government in promoting a greater role for French Canadians in Quebec's economy. Recognizing that the modern firm needed access to technology as well as capital, it began in 1957 to suggest that the provincial government create a research council. It would support and co-ordinate research in the universities, in government laboratories, and in industry, with the objective of developing technology related to exploitation of the province's natural resources.[12] The CCPQ emphasized particularly the need for intensive research connected with the use and production of forest resources. Toward the end of the decade, the CCPQ began to press the government to create a centralized planning agency, with industry and government representation, to draw up proposals for new projects based on the province's resources and to co-ordinate the financial and industrial sectors of the French-Canadian community in the pursuit of these projects.[13] Again the Parti libéral showed itself to be attuned to issues of this kind when it incorporated into its 1960 electoral program a proposal for the creation of a Conseil d'orientation économique with some of these planning functions.

Third, organized labour was developing proposals complementary to those of the nationalists and of the business class. The Confédération des travailleurs catholiques du Canada (CTCC) and to a degree its counterpart, the Fédération des travailleurs du Quebec (FTQ), began in the 1950s to promote strongly the idea that the secondary manufacturing sector needed to be expanded.[14] They argued that this expansion was needed in order to reduce unemployment, which had reached a post-war high in the late 1950s. It was to be based on increased processing of Quebec's own natural resources, a concern shared with the other two groups. Many of Quebec's natural resources were being exported in raw form. The case of iron ore was not untypical. Between 1957 and 1960, when production of iron ore in Quebec began to expand rapidly, 90.9 per cent of the ore mined was shipped abroad unprocessed.[15] Despite being the largest producer of iron ore among Canada's provinces, Quebec did not have a single blast furnace and produced only 4.3 per cent of the steel manufactured in Canada in 1958.[16] Over the years there had been several proposals for a steel industry from figures as different as Cyrus Eaton and Bishop N.A. Labrie of the diocese of the Gulf of St Lawrence, but no action was ever taken.[17]

The CTCC, which pushed systematically for increased processing of Quebec's natural resources in Quebec, was by no means alone in this struggle. Its proposals were similar to those made by the Fédération des unions industrielles du Québec (FUIQ) in the early 1950s, by the Canadian Manufacturers' Association (CMA), and by the CCM in its submission to the Tremblay

Commission. This refrain was increasingly sung by the Parti libéral as well. It was a major theme of the campaign of Georges-Émile Lapalme, the party's leader during the 1956 election. The language used by the Liberals when speaking of this issue drew from the imagery of colonization. An editorial in *La Réforme*, the party's newspaper, in 1955 said: 'Le drame du Canada français réside dans le fait qu'il a toujours été une sorte d'Afrique polaire pour les grands syndicats étrangers qui, dans le contexte nord-américain, ont voulu exploiter nos ressources naturelles dans les mêmes conditions qu'ils profitaient des pétroles du Moyen-Orient, des sulphates africains et des minérais d'Amérique latine.'[18] The Liberals echoed demands of the CTCC for more local processing of asbestos, forest products, and iron ore. In doing so, the party was becoming the link between organized labour on the one hand and the indigenous small capitalist class and the nationalists on the other. The CTCC was not politically radical in its orientation on economic issues. It rejected the extensive use of nationalization advocated by the FUIQ in its 1954 manifesto and later by the early independence groups, the Alliance laurentienne and the Action socialiste pour l'indépendance du Québec (ASIQ). Its advocacy of rationalization was limited to hydro-electricity, which complemented that of the SSJBM noted above. It probably still shared the views of such traditional thinkers on this matter as F.–A. Angers, who argued that nationalization was profoundly in disaccord with Catholic culture.[19] It would also lead to a socialisme niveleur that would destroy individual liberty. These arguments were amplified by Père Arès in an editorial written for *Relations* in December 1959.[20]

The CTCC's perspective on the economy drew more from liberal circles of Catholic thought that had begun to develop shortly after the war. This perspective brought it rather close to the other two classes in the coalition on the role of the state. In 1947, a group of clerics calling itself the Commission sacerdotale d'études sociales issued a report on the participation of workers in the life of the enterprise.[21] Most members of the group were chaplains attached to trade unions or the Action catholique movement. In their report, they attacked the existing economic system vigorously: 'Le régime économique et social dans lequel nous vivons a donné lieu à des abus qui ont porté atteinte à la dignité de la personne humaine, à la justice et à la charité.'[22] In considering measures to reform this system, they seized upon an idea that traced its roots to Pius XI's encyclical *Quadragesimo Anno*. They called for co-management between workers and employers in order to improve the conditions of work and to assure a fairer monetary return to the workers. These ideas were to be promoted by the Commission and by Abbé Gérard Dion, who taught industrial relations at Université Laval. He was to use for these purposes the journal *Ad Usum Sacerdotum* which circulated in clerical circles. Three years later, in a remarkable document, *Le Problème ouvrier en regard de la doctrine sociale de l'Église,* the province's bishops gave further legitimacy to demands for reforms in the direction of co-management.[23]

Early in 1949, the CTCC began to promote this notion, calling for the creation of comités mixtes de production. Initially the CTCC saw these committees as a means to increase the awareness of employers of certain of the human aspects of production. The series of difficult labour disputes involving the CTCC that began with the famous strike at Asbestos in 1949 prodded the union's leaders to expand their critique of the capitalist system and to lay more importance on co-management. In his rapport moral to the annual convention of the CTCC in 1951, its president, Gérard Picard, called for increased responsibilities for workers. He expanded the notion of co-management to include activities governing the industry as a whole and even the national economy. Throughout the 1950s, the CTCC developed these ideas until in its 1957 convention it called for the creation of an economic planning commission.[24] This commission was to be a state agency with representation drawn from labour and employers and was to be charged to watch over the conservation and rational exploitation of Quebec's natural resources. It was to see to the replacement of private monopoly concerns in the resource industries by state enterprises that could be structured as co-operatives, or co-managed by employers and workers, or run simply as crown corporations. The commission was to promote the establishment of industries that would process Quebec's mineral products. While the responsibilities of this commission were perhaps broader than those envisaged by the CCPQ, one cannot help but be struck by the similarity between the two proposals.

Such proposals by the CTCC were bound to have an impact upon the Parti libéral. The CTCC had fought a series of strikes at Asbestos, Louiseville, Klasson Mills, and Dupuis Frères that had brought it directly into struggles with Duplessis and his Union nationale government. As early as 1949, the CTCC created a comité d'action civique later renamed the comité d'orientation politique. These organizations co-ordinated the public participation of the CTCC in the 1952 and 1956 election campaigns, whereby it sought to support candidates, always Liberals, who were favourable to its cause. In 1958, the CTCC expanded its political activity further by instituting a commission d'éducation politique which was assigned responsibility for the political education of its members.[25] All these political actions tended to the creation of more and more tangible ties to the Parti libéral.

While expanding its political activity, the CTCC moved also to confirm its independence from the church and thus the old régime. The union central was tied to the church through its name, its formal allegiance to the social doctrine of the church, and the presence of chaplains within its ranks. In his last rapport moral in 1958, Picard recommended that each of these ties be revised. After a bitter dispute involving conservative elements in the church, the CTCC changed its name to the Confédération des syndicats nationaux (CSN) in 1960.[26] Chaplains were retained but in a strictly advisory capacity on moral questions. A formal statement supporting Christian social doctrine was also written into the organization's Declaration of Principles.

Thus the CTCC that was proposing the economic planning commission in 1958 was viewed as an independent force of a new kind. Its demands for increased control over the economy by French Canadians and for more processing in Quebec of the natural resources of the province complemented those of the indigenous francophone business class. These small capitalists saw the kinds of industries proposed by the CTCC and others as areas where they could themselves expand. They were not interested in direct state intervention but certainly welcomed state support of private initiatives. The corporatist planning mechanism proposed by the CTCC was also not foreign to the thinking of more liberal elements of the church hierarchy in the late 1950s. In 1959 Cardinal Léger, archbishop of Montreal, and in 1960 the Canadian episcopate had called for the creation of similar bodies in order to fight unemployment.[27] The idea of collaboration among major social groups in economic planning was very much in the air.

The Parti libéral became a potentially important actor because it had ties to the CTCC and had made programmatic overtures to some nationalists and to the indigenous employers. It was thus in a position to put together a platform that would promote increased integration of the francophone community into the North American capitalist system. It was prepared to use the provincial government and its powers to facilitate this process. Such a move was viewed favourably by the dominant non-francophone élites because it was understood to involve the 'modernization' of Quebec. Profiting from this support and the agreement among the francophone working class, the francophone small business class, and elements of the traditional middle class, the Parti libéral and its program were seen to promise a new beginning when it took power in June 1960.

The pursuit of a new economic order

The overall objective of economic policy during the Quiet Revolution was to obtain significant control over production in Quebec for the francophone business class. The proposals of the 1950s for reaching this objective emphasized the creation of large, modern enterprises controlled by franco-phones and concentrated in the production and processing of natural resources. Specific recommendations on how such enterprises might be formed were to come from a central planning body that brought together major social groups in the francophone community. The first priority of such a group in the view of the business class was to devise a means for bringing together the capital needed for supporting the creation of larger firms. The problem was generally perceived to be one of gaining the release of savings held by a myriad of small credit institutions in the province and not one of developing the capital itself.

Upon its election, the Parti libéral began to try to move toward these objectives by creating a central planning body, the Conseil d'orientation économique du Québec (COEQ), early in 1961. The membership of the COEQ reflected to an important degree the coalition of the three groups I argue was crucial to the Quiet Revolution. It was headed by René Paré, former president of the Montreal Chambre de Commerce. It had representatives also from the CCPQ and the CTCC. It counted among its members from the traditional middle class Esdras Minville and F.-A. Angers, whose ideas were so influential in the Tremblay Report. It included representation from the Mouvement Desjardins, the largest credit union organization in Quebec, and hence a significant source of capital for investment. Brunelle emphasizes that the entry of the Mouvement Desjardins into the proposed system of planning was an important step and distinguished the COEQ from its earlier private versions. The government created the Department of Natural Resources which had been requested by the nationalist societies, and it reorganized the Department of Industry and Commerce. Mechanisms were thus put in place to develop a new economic policy.

In this section of the chapter, I will survey three aspects of this new economic policy: attempts to consolidate large pools of capital for investment in francophone enterprises, efforts to promote adoption of a more modern firm structure, and moves to increase the indigenous processing of natural resources. None of these initiatives was as successful as had been hoped. Their failings were an important factor. I shall argue, in the break-up of the Quiet Revolution coalition and in the movement of organized labour and elements of the old traditional middle class to the independence option.

The consolidation of capital

Phase I, 1960–72
In an important brief to the Department of Industry and Commerce and the newly created Department of Natural Resources in May 1961, the CCPQ reiterated its call for the creation of a 'banque de financement à long terme.'[28] It emphasized that such an institution would be important for the economic emancipation of French Canada and a good avenue for investment for French Canadians with a minimum of risk. A month later, in a speech to the Fédération des Sociétés Saint-Jean-Baptiste du Québec (FSSJBQ), Premier Lesage presaged the form that such an entity would eventually take when he suggested the

creation of a series of mixed enterprises, owned jointly by the government and private concerns, to develop Quebec's economy.[29] The government turned the proposal for a 'banque de financement' over to the COEQ for consideration. In an article in *L'Action nationale* in December 1961, René Paré articulated further the philosophy that would inspire the approach of the COEQ to this matter.[30] He pointed out that some involvement by the state was necessary if French Canadians were to prevent their firms from continuing to fall into foreign hands; this involvement would in some cases need to be direct if new industries were to be founded and new avenues of trade discovered. Thus a future Société générale de financement (SGF) should seek to establish an iron and steel industry in Quebec, an idea popular with both labour and the business class. The state, however, would remain involved in such ventures only until the private sector could take over.

In June 1962, the work of the COEQ bore fruit with the introduction of legislation establishing an SGF. It was to support and favour the formation and development of enterprises in Quebec and was to involve the province's people by selling shares and encouraging their purchase. The provincial government purchased 5 million shares, as did the Mouvement Desjardins. The large pool of savings in the caisses populaires was thus finally brought into the investment picture. The SGF was greeted warmly by the representatives of Canadian business, by the labour centrals, and even, almost unanimously, by traditonal nationalist circles. The virtually complete acceptance of the SGF by the latter groups may appear somewhat surprising, because, as we saw in chapters 2 and 3, many in these groups were most suspicious of any involvement by the state in the economy. This change of heart can be partially explained by a shift in Catholic social thought that occurred almost simultaneously with the Quiet Revolution.

Virtually all discussions of the change in ideology by intellectuals and political élites in Quebec in the early 1960s have ignored the impact of Pope John XXIII's encyclical of 1961, *Mater et Magistra*. This encyclical, published on the seventieth anniversary of *De Rerum Novarum* by Leo XIII and the thirtieth anniversary of *Quadragesimo Anno* by Pius XI, broke new ground in its depiction of society and the state. In doing so, it gave an added legitimacy to direct state intervention in society. It caused a stir in intellectual circles in the province, particularly among traditional thinkers who had viewed any state intervention as socialistic and hence atheistic. The idea of using the provincial government as a tool for promoting the francophone collectivity in Quebec could now be seen as quite consistent with Catholic thinking. The pope's message was widely analysed – from Jean Marchand's moral report to the special 1961 convention of the CNTU to a series of tortured articles by former Tremblay commissioner Père Arès in *Relations* in 1961 and 1962.

In the encyclical, John XXIII paid considerable attention to the vast increase in social relationships entered into by men in the modern age.[31] These relationships are usually established for limited private ends, not the general good. Accordingly, the pontiff argued, there was an increased need in the modern age for the intervention of the state in order to establish policy for the whole and to favour the co-operation of all. He added, in a sentence that could hardly be more pleasing to the COEQ or the CNTU: 'Que cette politique d'ensemble se traduise concrètement par des *plans* ou par une certaine planification de l'économie, c'est là, semble-t-il, une exigence du temps présent.'[32]

He made suggestions that appeared particularly fitting for the francophone community in Quebec. Public authorities must intervene to correct regional inequalities; the structure of the economy must stimulate the spirit of enterprise; and the state must be ready to intervene where private initiative has been lax or has failed. Further, the development of science and technology afforded the state new opportunities to reduce unevenness in the development of different zones, communities, and countires. What better justification for the creation of the SGF could be written! How closely its objectives and causes approximated the situations described by the pope! What could be more convincing for uneasy Catholic conservatives than these words from the bishop of Rome?

Despite this favourable beginning, for the first ten years of its existence the SGF was a failure. It became a place of last resort for a series of small French-Canadian firms on the verge of bankruptcy. It acquired in this process a series of businesses in sectors as widely dispersed as food processing, forest products, heavy machinery, automobile assembly, and clothing. It spawned no new avenues for French-Canadian capitalism and year after year recorded losses on its investments, which eventually totalled over fifty million dollars. It provoked no great spirit of co-operation among the public. In 1971, only 4.5 per cent of its shares were held by the public at large, the rest being in the hands of the provincial government or the caisses populaires. The only positive part of its performance was the acquisition of some companies that had potential for growth – Marine Industries (shipbuilding, heavy machinery, turbines), Forano and Volcano (heavy equipment), and Donohue (newsprint). The reprise of the SGF however only took place after a change in government policy to which we shall return below.

A second means for capitalization of indigenous entrepreneurs that evolved out of the discussions of the COEQ was the Caisse de dépôts et de placements du Québec. The caisse was created only after a bitter dispute with the federal government over pensions that will be examined in the next chapter. It was set up in order to administer funds coming initially from Quebec's pension plan. Besides making certain that these funds were profitably invested, the caisse used its capital to assume two further functions. It relieved the provincial government of some of its dependence on the English-Canadian capital market, which was controlled by a financial syndicate. In particular instances, notably the nationalization of Hydro-Québec and following the election of Daniel Johnson on a strong nationalist platform, the government of Quebec had some difficulty floating bond issues because English-Canadian banks were reluctant to buy before wringing concessions from the government.[33] The caisse quickly became a source of capital independent from that of the Canadian grande bourgeoisie and has invested over 60 per cent of its funds in bonds issued by the provincial government and other public corporations.

The caisse was also seen from the beginning as a source of capital that could be used to advance Quebec's economic development. By 1975, 17.85 per cent of its investments were in shares of companies active in Quebec. However, these investments were limited in scope by the charter of the institution. The caisse was proscribed from holding more than 30 per cent of the shares of any company and could not invest more than 30 per cent of its capital in this manner. In general, until the mid-1970s, the caisse had a minimal impact on indigenous capitalist development. It invested in both English- and French-Canadian companies. Although it came to control an increasingly significant pool of capital, it had done relatively little to advance the interests of the indigenous capitalist class which had inspired its creation.

In light of the minimal impact of the SGF and the caisse, the provincial Chambre de Commerce in 1974 again asked the provincial government to create special institutions for providing risk capital for small and medium-sized enterprises.[34] In 1976, the Liberal government passed a law creating the Sociétés de développement de l'entreprise québécoise (SODEQs). Such corporations were to invest capital in small and medium-sized manufacturing firms and to provide management assistance. Among the conditions for the creation of SODEQs were several standards that heralded a more aggressive approach to promoting an indigenous Quebec-based capitalist class. Investments had to be in a manufacturing firm with production mainly concentrated in Quebec. If the firm was owned by one person, that person had to reside in Quebec; if it was a partnership, the partners holding a majority interest had to reside in Quebec; if it was a company, a majority of its voting shares had to be held by Quebec residents.[35] This direct approach to the creation of an indigenous capitalist class grew out of disappointment with the mixed public-private approach advocated during the early 1960s and out of the realization that such a class should not be created to challenge the dominant capitalist fractions but to complement it.

Phase II: 1972–80

In the early 1970s, discontent with the policies on economic development begun in the early 1960s emerged in the public service and particularly the Department of Industry and Commerce. A series of papers both unpublished and published gradually outlined new strategy for economic development.[36] The most notable public documents were the report of the Interdepartmental Task Force on Foreign Investment (Tetley report) and the report *Bâtir le Québec* published by the Ministry of State for Economic Development under the Parti québécois government in 1979. These documents retained the same overall objective that had been pursued during the Quiet Revolution – the creation of viable capitalist enterprises controlled by members of the francophone community, thereby assuring that community greater control over economic development in the province. The situation that had to be changed was not much different from before. The modern, expanding sectors of the provincial economy were still under outside control and being developed in response to outside needs. Accordingly, the massive foreign investment in the province had had few beneficial spread effects. Local entrepreneurs were still operating small, relatively labour-intensive firms.

The strategy devised during the Quiet Revolution had been to create institutions parallel to the foreign corporations and with the help of the state to strengthen these institutions to the point where they could be competitive. The new strategy, argued the Tetley Report, had to accept the foreign-controlled sector and seek to promote the growth of industries that complemented this sector.[37] Emphasis could be placed upon creating sectors that could be integrated with these corporations. The first change in policy was a decision to co-operate rather than compete with the modern foreign-controlled sectors. An important second change was the decision to place a greater emphasis on strengthening the private sector directly for this task, rather than relying so heavily upon the state. This change in emphasis was articulated first in a working paper in the Department of Industry and Commerce: 'L'état de santé de l'économie du Québec dépendra de plus en plus dans le futur du degré de dynamisme des Québécois. Tout politique économique doit donc comporter comme première préoccupation celle de privilégier les autochtones, voir à l'éclosion d'une classe d'entrepreneurs et d'innovateurs, de favoriser une présence des Canadiens français, qui constitue le group majoritaire, dans tous les secteurs vitaux de l'économie.'[38] The same stress on creating strong Quebec-based private firms is found in the PQ government paper *Bâtir le québec*. It argued that previous policies had failed to foster a Quebec-based entrepreneurial class.[39] The continued strength of the foreign-controlled sectors under the old policy had hindered indigenous entrepreneurship. *Bâtir le Québec* thus assigned great importance to the private sector. It was to be primarily responsible for assuring economic development; it would decide where to start up an enterprise, where and when to invest, and which new markets would be tackled. The state would play a facilitating role, subsidizing the development of transportation networks, providing energy, and, where necessary, regulating foreign investment. The continuity with earlier government documents on the subject is noteworthy, because this policy contradicted the PQ platform,[40] which, in a spirit more in tune with the orientation of the early 1960s,, emphasized the state as the motor of economic development.[41]

The nationalist ideology of the Parti québécois, however, coloured its presentation of economic policy. The document emphasized the government's desire to create a strong, Quebec-based, francophone capitalist class which would acquire control of Quebec's internal market. Yet doing so without displacing the large foreign concerns meant controlling the market created by these concerns – the objective outlined in the Tetley Report. In the eyes of the Parti québécois, the strategy required as well an attempt to 'créer chez tous les agents économiques une conscience nationale.'[42] Unlike its predecessor in government, however, the Party did give greater importance to the co-operative movement. It thus revived the idea popular at the outset of the Quiet Revolution of drawing upon the largely untapped but indigenously controlled pools of capital that had grown in the thousands of caisses populaires in the province.

This new delegation of responsibility to the francophone private sector was possible in part policy-makers thought because a new class of entrepreneurs had developed in recent years. It came out of the revitalized educational system (to be discussed in chapter 6) and eschewed traditional behaviour by emphasizing growth and penetration of markets rather than short-term profits and familial security. It was ready to arrange for the merger of small and medium-sized firms in order to create the revitalized firms needed for dynamic growth.

With this change in economic policy, emphasizing growth complementary to the foreign-controlled industries and placing greater responsibility on private agents, came a change in the objectives and behaviour of the public corporations created during the 1960s. These were now encouraged to co-operate with the private sector, including foreign firms, and to enter into joint ventures where it was deemed suitable.

The revision of economic policy being considered in the 1970s had its effects on both the SGF and the Caisse de dépôts et de placements and was complemented by a rapid increase in the centralization of the francophone community's private financial institutions. In 1973, the legislature passed Bill 20, which changed the SGF from a mixed enterprise to one wholly owned by the government. The new public corporation was given a transfusion of capital and this, along with the removal of several losing investments, changed the orientation and function of the enterprise considerably. It came to resemble more a holding corporation and by 1980 had rationalized its subsidiaries to give it strength in heavy machinery and the forest industries in particular. It also became more independent of the state in its activities.

While the corporation began finally to build large, viable enterprises that were under French-Canadian control, it increased its ties with large firms outside the francophone community. Its development of the large Donohue-St-Félicien pulp and paper complex in the Saguenay was done jointly with British Columbia Forest Products. The SGF entered into an agreement with Gulf Canada and Union Carbide Canada to form a new corporation called Petromont, which would build a large petrochemical complex outside Montreal. The expansion of the particle-board firm Sogefor is to be carried out in partnership with the Noranda Group. Only the recent new forestry project at Amos was to be created in partnership with a French-Canadian firm – Normick Perron Ltd, the province's largest sawmill company.

The nature of the economic activity of the SGF thus differed somewhat from that of the earlier period. Rather than controlling and managing companies on its own, in its newer projects the corporation would share control and usually let the partner manage and run the new project on a day-to-day basis. Using this strategy, the financial balance sheet of the corporation improved immensely, with large profits being turned by the corporation. French-Canadian enterprises of the size and capacity that had long been desired were beginning to take shape. Admittedly the SGF was not itself developing and providing the personnel for managing these enterprises; this was coming more from its partners. Still, it had a sufficient say to see that these partners trained and used francophone personnel. By the late 1970s, the corporation was contributing to the development of an indigenous capitalist class in the francophone community. It was also forging links between this class and dominant fractions of the capitalist class in English Canada and the United States.

A similar picture emerges from a survey of the activities of the caisse in the 1970s. The election of the Parti québécois in 1976 brought to political power several individuals who agreed with the thinking in the Industry and Commerce bureaucracy that the caisse needed to be used more actively in support of indigenous capitalist development. Under the Parti québécois, the caisse became more active. It purchased shares in Quebec-based firms wanting to expand or being threatened with takeover by a non-Quebec firm. The most publicized example concerned Provigo, the large retail food store company. Through buying some of its shares, the caisse made certain that Sobey, a Nova Scotian firm, failed in a takeover attempt in 1977.[43] It also helped Provigo in its purchase of M. Loeb Ltd, a large food wholesaler in English Canada. However, the pressure on the caisse to intervene more extensively in the marketplace was resisted somewhat by the institution's management. Three administrators eventually resigned in 1978, and Marcel Casavan, who had headed the caisse since its inception, was replaced in 1980. His successor, Jean Campeau, was deputy minister in the Department of Finance, which was headed by Jacques Parizeau, long an advocate of a more activist caisse. Earlier, Eric Kierans had resigned from the board of directors in protest against the new activism of the caisse.[44]

By the end of the decade, the caisse held shares in 179 enterprises, mostly large Canadian corporations. The caisse used its position there to push the promotion of French Canadians to the boards of directors of these firms. It presumably obtained an opening for French Canadians into the activities of the dominant corporations operating in Quebec. It appeared unwilling to push matters further than this, however. Although it was the largest shareholder in Domtar, a company active in Quebec's forest industry, it did not or could not do anything to prevent this company from transferring a number of positions to Ontario.[45] The caisse also has tended to avoid investing in smaller enterprises, considering them too big a risk.[46] The results are the promotion of French-Canadian capital and of large, viable French-Canadian firms, but also, as in the case of the SGF, the promotion of that capital's integration with Canadian and American capital writ large.

In bringing to a close this discussion of the capitalization component of economic development since the Quiet Revolution, we should note that the desire for large sources of capital, which emerged in the 1950s, has been realized to an important degree. The Caisse de dépôts is one of the three large centralized pools of capital now controlled by the francophone community. The other two are the Banque nationale du Canada (BNC) and the Mouvement Desjardins. The BNC was formed in 1979 following a fusion between the Banque canadienne nationale and the Banque provinciale du Canada. At the time of its formation, the BNC had assets of over fifteen billion dollars, bringing it closer than any bank in French-Canadian history to the size of the 'big five' chartered banks in English Canada. It was well positioned to expand even further, having recently purchased the assets of Crédit foncier, which had a network of branches across Canada. The BNC is the only institution controlled and managed by francophones capable of offering the full range of industrial and commercial banking services. In a manner complementary to the SGF and the caisse, it clearly saw its sphere of operation to be Canada, not just Quebec.

The Mouvement Desjardins is the largest of several financial co-operatives active in Quebec. Controlling assets valued at 10.3 billion dollars in 1980, it, like the banking sector, has been involved in a process of centralization in recent years. This process has led to the constitution of a significant pool of capital controlled from a central position. The Caisses populaires Desjardins have also joined a new body, the Confédération des caisses d'épargne et de crédit. It includes the Fédération des Caisses d'économie, the Ligue des Caisses d'économie, the Fédération des caisses d'établissement, and the Fédération des caisses d'entraide. Like the Mouvement Desjardins, each of these groups has become more active in industrial investment in recent years. The Mouvement Desjardins created the Société d'investissement Desjardins (SID) and the Crédit industriel Desjardins. The SID now controls Culinar (formerly Vachon), which has recently expanded into the northeastern United States and other enterprises.

The Caisses d'entraide have invested in tourist properties in the Laurentians. However, unlike the caisse and the BNC, the financial co-operatives have relatively few ties outside the province.

Each of these three financial groups has important ties to the other two. The Mouvement Desjardins is the largest shareholder of the BNC through its previous control of the Banque provinciale. The Caisse de dépôts has recently acquired 15 per cent of the Société d'investissement Desjardins and is also a large shareholder in the BNC. Together as a group, this financial trinity has power sufficient to place it on the same level as the English-Canadian banks. Two-thirds of the trinity, excluding the co-operatives, are more and more integrated into the financial community which the English-Canadian banks dominate. The various components of the trinity show a continued willingness to co-operate with each other. The recent decision by the BNC and the caisse together with the SGF to create a venture capital company to encourage the growth of high-technology industries is a good example.[47]

The original vision of the provincial Chambre de Commerce of a banque de financement à long terme has not emerged in the form originally outlined. Rather, the spirit of the proposal, the need for a large pool of locally controlled capital in order that indigenous capitalists could make their operations viable, has been partially realized. By 1980, the three major sources of local capital had become more oriented to promotion of local capitalist development and sufficiently integrated to do this on a large scale. The original SGF had become a holding company maintaining local control over certain industries and forging ties between its sponsored entrepreneurs and English-Canadian capital. The Caisse de dépôts sponsored the expansion of a number of francophone-controlled firms and increased the involvement of francophones in major Canadian corporations. Thus the growth of French-Canadian industry that resulted from the centralization of capital involved the development of complementary, not competitive, ties with English-Canadian capital. In reviewing business activity in Quebec for the year 1980, Michel Nadeau, economics specialist for *Le Devoir,* summarized it with the phrase 'la nord-américanisation de l'entreprise québécoise.'[48] This continental orientation of business in French Quebec has consequences for the independence movement, as I shall explain more fully in the conclusion to this chapter.

Fostering the modern enterprise

The need to develop larger pools of capital was not the only objective outlined by the francophone business class in the 1950s. These pools of capital, it was argued, could be used effectively only if there was a reorientation of the traditional French-Canadian firm. The firm had to move away from its small familial character and its conservative investment tendencies to become larger, more entrepreneurial, and more willing to take risks. Bringing about such changes may be left to the whims of the market, to business associations, or to the state. Perhaps because leaving matters to market forces would have seriously undermined the francophone business class, and because business associations were unaccustomed to assuming such functions, the provincial government, when pressed, responded by introducing several measures in these areas. In the end, these policies contributed to the development of a stronger business class but did so by promoting its integration with the dominant fractions of capital in Canada and the United States.

The first kind of response involved changes in the Department of Industry and Commerce. In 1961, the department set up a Regional Studies division in its Economic Research Bureau. This was followed by a series of steps attempting to set up a regional structure for the department through which it could reach entrepreneurs at the local level. These moves culminated in a plan jointly developed by the department's Economic Research Bureau and the COEQ to divide Quebec into ten administrative regions and to set up offices of the department in each.[49] In subsequent years, the delegates in these offices conducted training seminars on various topics for business leaders and their staffs. The department also supported the Centre des dirigeants d'entreprise, a business association representing small and middle-sized francophone firms, which was conducting a program to encourage mergers and regroupings of small and medium-sized enterprises. The department saw the mélange of firms in this category as a possible basis for the development of an efficacious private sector. Such firms could concentrate on obtaining technological advances in a very specialized area. This new technology could then serve as a means for integrating these firms' activities with those of large firms, including foreign-controlled ones, and thus as a basis for the creation of new jobs and regional development. Such an emphasis on the growth of small firms with advanced technological expertise was, of course, perfectly consistent with the department's new orientation in policy in the early 1970s, described above.

The regional structure put in place by the Department of Industry and Commerce in the mid-1960s quickly became a means for collecting information and disseminating financial assistance. Through its 1967 Quebec Industrial Credit Bureau Act, the government took from the municipalities responsibility for disbursing aid and placed it in the hands of the new Office du crédit industriel du Québec. This corporation was given the objective of promoting the development of the manufacturing industry of Quebec. These structures were supplemented in 1968 by new programs designed to encouraged implanation of industry outside the Montreal and Quebec City metropolitan areas and to foster the growth of high-technology industry in the province.[50] Grants in the latter program were made conditional on the hiring of engineers, technicians, administrators, and scientists who held degrees from Quebec universities. These programs were revised further in 1971 with the passage of the Quebec Industrial Development Assistance Act, which created a new Société de développement industriel (SDI) to succeed the Office de crédit industriel. The SDI was given the power to acquire up to 30 per cent of a business's capital stock and up to 10 per cent of its total assets.

Generally, prior to 1973, the funds disbursed by the SDI continued to go to the larger, mostly foreign-controlled corporations. Fournier reports that in 1973, the SDI took a more nationalistic turn and sought to promote the growth of indigenous capital, specifically small and medium-sized firms.[51] Formal agreements began to be signed with corporations that tied grants to the hiring of graduates from Quebec's universities, to increased efforts to have francophones represented at management levels, and so on. This shift in direction by the SDI was accompanied by the new programs in the Department of Industry and Commerce to support small and medium-sized firms.

The change in the orientation of the SDI, of course, corresponded to similar shifts in direction in the area of capitalization which we have already discussed. The policy of promoting the growth of an indigenous capitalist class was also supported by two other government-created institutions. In 1969, the government of Quebec had set up a Centre de recherche industrielle du Québec (CRIQ). The objective of the centre was to provide research services to smaller firms that could not afford their own research operations *in situ*. Gradually, throughout the 1970s, the budget of the CRIQ increased. By 1977–8, it employed 217 people and reported that over 90 per cent of its work was done for firms with fewer than 500 employees.[52] Shortly after taking power, the Parti québécois created the Société de développement coopératif to provide the same kind of financial support to co-operative undertakings as the SDI did to private firms. The government continued the pattern of supporting indigenous firms by subdividing the SDI into two parts, one being a separate SDI-Exportation which was to manage and expand programs promoting exports.[53]

In closing this discussion of the policy designed to modernize or expand the indigenous firms of the province, I would emphasize two points. First, the objective was not to supplant the large foreign-controlled firms but to build a series of smaller, modern, technologically advanced enterprises that could complement the foreign sector and expand on the basis of their complementarity. The policy was integrationist and hence very much in the spirit of the 1970s. Second, to the extent that such a policy is successful, to the extent that firms are developed that are more and more integrated into the existing corporate structure, the basis for nationalism in the indigenous capitalist class becomes weaker and weaker. What is more, and this point is often overlooked, an important means for rallying working-class support to nationalism is also attenuated. Hence the economic policy of the various governments was creating the basis for divisions within the working class based on whether the individual worker was in the private or the public sector.

Indigenous processing of natural resources

One of the major points of agreement among the francophone business class, the members of the nationalist societies, and organized labour during the late 1950s was that Quebec did not transform sufficiently its natural resources into finished products. They saw the continued export of natural resources in brute form as severely weakening the already underdeveloped economy of French Quebec. Further, in the views of each of the class fractions articulating positions on these points, the development of a manufacturing industry that was integrated with Quebec's resource wealth required some kind of planning or a coherent government strategy. In the early 1960s, the COEQ received the support of each as the body that could articulate such a plan or strategy. Before it began to wane in influence in the mid-1960s, it did make several sweeping proposals in this direction, and to a degree these were initiated. However, as the 1960s progressed, the government slowly abandoned this global approach to the problem and adopted a more piecemeal approach, whereby it sought to develop particular sectors. In all cases, it can be said that policy had a limited impact on the basically dependent structure described in chapter 1. However, by 1980 there were in place some institutions that could help make a dent in that structure.

COEQ and the development of a steel industry

By 1960, Quebec produced more iron ore than any other province. Yet it had not a single blast furnace or any primary steel industry. Perception of these facts as an anomaly was not new. Duplessis had scoffed at ideas articulated in the 1940s for the development of a steel industry.[54] He had rejected the suggestions of Bishop Labrie for the establishment of a steel industry on the northern shore of the gulf.[55] The coming to power of the Parti libéral and its approach to economic policy created an atmosphere more favourable to these kinds of proposals. In May 1961, the CCPQ in its brief to the Department of Natural Resources renewed the call for a primary iron and steel complex in Quebec.[56] The matter was taken up by the COEQ, which recommended that a mixed corporation similar to the SGF be created. The argument for the steel industry given by the COEQ pointed to how such an industry could become the centre of a whole new series of industries that could be developed based upon it.[57] In 1964, the government obtained approval of legislation creating such a corporation, the Sidérurgie du Quebec or Sidbec.

During the next four years, a variety of studies were done and discussions took place, but the company remained essentially a paper entity. Impatient, the increasingly active independence party, the Rassemblement pour l'indépendance nationale (RIN), and the major labour centrals called for an end to the mixed corporation and for a fully publicly owned entity.[58] Others, including Eric Kierans, also suggested this approach, In 1968, the company's status was changed to that of a public corporation, and it purchased the assets of Dosco, a steel subsidiary of the British company Hawker Siddeley, to provide it with a base for growth. Dosco, it was felt, already had developed markets and possessed certain managerial and technical human resources that Sidbec lacked. This strategy of purchasing a significant private actor in an industry and building upon it was to be repeated in the asbestos industry.

Sidbec immediately embarked upon a major project to modernize the Dosco plants and built a new furnace to complete the Dosco holdings at Contrecoeur. As these revamped plants came on stream, Sidbec found itself more and more short of iron ore and had to import the mineral from outside the province. Virtually all of the province's best and most accessible reserves were controlled by foreign-controlled corporations, especially Iron Ore Company of Canada. To remedy this problem, Sidbec began to develop its own mines at Fire Lake and Port Cartier in partnership with British Steel and Quebec Cartier Mining Company. These developments required investments well in excess of 200 million dollars but helped the corporation to become more vertically integrated and thus stronger. The coming to power of the Parti québécois in 1976 changed little in the company's path of development, save perhaps to reinforce its publicly owned character. Jean-Paul Gignac, the president of Sidbec, who had overseen the company's rapid rise to prominence, was replaced in 1979. Gignac had at times felt uncomfortable with the public character of Sidbec and had hoped to turn it over eventually to private interests. Following the pattern established with the caisse de dépôts, Gignac was replaced by a public servant, Robert de Coster, president of the Régie d'assurance automobile created by the government in 1977. The move was seen by some as an attempt by the government to assume greater control of the corporation.[59]

By the first quarter of 1980, Sidbec's manufacturing operations had reached the level of profitability.[60] Overall, the company was still in the red because of difficulties in its mining operations. These difficulties, it was expected, would be short term. Concerning the original notion of encouraging more indigenous processing of natural resources, Sidbec cannot as yet be said to have had a large impact. In 1968, the year Sidbec took control of Dosco, Quebec accounted for 7.8 per cent of the value added in Canadian iron and steel production. In 1977, after the modernization of the old Dosco facilities, Quebec accounted for 10.18 per cent of the value added.[61] Thus Quebec had increased its share of Canadian production by about 2.4 per cent over the first ten years of Sidbec's existence.

These figures may appear promising but they must be considered along with information on exports of Quebec's iron ore. In 1957, when the first major shipments of iron ore from the Ungava region were made, Quebec shipped 93.8 per cent of the mined ore directly for export. At late as 1976, 97.6 per cent of the ore mined was exported. In 1978, the figure was 89.7 per cent, only 4 per cent below that of 1957 when large exports began.[62] Another hope of the COEQ was that an indigenous steel industry would have spread effects to other industries. Fournier writes that there is no evidence that this has occurred yet.[63] He does note, however, that Sidbec brought francophones into senior levels of management in the industry, where there had been few of them before.

Asbestos
Asbestos occupies an almost mythical position in the culture of francophone Quebec. The famous strike of 1949, its retelling in fiction and on the stage, and the huge depressions in the soils of L'Estrie left by the mines are well known. The mineral has also come to symbolize, as iron once did, the weakness of Quebec's economy. Virtually all the asbestos mined in Quebec is shipped abroad unprocessed. In 1975, over 95 per cent of that extracted was exported in this condition. Quebec was the largest producer of asbestos in the non-communist world and manufactured virtually none of what it produced. Annually, as Quebec's leading exports were surveyed, raw asbestos was seen among the top ten.

    Although asbestos was in the forefront of concerns about the lack of manufacturing of Quebec's natural resources, it did not become a pronounced object of public policy in the 1960s as did iron ore. In the late 1960s, the CSN and later the Parti québécois began to question more stridently the use of the asbestos resource. Evidence of a similar questioning in the public service emerges in 1973 just when the concerns about capitalization discussed above were being raised. In July 1973, under the aegis of the Direction générale des mines in the Department of Natural Resources, a study program on asbestos was created. From it there emerged a working document by Normand Alexandre that provided the blueprint for the policy that eventually emerged.[64]

    Alexandre focused on the problem of increasing the processing of asbestos in Quebec. He noted that the asbestos mining industry was controlled largely by multinational corporations. The logic of profitability for these corporations was to extract the ore in Quebec and to export it to those areas in the world where labour was cheap. Under these circumstances, in Alexandre's view, there was virtually no chance that a significant manufacturing industry would develop with the existing corporations in the industry. Some more exceptional means would be needed to create such an industry. In developing such a means, care would need to be taken because the organization of the asbestos industry was very structured. It was highly concentrated, with four companies – Johns

Manville, Turner and Newall, Cape Asbestos, and Eternit – responsible for the production and distribution of more than 50 per cent of the fibre mined in the non-communist world.[65] These companies did not really compete with each other – they simply divided up the markets. Alexandre argued that any policy would need to take account of this organization.

The Parti québécois had proposed the creation of a government-controlled marketing office for asbestos.[66] This office would be the exclusive agent for buying and selling the mineral mined in the province and would be given the powers needed to increase the manufacture of the mineral locally. Alexandre argued against this policy; he felt that it would disturb unduly the market positions held by Quebec in the world. Quebec might lose its position and not be able to regain it. The CSN favoured the nationalization of the mines. Alexandre rejected this proposal; he saw it as being difficult to carry out and possibly futile. In nationalizing the mines, the province would still lack the marketing organization of the companies. Again the penetration of the world market achieved by the Quebec industry would be threatened, and these losses could hardly be compensated for by producing finished products for the Canadian market.

Alexandre recommended another policy. He suggested that the province seek control of a slice of the industry and use this position as a base for increasing the manufacture of the mineral. He argued that, in order to conserve time and money, the province buy an existing corporation with extensive mines and use that company as its base. This strategy is not unlike that used by Sidbec in purchasing Dosco. Which company should the government purchase? Alexandre reviewed the possibilities. Johns Manville, the company involved in the famous strike and the largest in the province, might have seemed the best candidate. Alexandre argued that its bad reputation was largely undeserved:

On se demande pourquoi on s'en prend si souvent à la Johns Manville lorsque l'on parle de l'amiante au Québec (pays). Ses performances ne sont pas les plus mauvaises. Cela est d'autant plus vrai que nulle autre compagnie n'a contribué davantage à l'augmentation de la production d'amiante du Québec. Par ses investissements à l'étranger, la Johns Manville a contribué et contribue toujours à l'expansion des marchés existants et au développement de nouveaux. Elle est en quelque sorte monitrice de la production québécoise dans laquelle elle joue un rôle de première importance.[67]

He recommended Asbestos Corporation, owned by General Dynamics of St Louis, Missouri. Unlike Johns Manville, it had made no effort to process the mineral in Quebec. It had recently opened a new mine in the Ungava region and shipped all the mineral mined there to a plant in Nordenham, West Germany. He described its behaviour as a 'contreperformance.'[68] It possessed good mines, being able to offer a virtually complete selection of chrysolite fibres, which accounted for 95 per cent of the world's production.[69] Purchasing the company would not affect at all Quebec's positions in the world market.

When the Parti québécois came to power, it was apparently persuaded by Alexandre's logic and abandoned its own more radical proposals. During its first government, it gained passage of a law bringing into being the Société nationale de l'amiante. (SNA). The SNA sought to purchase Asbestos Corporation, a move that the latter fought in the courts. In March 1981 the courts made it clear that the expropriation could not be blocked by the company. The agreement to purchase the corporation was finally reached later that year. While the struggle was in the courts, the SNA sought to put in place the infrastructure it would need to begin a processing industry, most significantly by purchasing Bell Asbestos from the British firm of Turner and Newall. Bell Asbestos possessed the largest plant for the secondary processing of the mineral in the province and a well-developed sales department. The SNA thus seemed poised in the early 1980s to develop a secondary asbestos industry.

Other examples of attempts to improve the manufacturing base of the province through the development of natural resources, such as that of the Société québécoise d'exploration minière (Soquem), could be cited, but they would only amplify what is clear from the study of Sidbec and the SNA. The government has sought to increase the amount of indigenous processing of resources, following strategies that emerged originally from the COEQ. These strategies are designed to integrate public corporations as viable players in the private markets. These corporations co-operate with the private sector entering into business arrangements with them and respecting the existing market structure. The emphasis has been again on integrating the francophone entrepreneurial class into the continental capitalist system. The policies followed show some promise for eventually constructing a more autocentric economy in the province. At the same time, valuable time and resources have been lost to the province since the hue and cry of the 1950s. The disposal of resources lamented at that time has scarcely changed since. The somewhat slow development of a viable private sector in the francophone community as the means for increasing control over the province's resources has continued to be supported by the business classes both within and outside the francophone community. However, the remaining partners in the Quiet Revolution coalition have become disenchanted with the economic policies begun in the early 1960s. For the working class, the labour market remains highly unstable, and unemployment has not eased. For the nationalists, the advances in economic control for francophones have not prevented the erosion of a distinctive French-Canadian culture. Accordingly, the original coalition began to break up after 1965, and with it also went the sense of unity and strength that characterized the early 1960s.

Economic control: Public or private

By the end of the 1950s, there was general agreement among the members of the francophone business class, the organs of labour, and the nationalistic middle class on three points. First, French-Canadian participation in the economy of Quebec had to be strengthened. Second, in moving to increase participation, special emphasis had to be placed on increasing the processing in Quebec of the province's resource wealth. Third, movement toward these first two objectives would require planning and thus an increased role for the provincial government. Agreement on these three issues helped to bring about their inclusion in the 1960 electoral program of the Parti libéral and perhaps contributed to the sense of societal unity and promise of fast progress that characterized the early 1960s. None the less, this agreement was based on the differing needs of the three classes involved. The business class was concerned about the increasing lack of viability of small, family-owned firms in the post-war corporate economy and feared that its already weak position was going to deteriorate further. The concerns of labour were jobs and the lowering of unemployment, which were linked ideologically with the stabilization of what it perceived to be a chaotic, resource-oriented economy. Nationalists saw increased economic control as a precondition for the maintenance of a distinctive French-Canadian culture.

These differences among the three groups were reflected in slight differences in emphasis on these points. The CTCC/CSN desired a more elaborate state planning apparatus, complete with public corporations. The business class wanted a less elaborate mechanism that drew from and relied upon the private sector. The middle-class nationalists appeared willing to accept either approach if their goals were realized.

These differences, muted in 1960, became accentuated and much sharper as the working class in particular saw the government adopt the emphasis of the business class and saw its economic problems remain unsolved. A variety of factors brought organized labour and the patronat into conflict after 1965. Many related to the unionization of the public sector that took place following adoption of a revised labour code in 1964. The differences over economic policy also became a part of the struggle between classes and thus were a force in the process of class formation and the development of articulated class ideologies. The middle classes tended to be caught in the cross-fire of these struggles, now leaning one way, now the other.

This section of the chapter will begin with a description on a general plane of the process of class formation and of ideological development. It will be followed by a discussion of two cases relating to economic policy that became part of the struggles and thus factors in the process of class formation. The first case is the nationalization of hydro-electric power companies in 1962, and the second is the debate that developed over the proper policy for developing the forest resource in Quebec.

Ideological divisions emerge

Already, in the early 1960s, the divisions between the working class and the business class over economic policy were presaged. The moral reports given by Jean Marchand, then general president of the CSN, to its 1962 and 1964 conventions were characterized by an increasingly intense critique of the workings of the capitalist system and particularly of the effects of foreign ownership. Marchand upbraided the labour movement for its haphazard analysis of the economy and for its lack of an ideology from which a systematic critique could be developed. When Marchand entered federal politics in 1965, he was succeeded by Marcel Pepin, who sought to remedy the problem defined by Marchand.

Starting in 1966, with a series of moral reports, 'Une société bâtie pour l'homme,' 'Le Deuxième Front,' and 'Un camp de la liberté,' Pepin began to sketch out the bases of an ideology. Following, in part, the humanist tradition inherited from Catholicism, Pepin reiterated the long-held belief of the CNTU that society must be centred on man and his fulfilment, not on profit. He described grimly the growing corporatization and integration of capitalist enterprises and the chaotic way in which this growth was proceeding.[70] His critique extended to the state as well, emphasizing the oppressive way in which it treated its workers. By 1970, he was describing an alliance between the state and employers against the workers. He argued that the provincial authorities and employers were united as they had been at Asbestos in 1949 and together formed a new superman ('surhomme') fighting the working man: 'Nous nous sommes retrouvés dans le même entonnoir avec l'État et l'entreprise contre nous. Il en était ainsi en 1949, mais aujourd'hui, les deux sont coordonnés, conjugés, concertés par des moyens techniques puissants qui en font un seul pouvoir, un nouveau surhomme: un bras économique, un bras politique, mais un seul cerveau.'[71] Such an analysis indicates that a substantial gap had developed between labour and the patronat by this time.

Pepin's solution to the problem was also firmly in the tradition of the CTCC/CSN – open a second front using the labour movement as a tool of critique. In 1966, he stated, 'La plus grande mission du syndicalisme consiste à faire une critique approfondie des maux de la société, a préciser les remèdes qu'elle entend y apporter et à faire le nécessaire pour qu'ils soient appliqués.'[72] In 1966 and 1967, the FTQ showed little enthusiasm for a second front.[73] However, as the unemployment picture darkened and the political leaders of the province hardened their response to labour demands in the public sector, the FTQ began to look more to co-operation with other labour bodies and eventually participated in a series of regional colloquia with the CSN and the Centrale de l'enseignement du Québec (CEQ) early in 1970. There was growing concern emanating from the leadership of the FTQ that the labour movement had become moribund, out of touch with the poor, 'bourgeois.' This kind of criticism was also made by socially radical clerics in the Mouvement des travailleurs chrétiens (MTC), formerly the Ligue ouvrière catholique, who tended to work among the poorer, usually unorganized members of the working class. Thus Laurent Denis, an Oblate and national chaplain of the MTC, wrote: 'Or si nous jetons un regard réaliste sur le monde ouvrier tel qu'il existe chez nous, sur l'ensemble des travailleurs à qui s'adresse le MTC, on est contraint de reconnaître que les engagés sont en très petit nombre, que la conscience ouvrière existe peu, et que le militantisme est à peu près absent même a l'intérieur du mouvement ouvrier.'[74] Thus it was more and more realized that opening a 'second front' would require a major revitalization of the institutions of organized labour.

When economic conditions continued stagnant through the early 1970s, further impetus was given to this process of critique. As factories closed in somewhat disturbing numbers, particularly in the metallurgy industry, the CSN produced a document called *Il n'y a plus d'avenir dans le système économique actuel.*[75] It was followed by the manifesto *Ne comptons que sur nos propres moyens,* which called upon the workers of the CSN to strive for the realization of socialism in Quebec. *Il n'y a plus* was approved by the 1972 convention of the CSN, although the same group also rejected Marxism as an appropriate ideology for the CSN.[76] Similar ideological developments took place in the FTQ and the CEQ. Each issued important statements calling for some variant of socialism.[77]

The idea of socialism was, of course, not new to Quebec. What was new was its open espousal by organized labour. Socialism had been promoted as early as 1954 by industrial unions in Quebec, and a Ligue d'action socialiste had been formed.[78] This tradition was carried on in the FTQ in the form of support for social democratic parties but never as open endorsement of socialism. The brand of socialism that came to be espoused by the labour movement in the early 1970s was much closer to Marxist socialism and more radical than the social democracy promoted by the FTQ and the New Democratic Party.

None the less, striking out on the road to socialism generated heated debate and finally fission within the CSN. In the spring of 1972, Paul-Émile Dalpé, vice-president of the CSN, Jacques Dion, treasurer, and Amédie Daigle, service director, led between thirty and forty thousand workers out of the CSN into a new organization, the Centrale des syndicats démocratiques (CSD). The move appeared to be precipitated by two factors. First, there was disagreement over the role of the labour movement in society. The dissidents, usually referred to as the 'Three Ds,' regretted the increased politicization of the CSN. They argued that unions should devote themselves more to the immediate interests of workers, rather than worrying about mobilizing them politically. Second, they suggested that the CSN had been captured by 'anarchic intellectuals' who sought to constrain the movement within the confines of a dogma, an action which, in their view, was alienating the rank and file from the leadership. However, it was not only a break over ideology. Two further dimensions characterized the dispute. First, the overwhelming majority of the departing workers were from the private sector, in particular from textiles, metallurgy, and woodworking industries.[79] These workers had long constituted the core of the CSN's private-sector unions and resented the latter-day rise in strength of public employees in the organization. Second, the departing workers were largely from outside Montreal and were somewhat hostile to the radicalism of the Montreal Central Council.[80] One finds, accordingly, that by December 1973, 100,000 of the remaining 173,000 workers in the CSN were employed in the public sector.[81]

The response by private employers to these positions was primarily organizational. The ideology of free enterprise that came from this class was well established. In the view of some, what was lacking was the effective presentation and defence of that ideology, and as labour radicalized steps were taken to remedy this weakness. In Quebec, a small francophone employers' group, the Association professionnelle des industriels, (API) had long promoted greater unity among employers, based upon its belief in Catholic corporatism. The API, which changed its name to the Centre des dirigeants d'entreprise in the late 1960s, continued to promote such unity even after the enthusiasm for corporatism waned. Its ideas were largely ignored until 1966, when the Conseil du Patronat du Québec (CPQ) was formed. The CPQ, however, remained a paper organization until 1969, when a permanent secretariat was established. The CPQ has a mixed structure, having as its members other business interest associations as well as individual corporations. It was set up to study, promote, and develop the economic and social interests of employers, to co-ordinate patronal activities in the province, and to communicate employers' interests to politicians and to the state. The CPQ has strong backing from the English-Canadian and French-Canadian fractions of the capitalist class in Quebec. It has quickly achieved a position of influence, commenting widely on public affairs, having an annual meeting with the cabinet on the budget, and having three representatives on the Quebec Planning and Development Council, a successor body to the COEQ.

At the same time as the CPQ was being formed, the provincial government formed the General Council of Industry (GCI). Set up in February 1969, the GCI is made up of the top industrialists and financiers in the province. Its function is to advise the minister of industry and commerce on business opinion and to make proposals about government economic policy. Fournier reports that the GCI has a significant influence on the Quebec Planning and Development Council.[82] It has continued to function throughout the Parti québécois's years in power.

These two institutions made more certain that the formulation of a more coherent, radical ideology by organized labour would be effectively countered in government circles and in society at large. In countering the proposals of labour, these groups have stressed that the private sector must be given the opportunity to develop an industry or economic sector before any public involvement and without any competition from the public sector. This primacy of the private sector has been repeatedly recognized by governments. Guy St-Pierre, minister of industry and commerce, in a speech to the CMA in May 1972, after stating how such government corporations as Soquem, the Société québécoise d'initiatives petrolières (Soquip), and Rexfor existed to serve private enterprise, concluded: 'L'entreprise privée, encadrée dans une législation progressiste, demeure le meilleur champ pour le développement industriel du Québec.'[83] We have already noted similar professions of faith in the PQ policy document *Bâtir le Québec,* published in 1979.

The position of the Parti québécois in power was not the one it promoted prior to its election victory. Throughout the early 1970s, it reflected a more typical petit bourgeois position in calling for significant extension of the public sector as the major form of involvement of the state in the economy. In its 1973 program, the party was obviously influenced by the radical turn in labour and called for the subordination of profitability to social welfare in the orientation of the economy. It hoped that an economic system would be established 'éliminant toute forme d'exploitation des travailleurs et repondant aux besoins réels de l'ensemble des Québécois plutôt qu'aux exigences d'une minorité économique favorisée.'[84] Such more socialistic sentiments were echoed by church militants active among the poor and even found their way temporarily onto the editorial pages of the formerly staid, conservative Jesuit journal *Relations.*[85]

What should be clear, therefore, is that on an ideological plane, the coalition of classes that had spurred the Quiet Revolution of the early 1960s quickly fell apart. As the decade progressed, the organized trade union movement and the employers took their distance from each other on the political plane and reinforced their organizations for intense ideological struggle. The nationalistic elements of the middle classes tended to move left in their orientation, although they remained more reformist and confident in the state as a potential neutral arbiter than did their labour counterparts. These divisions, which became more and more magnified through ideological struggle, were also sharpened in political struggles. Two of these political struggles serve to illustrate how these divisions were developed.

The nationalization of electricity in 1962

An important area of the post-war economy where the French-Canadian community had significant economic power was the production and distribution of hydro-electricity. In 1944, under the Liberal government of Adélard Godbout, a public corporation, Hydro-Québec, had been created and took over the company of Montreal Light, Heat, and Power. The Montreal market in the ensuing years was strong, and Hydro-Québec grew in strength. By 1960, it, along with Shawinigan Power, Gatineau Power, and Alcan, produced 89.5 per cent of the power in Quebec.[86] It was becoming clear that the next step in the development of electricity in the province was the building of dams on the Manicouagan and Outardes rivers. The investments required were massive.

While these economic developments were taking place, concern about control over the generation and distribution of electricity was being voiced at the political level. A call for the nationalization of the electricity 'trusts' in the province had been raised by the Action libérale nationale in the 1930s. In the 1950s it was increasingly raised again. In 1954, in its brief to the Tremblay Commission, the SSJBM called for an extension of Hydro-Québec. In 1949, 1955, and regularly from 1958, the CTCC resolved at its annual meetings that the production and distribution of electricity in the province be state-controlled. The FTQ began a similar series of resolutions starting with its 1960 convention.

Shortly after the Parti libéral came to power in 1960, it became clear that this proposal enjoyed some currency with René Lévesque, minister of natural resources. It was evident that with labour and groups such as the SSJBM supporting the idea, it might be politically feasible. Two-thirds of the Quiet Revolution coalition were in favour. The other third is more difficult to gauge but was probably opposed. The CCPQ, in a brief to Lévesque in July 1961, recommended against the use of nationalization as a means for recapturing parts of the economy, including the production of electricity. In an editorial in its journal *Faits et tendances* in April 1962, the CCPQ repeated its message.[87] It argued that nationalization was contrary to the fundamental principles of a free-enterprise economy. The opposition by the CCPQ was matched by the opposition of English-Canadian capital. The CMA sent several messages to the government warning against such an action.[88] After nationalization had taken place, the English-Canadian banks, through their syndicat financier, made things very difficult for the government when it sought to raise the capital required for the transaction. Thus, unlike the other economic policies pursued in the early 1960s, the nationalization of Hydro-Québec did not enjoy the full support of the Quiet Revolution coalition. Yet the government persisted. Why?

Three possible explanations have been given. The first and most usual is that nationalization was a logical outcome of the new nationalist ideology that was sweeping élite circles and the new middle class. A fundamental premise of this ideology was that the state should be given primary responsibility for giving French Canadians control of their economic destiny. A move to nationalize electricity was consistent with the assumption of such a responsibility. There are two problems, with this explanation. First, there was no such ideology in any elaborated sense shared by the three groups motivating the Quiet Revolution. The issue of state involvement separated rather than joined them. Second, the government showed only flashes of such beliefs, being somewhat more attuned to the business class than to labour. In short, once one replaces the new-middle-class theory of the Quiet Revolution (noted in the Introduction) by the coalition theory, this kind of explanation becomes less tenable.

Carol Jobin has proposed a second kind of explanation that draws from a particular Marxist theory about economic development in advanced monopoly capitalism.[89] The logic of capitalist development in general was toward greater concentration in ownership, and as these processes continued, pressure was placed on the electricity industry to become more concentrated as well. Concentration in ownership was required if sufficient pools of capital were to be found to finance the further development of production sites. However, Jobin notes, the low profitability of the industry meant that the private sector was less than enthusiastic about assuming the risks involved. In such instances during the advanced monopoly stages of capitalism, the state is called upon to intervene directly and to assume responsibility for the high-risk sectors. The provincial government, Jobin argues, felt such pressures, nationalized electricity production, and thereby provided power at cheaper rates, using a more rational grid than the dominant corporations in the economy.

There are several problems with this explanation. First, it states that nationalization was in the interests of the capitalist class, while in fact members of that class actively opposed it. Hence one needs to argue that the state knows the interests of the capitalist class better than do its members. Second, the theory of monopoly capitalism upon which it is based has been roundly criticized by other Marxists in debates the substance of which is beyond this study.[90] Third, Faucher and Blais have suggested that profit rates in electrical production were not as low as Jobin assumed.[91] Further, they do not find any evidence that large monopoly corporations benefitted more from the action than did others. Accordingly, nationalization was not necessarily done in order to benefit large capital, and there might have been sufficient profits avaialble to incite the private sector to expand hydro-electric facilities.

This leaves a third possible explanation. Hydro-Québec, with its control of the Montreal market, enjoyed an increasingly dominant position in the provincial system. It was in a good position to expand its control of production and to cement its dominance by developing the Manicouagan. In order to build up its strength for such expansion, it felt more and more a need to absorb one of the larger private companies in the field. Such expansion – the logical product of the operation of normal market forces – converged well with the overall objectives of the Quiet Revolution. It brought francophones increased economic power; it did so through more intensive exploitation of natural resources; and it gave the state an additional instrument that could be used to plan further development. The market competitors of Hydro-Québec – the private sector – were opposed. The francophone business class, which adhered to a strict free-enterprise ideology and feared monopoly power, was also opposed. The government was able to play upon the nationalistic aspects of the proposal and its probable spread effects throughout the economy to swing labour and the middle classes behind it. Spokesmen for both of these groups were much more willing to tolerate monopoly if it were public and if it meant increased indigenous control of natural resources.

Whatever the economic effects of the nationalization, politically it drove a wedge into the Quiet Revolution coalition. The intense politicization of the issue through an election campaign made clear to the élites involved that there were opposing sides, with labour and elements of the middle class on the one side and business and other elements of the middle class on the other. The class conflict here anticipated the ideological conflicts and splits that were soon to follow.

Control and development of the forest resource

Quebec's most important resource-based industry is the manufacture of pulp and paper. The production of pulp and paper has been traditionally in the hands of a small number of large companies controlled by interests outside the francophone community. These companies did not own the majority of the forests they logged but had contracted with the provincial government to farm large tracts of forest called timber limits. Through these timber limits, they effectively controlled the public forests. Traditionally, significant amounts of the logging done for the industry had been contracted out to small entrepreneurs or co-operatives which had in turn drawn their manpower from the farming communities of rural Quebec. The logging had been carried out in the winter when snow facilitated the dragging of logs and manpower was available.

Increasingly after the war, with the advent of power saws and logging trucks, there was a tendency toward professionalization of the bûcheron, with work taking place year round and most intensively in the spring and summer.[92] Still, the exploitative situation of the woodcutters and the overall absence of francophone control in the province's largest industry meant that it would become an object of policy in the early 1960s. We have already noted above the concern of the CCPQ that greater returns be brought to French Quebec from the forest resource. The strategy that was adopted was to use the SGF, which was after all a mixed public-private enterprise, as a means for entering the industry. The SGF created a holding company, Sogefor, in the pulp-and-paper sector in 1963. Sogefor purchased three small plants, Albert Gigaire, the Dubé mill, and Maki and built another one, Dupan. None of these was very successful. By 1972, Gigaire and Maki had been sold off and Dubé shut down, and Dupan was operating shakily after already closing down once. The strategy developed by the government through the SGF in tandem with local business élites was obviously not working.

In the early 1970s, the Department of Lands and Forests sought to develop a new approach to the forests. Upon examining the department's consultations with the various parties concerned, it is evident that there was little common ground among them. The basis for consensus that had existed in the late 1950s no longer existed. The issues of who should control the forest resource and how that resource should be exploited were major points of division. The Fédération des travailleurs des pâtes et du papier (CSN) called for the abolition of timber limits and for a return to some sort of popular control of the forests.[93] For this policy, it suggested a public corporation to oversee and plan the exploitation of the resource and a board to manage the forests. It requested as well the creation of a second public corporation that would be engaged in the manufacture and processing of the timber and pulpwood. These positions developed by organized labour also came to be part of the electoral program of the Parti québécois. They implied that the provincial government would plan and direct the exploitation of the resource, thereby relieving the private companies of their initiative in this regard. Although it was not yet clear how large a role it would be, the province was also to become more involved in the processing of the resource.

The Fédération des producteurs de bois du Québec, an autonomous subsidiary of the Union catholique des cultivateurs and a representative of the small contractors and woodcutters, called for a different reorganization of forest activity.[94] It noted that about 180,000 proprietors owned on average sixty acres of forest. This acreage compared poorly with the 500 to 1500 acres that formed the basis of a profitable operation. It called upon the government to redistribute and integrate forest properties so that a viable small-proprietor class could emerge. It pointed to waste and to irrational allocations of land under the existing timber limits and asked that these problems be eliminated. It thus agreed with labour and with the Parti québécois that the provincial government, rather than the large companies, should have more control over forests. However, it was not anxious to see the province involved in the primary production of the resource, a task that could be assumed by the independent producers with proper planning.

Pulp and paper companies were opposed to further involvement by the provincial government in the forestry industry. They preferred the status quo, where public involvement was restricted to building roads and reforesting blighted areas. The government, however, did not conclude that it could abstain from further involvement in the industry. Two considerations motivated its decision. First, the existing system of timber limits was becoming more and more a tangled web of jurisdictions, interfering with rational exploitation of the forest and prohibiting systematic reforestation policies. Second, the forestry industry, like other resource industries, remained outside the control of francophones and was being exploited in response to the needs of mainly foreign interests. In 1972, the Department of Lands and Forests published a green paper which contained the nucleus for the policy that was to emerge.[95] In noting the need for greater planning in the development of the forest resource, the paper argued that the government had to assume a greater role in the management of public forests. It suggested that the government might enter into contracts with smaller producers in agricultural areas for managing some smaller tracts of land. The vehicle for this increased role was to be a new managing corporation that would allocate forests to companies and prepare plans for their rational harvesting. Once forests were allocated, the government was also to contract with the companies involved to ensure that the logged areas were properly reforested.

The paper also recommended a greater role for the province in the exploitation of the resource. Through a public corporation, the government would consolidate many of the small French-Canadian enterprises involved in the cutting and preparing of wood. The ideal vehicle for this purpose, it felt, was the existing public corporation, Rexfor, created in 1969 to reclaim forested areas and to sell salvage wood left from logging operations.[96] The insertion of an expanded Rexfor into the industry was seen as a means to begin to force the industry to work more in the interests of the people of Quebec. The role proposed for Rexfor was similar to that of both the SNA and Sidbec – to obtain a share of the industry for Quebec but not to distort the existing market structure. The goal was not to supplant private enterprise but to find a place through a public vehicle in the existing industry: 'Il n'est pas question que cette Société se substitue à l'entreprise privée, mais bien de lui faire jouer un rôle de complémentarité et d'agent "moteur" pour le développement des ressources forestières.'[97]

These policies did not satisfy organized labour in its desire for public control of the forest resource. In a brief to hearings on the future of the pulp and paper industry in Quebec held in the fall of 1977, the Fédération des travailleurs du papier et de la forêt reformulated its position.[98] It argued that the government had to become the sole producer of wood on all pieces of land larger than 2,000 acres through a new Société d'exploitation forestière. This corporation would sell wood to interested parties and use its power to strengthen public involvement in the manufacturing sector. If it became necessary, certain profitable manufacturing firms would be nationalized to ensure a full return to the people of Quebec for the use of the forests. Such measures would have involved the transfer of considerably more control from the private to the public sector than the green paper had proposed. Such a policy would be strongly opposed by large companies in the forest industry, some already unhappy with the disappearance of the timber limits system.[99]

In subsequent years, both Rexfor and the SGF have brought a greater francophone presence to the industry. Upon being allocated lands to engage in forest production, Rexfor has followed the pattern of operation developed by public corporations in other industries. It has secured a partner in the private sector which has often supplied the management for the new complex. This was the pattern, we have seen, that the SGF used in contructing its Donohue-St-Félicien complex. It was used by Rexfor, for example, in 1981, when it announced a new forestry complex to be built in the area of Maniwaki in the Outaouais.[100] The project was to involve a new method of cutting on a deciduous forest and the building of a factory for the manufacture of various grades of lumber. It involved a partnership between Rexfor and MacClaren Forest Company, owned by the Noranda Group, and was facilitated by the reclamation of timber limits from E.B. Eddy and International Paper.

These several differences, ideological and political, among the larger social classes in the francophone community illustrated by the examples of Hydro-Quebec and the forestry industry are deep and do not facilitate co-operation. One is talking about differences in the view of the orientation and dynamic of economic development. On the employers' side, there is a strategy of economic integration with the rest of North America. On the other side, there is an orientation toward economic separation and reclamation. What is common is only the sense that the francophone community is in an economically disadvantaged position that needs to be changed. In 1960, the three classes had this latter perception in common along with an economic strategy. Without this agreement on economic strategy, the means for possible unification had to be a more intense nationalist appeal, which we shall see was only spasmodically successful and always fragile.

Conclusion

The series of economic policies developed in Quebec in the early 1960s shared two properties: they were capitalist and they were integrationist. First, stating that they were capitalist is to emphasize that the primary objects of the policies were smallish, mainly francophone capitalists. These individuals were trapped in marginal industries and wanted a larger share of the economic pie in the province. The policies developed had the ultimate objective of placing such individuals where they could play a more central role in the economy of the province. Second, aside from perhaps some initial ambiguity, it became more and more clear that the promotion of an indigenous entrepreneurial class had to be accomplished through the establishment of stronger links between this class and the dominant fractions of North American capital. To the extent that these policies had any success, they further integrated French-Canadian capital into the North American markets.

The major projects of the late 1970s involved partnerships between the economic institutions created in the 1960s by the provincial government and such English-Canadian and American companies as Noranda, US Steel, and Gulf Canada. Two consequences of this economic policy are worthy of note. First, the sustenance and expansion of an indigenous capitalist class by the political leaders of the francophone community has complemented and supplemented the corporations already dominant in the province. The policy has not yet transferred significant economic power to the francophone community. Without such power, it is difficult to see how the structure of dependence described in chapter 1 can be reversed. Arnaud Sales, in his extensive studies on the relation among fractions of capital in recent years, has not found much encouragement for those looking for the beginnings of an autocentric economy.[101] He found that anglophones still occupied the majority of comprador positions, that is, management positions in branch plants of companies owned outside Canada.[102] Since Raynauld conducted his studies using the 1961 census, French Canadians had increased their ownership in primary metals, metal products, and transportation materials. Still they hardly enjoyed a dominant position in these industries, controlling 30.3 per cent, 38.7 per cent, and 44.5 per cent respectively.[103] Sales concludes that in the absence of a better-formulated industrial strategy, French Canadians are unlikely to regain control over the Quebec economy.

A similarly discouraging picture emerges from a study of recent export patterns. Of the province's ten top exports in 1978, four are minerals in raw form: iron, asbestos, copper, and precious metals; two are partly processed, intermediate products: aluminum and timber; and four are finished products: newsprint, vehicles, airplanes and their parts, and industrial machinery. Many of the exported vehicles are automobiles assembled in Quebec with many of their parts imported from the United States. The inclusion of industrial machinery and aircraft does mark an advance from earlier periods, particularly if one examines the evolution of value added in production from 1961 to 1974.[104] The primary metals industry rises from a rank of 14 to 12 among economic sectors, and metal products from 18 to 13. These several changes may reflect the progress achieved by the SGF in heavy machinery resulting from the growth of Hydro-Québec and that achieved by Sidbec in steel manufacturing. However, these are simply trends and do not reflect as yet a significant departure from dependence. In 1976, inedible raw materials still accounted for 24.73 per cent of Quebec's exports, fabricated materials 41.82 per cent, and inedible end products 27.35 per cent.[105] In the period 1969–76, exports of raw materials rose by 5.7 per cent, and fabricated materials declined by 7.4 per cent. What is more, the data indicate that French Canadians participate relatively little in export markets.[106]

This relative lack of control over the province's economy by the francophone community has been one factor producing a split among classes in that community. The short-lived consensus of the late 1950s and early 1960s on policies to reverse this situation has since foundered on the issue of the means to increase control. The degree of direct government involvement required to reverse the weak economic position of francophones and to restructure the economy has become a class issue. The policy of minimal intervention that has been followed has alienated sections of the working class which have been buffeted by layoffs and instability characteristic of an underdeveloped economy. It has given rise also to some discontent among the middle classes who either find positions in the private sector closed to them or find that their own language and culture continue to be compromised by the presence of outside economic power. In certain instances, the disaffected classes have sought compensation in other areas, particularly through trying to increase the provincial government's power even to the point of making it sovereign.

These economic policies also had important consequences for culture and its preservation. The stronger and more successful the francophone business class becomes in Quebec, the more likely it is that it will want to expand its operations beyond Quebec. Capitalist enterprises grow by extending their markets; increases in profits facilitate increases in investment, and such investment will be increasingly directed toward the larger markets outside Quebec. The more success entrepreneurs have in reaching these markets, the less likely they are to see Quebec as being separate from the other territories in which these markets are found. The more developed the francophone capitalist class becomes, the less interested in nationalism it is likely to be.

An interest in broader markets has cultural implications as well. To the extent that culture in a capitalist society is expressed through the purchase and consumption of commodities (and William Leiss presents a persuasive case for such an argument), the more extended markets become, the weaker will be the position of a minority culture.[107] The advantage of a larger market is that more of a product can be processed at a smaller unit cost. Invariably, the products become tailored to reach the largest market possible and hence less adapted to the market of a minority culture. The minority's needs are constrained to be similar to those of the majority. At the level of consumption at least, the economic policies of the 1960s and 1970s have narrowed the differences between francophone Québécois and other North Americans.

These sorts of changes have an impact on the political thinking of sections of the working class and of what I have called the nationalist portions of the traditional middle class. Some workers in the private sector have of course benefited from the expansion of francophone enterprise. Others who work in the resource sectors or in stagnant industries such as textiles and clothing are more open to appeals for greater francophone control and for sovereignty. The North Americanization of the French-Canadian consumer is not welcomed by the traditional middle class. From the perspective of its nationalist leaders, the economic progress of francophones has not brought the cultural security for which they had hoped. In short, the economic policies of the 1960s and 1970s created the basis for significant alienation from political institutions for selected social groups. This process of alientation takes place in cultural development, educational and social welfare reform, and language protection. These fields will be examined in the following three chapters.

5

Political control of cultural development

The summary description of the economic policies of the government of Quebec as capitalist and intergrationist found at the end of chapter 4 suggests immediately an apparent paradox. We have seen that Quebec was moving to become more similar economically to *les autres*. There was a concerted push to develop larger pools of capital, to increase the size and capital intensity of enterprises, and to plan economic activity so as to facilitate greater participation by francophones in the direction of the North American economy. The economic emphasis was, to use Canadian political jargon, to 'opt in.'

Yet in other areas a different picture emerges. Over the same period there was a series of pitched battles between the government of Quebec and the federal government in which Quebec sought the political power and fiscal capacity to define its own social policies, to control the flow of immigration to its territory, and to control and administer radio and television broadcasting. It sought the right to conduct many of its own affairs in the sphere of international relations and to set up the equivalent of embassies and consulates in several foreign countries. It set up its own Department of Cultural Affairs and defined its own policy on culture. All these activities appeared to be attempts to separate Quebec from Canada, to break ties and established practices, to 'opt out' of national affairs. Why did a society and a government moving to break down barriers on the economic plane erect new ones on the political, social, and cultural planes? The relationship between economic policy and these other policies is the subject of this chapter and the two chapters that follow.

In beginning to explore this paradox, it is helpful to return to the report of the Tremblay Commission. This report, it will be remembered, was concerned about the onset of advanced capitalism in Quebec. It saw this change in the orientation of the economic system as undermining the traditional values and institutions of French Canadians in Quebec. The institutions that existed for the delivery of social services and/or the education of the young maintained at their centre traditional values and practices. On the fringes of this nucleus, however, were developing new institutions in response to industrialization that were mainly under state control. Accordingly, the commission had recommended that conscious steps be taken to develop an economic strategy based on small, family firms that was consistent with traditional values and yet that would generate sufficient wealth for society's needs. It also suggested that the government of Quebec be given full control over education and social policy in order that the new institutions sprouting on the edges of the old, often with federal government support, could be reformed in the appropriate manner.

Chapter 4 showed, however, that the economic strategy adopted by the government of Quebec was virtually the antithesis of that recommended by the commission. Rather than turning away from advanced capitalism, the government embraced it and sought a place for francophones within it. Such a policy had implications for social services and education. If the institutions in these fields incarnated values and practices contradictory to capitalist expansion (and the analysis in chapters 2 and 3 suggests this is a reasonable assumption), their operations will have been increasingly out of step with economic practices as the reforms of the 1960s proceeded. In a sense, they, not the economy, become the logical target of major reform, because their nucleus and their basic philosophy need to be fundamentally reshaped. Who was to carry out this reform? The church was committed to the existing structures and increasingly short of human resources. The task fell to the provincial government, which had primary constitutional responsibility for these areas. The sweeping character of the required reforms necessitated even more that the government of Quebec have increased fiscal capacity and full control over the policy areas if the reforms were to be successful. Thus the demands by the Tremblay Commission for increased fiscal resources and/or complete jurisdiction over social and educational policy were adopted by the government, which was acting in ways fundamentally opposed to the wishes of the commission.

The removal of the church from the centre of education and social services and the critique of traditional values and practices carried the seeds of a crisis of identity. Religion was the fundamental source of traditional French-Canadian values. Removing and criticizing the ideology and the system of thought that was anchored upon Catholic doctrine would inevitably force French Canadians to ask who they were and what distinguished them as a people. These new policies, which diminished the influence of the church and which for various reasons were not fought tenaciously by the church, were compounded in their gravity by two other trends in Quebec society.[1] The birth rate among francophones began to fall rapidly in the 1950s, rendering the community unable to balance the large influx of immigrants that came to Quebec between

1950 and 1965. The demographic position of francophones was perceived as weak within Quebec. Evidence suggests that the bulk of the francophone community was coming to embrace more fully the consumerist, materialist approach to life common elsewhere in North America. This development was leading the population away from traditional values and accentuating the crisis of identity. Pressure grew on the provincial government to play a more active role in the realm of culture and to obtain some control over immigration to the province.

Accordingly, the paradox noted above will be shown to be more apparent than real. The activism of the provincial government was precipitated by some of the same factors and groups that were the source of its economic policy and by the economic policy itself. In this chapter I will therefore explore the paradox by examining several areas of policy where the provincial government sought greater control over factors it perceived as important for the definition of a culture and for the demographic survival of a community. In particular, I will study the struggle for control over social policy, the founding and development of a Department of Cultural Affairs, the striving for stronger ties with France and for increased recognition on the international stage, attempts to gain greater control over immigration, and the growth in demands for provincial control over mass communications. The redefinition and reconstitution of the educational system will be examined in chapter 6, and the development of a global policy on language in chapter 7.

Introduction

It is not inappropriate to begin this study of the politics of culture with the following hypothesis: the more the francophone community becomes integrated into the North American economy at the level of management and of consumption, the more difficulty it will experience in defining for itself and maintaining a distinctive culture. Preliminary evidence in support of such a hypothesis may be drawn from an examination of the changes that have taken place in the definition by francophones of what constitutes their culture and what renders it distinctive. Since the comprehensive analysis of culture found in the report of the Tremblay Commission, there have been three further official attempts to reflect upon the bases of Quebec culture. The first was a white paper prepared in 1965 by a committee of scholars for the Department of Cultural Affairs and its minister, Pierre Laporte, which was never published.[2] The second was a green paper written by Jean-Paul L'Allier, minister of cultural affairs during the latter stages of the Liberal government of 1970–6, which died on the order sheet when that government was defeated at the polls in November 1976.[3] The third and most ambitious was prepared under the supervision of the sociologists Fernand Dumont and Guy Rocher for Dr Camille Laurin, minister of state for cultural development during the first term of the Parti québécois government.[4]

The social scientist, of course, must always treat such official documents carefully, because they are written often to advance the political fortunes of governments as much as to promote policy. However, the study of primary assumptions and basic definitions in these documents can be revealing and suggestive of changes that have taken place in certain social phenomena. In this spirit, a brief comparison of the approach to defining culture found in the Tremblay Report with that used in the PQ white paper, *A Cultural Development Policy for Quebec,* will be undertaken. This analysis will suggest that the francophone community in Quebec is having increased difficulty in defining its identity and in isolating its culture from others in North America.

It will be recalled from chapters 2 and 3 that the Tremblay commissioners defined culture to include three components: knowledge, means of communication, and values. They argued that the primary root or determinant of these components was religion. The Catholic religion, with its emphasis on the individual person and the supportive community, was understood by the commissioners to be a basic source of French-Canadian culture. The second root was the French national genius – a series of traits that included spiritualism and a capacity to work with abstract ideas – that had come to characterize those who were reared in and spoke the French language. Using as a basis these ideas, the commissioners pointed to a series of institutions and practices that were characteristically French Canadian. In particular, they emphasized that Quebec's educational and social welfare services reflected the essence of French-Canadian culture. They formulated a series of demands that spoke to a vision of the fiscal system and of the working of Canadian federalism that was consonant with French-Canadian culture. The approach developed had a classical form: basic definitions were made, implications of these definitions were noted, and political strategy, including political demands, was formulated on the basis of these implications.

The approach developed in the 1978 white paper was somewhat different. There culture was defined more generally to embrace virtually all a community's life: 'Culture designates certain ways of speaking, thinking, living, and, as a corollary, languages, beliefs and institutions common to a given group of people, small or large.'[5] The culture of Quebec as a specific instance of this definition is seen to have two roots. First, the individuals sharing in the culture draw upon a common history and experience of more than three hundred years. No attempt is made, however, to say what is most central or crucial in this history. Second, the individuals are part of a society of which the primary language is French. Language, in itself, is seen to give a certain form to culture:

'A language is not simply syntax or a string of words. It is an expression of the more meaningful aspects of community life.'[6]

In contrast, then, to the Tremblay Report, the white paper makes no explicit reference to religion as the foundation of French-Canadian culture. It does not explicitly emphasize ethnicity, the 'French national genius,' as its predecessor report had done. Culture is defined more vaguely than before. Language, previously one of several components contributing to a culture's distinctiveness, is given here an almost primordial role. None the less the general character of the definition of culture makes it difficult to point immediately to institutions and practices unique to French Quebec.

This difficulty is acknowledged in the white paper itself. Its authors write that Quebec's socio-cultural web appears to have been designed outside Quebec: 'Everything therefore suggests that Quebecers continue to draw much of what they require to satisfy the needs of community life from a wealth of foreign sources: they eat, dress, live, sing, count, work and pray in ways that are not their own but which they borrowed without hesitation, in part or in whole, from other cultures.'[7] A distinctive culture is thus no longer outwardly evident; distinctiveness, according to the white paper, is a quality of the soul; it is derived from inner psychological factors. This distinctiveness and this soul are no longer projected outward and internalized in major social institutions as the Tremblay commissioners had argued. 'The French-speaking Quebecers ... have not really succeeded in moulding the main structures and institutions of their collective life to satisfy their deepest aspirations. Quebecers have maintained and developed original attitudes and common features without the support and means of expression provided by those institutions which enable a culture to make full use of its potential.'[8] Since the time of the Tremblay Report, it appears that French-Canadian culture has ebbed slowly out of the visible manifestations of social life and remains strong only within the minds of individuals.

One further difference of some importance exists between the two documents. The reference group itself has changed. In the Tremblay Report, the reference group was delimited by ethnic criteria; it consisted of the biological heirs of the French 'national genius,' the French Canadians. The white paper defines its focal group using political criteria, viz all those who are residents of the province of Quebec, the Québécois. This group is multi-ethnic in character, dominated by francophones but including as well a number of non-francophone minorities. These minorities, it is hoped, will be an integral part of 'a Quebec entity that is primarily francophone.'[9] For the authors of the white paper, it is not expected that major institutions will appear as exemplars of the French-Canadian soul. These institutions must be structured so as to accommodate a variety of different souls.

A reading of these two documents would suggest that the processes affecting the existence of traditional French-Canadian culture and feared by the Tremblay commissioners have won out. In 1978, the traditional culture is no longer pointed to and no longer an issue of concern. Yet it would also appear that a new distinctive culture has not arisen to take the place of the old. No institutions or practices can be identified as distinctive or peculiar to the francophone community. The new way of life has come from the outside; it has been borrowed. If such a conclusion is correct, it has ominous implications for Quebec's francophone community. To the extent that it is sensed or believed, it will motivate many to search for radical solutions to repair the problem. In the remainder of this chapter, where we explore state activity in the cultural sphere, the likelihood of this conclusion will become evident.

Control over social policy

At the end of the Second World War, the institutions in Quebec providing health and social services were mainly in private, specifically clerical, hands. They were inspired by Catholic social thinking and were supported only indirectly by the provincial government. During the late 1940s and the 1950s, these institutions increasingly broke down. Designed to minister to smaller communities that could draw on an extended family and on ample clergy, they were inadequate in an industrial setting, where demand was higher, extended families disappearing, and clergy declining. Inch by inch the provincial government was forced to intervene, beginning with the creation of a Department of Youth and Social Welfare in the late 1940s. A series of commissions of inquiry over the next decade provided the francophone community with a listing of the areas of weakness in its social institutions.[10]

While the provincial government under Duplessis continued to adhere to the non-interventionist philosophy consistent with established Catholic thought and moved slowly and with reluctance in this field, the federal government was much more active. It had entered the field during the crises of the Depression and the Second World War and was reluctant to leave for a variety of reasons. After the war, it proposed a New National Policy wherein it would assume responsibility for ensuring high and stable levels of income and employment. It planned to assume the initiative in a comprehensive system of social security. The latter was seen as a means for developing the idea of a unified Canadian community and was a further manifestation, along with the creation of the Massey Commission, of the intention of the central government to construct a unified political community of 'non-hyphenated' Canadians. The federal government set up the National Health Programme in 1948, assumed a primary role in old-age pensions with the Old Age Security Act in 1952, expanded its role in the employment field with the Unemployment Assistance Act in 1955, and entered the hospital insurance field in 1958.[11]

There began to grow in Quebec some social welfare practices that originated and were based outside the province. Duplessis resisted these interventions by refusing grants and by not participating whenever it was politically feasible. This strategy helped to preserve part of the cultural heritage of the institutions of social welfare but in some cases compounded their difficulties by denying them access to funds they sorely needed. By the time the Liberals came to power in 1960 the need for some sort of change was pressing. The new government could follow two routes. It could take its lead from the Tremblay Commission and seek to control and orient economic development in a direction consistent with the traditional Catholic values. Or it could adopt fully the values of industrial capitalism and work to ensure that the francophone community would benefit fully from that system. I established in chapter 4 that the government chose the second route. In doing so, it set into motion certain pressures on the system for delivery of social policy. These pressures were to lead to a restructuring by the provincial government. They were also to produce a greater similarity between social services in Quebec and those in the rest of Canada. In essence, the cultural distinctiveness of the social institutions serving the francophone community in Quebec was to disappear. The agent for this change, however, was to be the provincial government.

Upon his election in 1960, Jean Lesage demanded that the federal government withdraw from all conditional grant programs, including those in social policy, and give over to the province sufficient tax room to allow it to recoup its financial losses, thereby enabling it to design its own programs. Following this demand, there ensued three years of often bitter struggle between the governments of Quebec and Canada. Finally, in 1964, the provinces and the federal authorities reached agreement on conditional grants. The Established Programs (Interim Arrangements) Act set out a series of programs from which provinces could contract out without financial penalty. Included were hospital insurance, blind person's allowances, disabled person's allowances, the welfare portion of general public assistance, health grants, non-capital expenditures on vocational training, the composite forestry agreements, and the roads-to-resources program. This proposal satisfied a large portion of Quebec's demands. However, it did not mean the full withdrawal of the federal government from social security which was demanded by the nationalists and which had been recommended by the Tremblay Commission.[12] The federal authorities excluded from this act areas of social welfare that it felt a need to control in order to regulate the national economy. Thus at the meeting of the Tax Structure Committee in September 1966, the federal finance minister announced the federal government's intention to vacate all social welfare programs where contracting out was permitted.[13] He indicated also the federal authroities' intention to continue to engage in shared-cost programs of an economic nature.

At the same meeting, the new premier, Daniel Johnson, presented the proposal of the Tremblay Commission for full provincial control of social policy.[14] At a later date and in terms clearly reminiscent of the Tremblay Report, he suggested that because social security measures touch the French-Canadian nation at its roots, they form a whole and must be administered as a whole by the government in charge of the nation's development.[15] The measures embraced by this whole included unemployment insurance, manpower policy, family allowances, old-age pensions, and even housing. The province now received support from the nationalists, the FTQ, and the CNTU in making these demands.[16] The support of both nationalist groups and of organized labour for more radical demands for control of social policy is an example of a new coalition of social forces destined to play an important role on the political stage. What is new here is the presence of middle-class elements in the nationalist groups – white-collar public servants, technicians,and business-service professionals such as advertising agencies and journalists.

In a constitutional document, *Income Security and Social Services,* issued in 1969, the federal authorities responded by rejecting these demands unequivo-cally.[17] Social security, it was stated, does not constitute a whole; rather it is composed of two parts–income security and social services. Responsibility for the latter was to remain exclusively with the provinces, providing that other areas of federal jurisdiction were not hampered. At the Tax Structure Committee meeting, Mitchell Sharp, on behalf of Ottawa, had suggested federal withdrawal from hospital insurance, the Canada Assistance Plan, and National Health Grants.[18] However, it claimed the power to make income support payments, exclusive power in unemployment insurance, and a prominent role in the fields of retirement and public income insurance.[19] In each case, the justification mentioned the necessity for an equitable distribution of income across Canada. In each case, as well, the federal authorities prevailed.

The Quebec authorities were hardly happy with this declaration of principles. After a massive study of social security by the Commission of Inquiry on Health and Social Welfare (Castonguay-Nepveu Commission), Claude Castonguay, the minister of social affairs, reiterated the traditional demands in this field. He recommended that section 94A of the BNA Act be revised to add to provincial powers those regulating family and youth allowances, occupational training grants, unemployment insurance, and the guaranteed income supplement to old-age pensions.[20] Intense bargaining followed these demands. The situation was perhaps opportune because federal officials, headed by Marc Lalonde, were revising their policies on social security. In doing so, they incorporated some of the philosophy of the Castonguay-Nepveu Report. In the end, however, the basic situation was not changed. McInnes, in his study of this federal-provincial dispute, sums up the end result aptly: 'Lalonde did not give Quebec its much wanted *primauté* in social security, and Castonguay came away with little of importance in contrast to what he had been bargaining for since 1970. The Orange Paper [the federal proposals] accommodated the language of the Castonguay-Nepveu Report, but little else. The long term effect of Castonguay's acquiescence was to reinforce rather than to break down federal dominance of social security, and it did little to make the Review a joint process.'[21] In the 1977 federal-provincial fiscal arrangements, the federal government abandoned all its conditional grants in the areas of hospital insurance and medicare and gave all the provinces additional tax points.[22] The other provinces thus were placed in a situation similar to that fought for by Quebec in the mid-1960s.

The government of Quebec was active not only on the constitutional plane in social policy. Beginning in the mid-1960s, using the additional funds it had won in its struggle with the federal government, it began to reform significantly the system of delivering social service. Gradually the church was relieved of its responsibility for hospitals and other social services such as orphanages and asylums. These were integrated into a single system under the control of the provincial government. Uniform standards were established, and supervisory bodies were rationalized. The new health care systems were less and less distinguishable from others in North America. By the late 1970s one never saw these institutions being held up as the incarnation of French-Canadian values. Complementing rationalized health care was a series of social programs still controlled by the federal government because it felt they were necessary to maintain a national economy. Both these governments' efforts in the social field complemented the new economic policy of the province. Health care was reformed in order to be adequate to the needs of an industrialized urban society. The federal policies, by helping to maintain a national economic structure, also were consistent with the orientation of the emerging francophone business class which was increasingly interested in markets outside the province.

The division of responsibility marked a defeat for the nationalist–organized labour demand for full provincial control of the field. These groups were less interested in preserving a national economy and were in the 1960s moving more and more toward the espousal of political separation from Canada. If their demands had been fully met, Quebec's economy would have been separated a little more from the Canadian economy. This fact was clearly recognized by the federal government, which systematically blocked any attempts by Quebec to gain control over policies that it felt might serve to disintegrate rather than integrate the national economy.

The Department of Cultural Affairs

Two important points made in chapters 1–3 will affect our understanding of the development of a cultural policy by the government of Quebec. The report of the Massey Commission made a series of recommendations designed to expand the role of the federal government in promoting cultural development. Following from the commission's report, the Canada Council was established, giving the federal government a major instrument for expanding and controlling the arts in Canada. In 1965, the secretary of state was given the powers necessary to become a de facto department of culture and thus represented a centralization of federal involvement in cultural affairs. If the federal government were normally perceived to act as a bicultural entity, that is, as an institution striving to encourage the development of both English-Canadian and French-Canadian culture, such changes would probably have been warmly endorsed by those most concerned with the culture of French Canada. However, a second point established in chapters 1–3 indicates that such a perception was not common among members of the French-Canadian intelligentsia. Intellectuals active in nationalist causes viewed the federal government as the national government of English Canada and the government of Quebec as the national government of French Canada. They saw the expansion of the federal involvement in culture as an intensification of attempts to impose 'Canadian' culture upon French Canadians. This was their view in the early 1950s as it was in the late 1970s. Speaking of the members of the francophone community in Quebec, the authors of the 1978 white paper write: 'Their dignity and their well-being make it impossible for them to live in a tributary society, a society that pays tribute to an overlord to enable him to develop his own culture.'[23]

Based upon such perceptions, counter-proposals were not long in coming. In its brief to the Tremblay Commission in 1954, the ssjbm articulated what came to be a standard nationalist position for countering the federal incursion. The group called upon the government of Quebec to fashion a policy of défense culturelle in order to prevent the federal government from becoming the cultural patron for French-Canadian artists.[24] This idea of a provincial counter-move to federal plans also entered the mind of Georges-Émile Lapalme, predecessor of Lesage as head of the provincial Parti libéral. In 1959 Lapalme wrote a long, two-volume work on policy, which was remarkable for its nationalism, and it served as the basis for the Liberal electoral program of 1960.[25] Lapalme proposed the creation of a department of cultural affairs with the following sections: the Office de la langue française, the Département du Canada français d'outre frontières, the Conseil provincial des Arts, a Commission des monuments historiques, and a Bureau provincial d'urbanisme. In 1961, a department with such components was created, with Lapalme its first minister and Guy Frégault, a noted historian, being lured from the academic world to serve as deputy minister. The new department was viewed as a symbol of Quebec's new drive to reorient its development and to adopt a new image. It showed that the French presence in North America was to be proudly strengthened. It was the logical sibling of the new Department of Natural Resources and the COEQ.

The proud and enthusiastic beginning for the department probably marked its apogee in influence until perhaps the late 1970s. Three years after its creation, Lapalme resigned his post in protest against the low priority given to the department by the government. His letter of resignation described a humiliating series of struggles between the department and the treasury, attempts by the department to secure rather small sums of money to support its activities.[26] Lapalme was succeeded as minister by Pierre Laporte, who commissioned a white paper on cultural policy. The document that emerged reiterated Lapalme's and the nationalists' desires for a strong department. It called upon the government of Quebec to take full responsibility for culture on its territory and to participate in the expansion and diffusion of the culture nationale. It warned that unless French-Canadian culture was strengthened, it was threatened seriously with anglo-americanization. It was never published, but its sombre warning appears to have been justified if one examines the remarks of Guy Frégault a decade later.

In September 1975, Frégault reviewed the performance of the department and the state of French-Canadian culture. He wrote that economic development and the mass consumer–oriented society it had brought in its wake had profoundly altered the way of life in Quebec. He concluded, after further analysis, that the cultural challenges imposed by these events could be met only with a global cultural policy: 'En bref, il s'impose de concevoir une politique culturelle globale, à la mesure des nécessités (personnelles et collectives) issues des agents de déshumanisation que sont: une croissance économique apparemment sans autre finalité qu'elle-même ... la dégradation du cadre de vie.'[27] After close to fifteen years in existence, the Department of Cultural Affairs still lacked resources and the mandate needed to act on a global policy on culture.

Frégault's assessment served as the basis for a second attempt by a minister of cultural affairs to set up the outlines of such a global policy. Jean-Paul L'Allier, who served in this position in the last year of the Liberal government of Robert Bourassa, published a green paper on cultural policy in May 1976. It was a compelling document, exhibiting L'Allier's passion for his position. It tried to be global, as Frégault had suggested, touching all bases, and in doing so weakened its impact. Its major proposal was the creation of a Conseil de la Culture du Quebec. Victor-Lévy Beaulieu, a noted author and publisher, described it as 'le Conseil des arts fédéral ... à la sauce québécoise.'[28] The council was to function much like the Canada Council, distributing grants to support the arts and letters. The paper retained the somewhat élitist proposal found in the Laporte white paper for the creation of an Institut d'histoire et de civilisation where intellectuals would be supported while they reflected on Quebec's culture. Beaulieu criticized the green paper for ignoring the question of the diffusion of culture.[29] He argued that the major foreign influences in Quebec would hardly be affected by the paper's proposals because these same proposals contained nothing about regulating the diffusion of foreign records, books, television programming, and cinema in Quebec. Thus its various attempts to preserve a national culture would amount to preserving folklore, which would be merely an adjunct to the dominant Americanized mass culture in Quebec.

It is perhaps already clear from this discussion that most of the activities of the Department of Cultural Affairs have scarcely touched the popular classes in Quebec. The cultural events that have been supported have been those of the haute bourgeoisie – the symphony, the established theatre, the fine arts – while the cultural activities of the working classes have been left in the hands of the Americanized cultural industries. Since the time of Laporte's white paper the ministry has had on its agenda the democratization of access to culture and has had since the early 1970s a Direction du développement culturel régional. Still, the creation of regional offices has been slow, despite a constant demand of the Parti québécois for more speed while it was in opposition. The 'culture' supported by the department has been that of the privileged few.

This is not to deny that the department has had an impact. It was under the aegis of the department that the first Office de la langue française began its pioneering work in the development of lexicons of French words appropriate for use in the industrial domain (see chapter 7). It has supervised the conversion of the Bibliothèque Saint-Sulpice in Montreal into the Bibliothèque nationale du Québec and the substantial and valuable bibliographical work carried out by the latter. The Office du Film du Québec, when transferred to the department's jurisdiction in 1967, began a period of significant growth and contributed indirectly to the development of a cinéma québécois. The latter, with the productions of Jutra, Carle, Arcand, Labrecque, Brault, and many others, grew out of the French section of the National Film Board (NFB). It reached new heights of popularity in the 1970s in Quebec. Nevertheless, the largest source of funds for film production in Quebec remained the federal government through the NFB and the Canadian Film Development Corporation.

Under the Parti québécois, the department has grown a little more rapidly. Major initiatives to create a new 'Musée de l'homme d'ici,' to expand the network of public libraries, to support authors and publication costs, and to revise the loi-cadre for films and the cinema emerged from the department during the party's first government. The government created the Société québécoise de développement des industries culturelles (Sodic) to support cultural operations poised for expansion or in need of start-up funds. It is difficult to say yet whether the Parti québécois has done significantly more for Quebec culture than its predecessors. It would appear that its tenure in office has not led to the flowering of culture many expected. Lise Bissonnette wrote near the end of the completion of the party's first government that the culture had become still more fixed and stagnant. Speaking rather critically of the party, she said: 'Ses performances, dans le domaine culturel proprement dit, non seulement ne passeront pas à l'histoire, mais sont au total d'une faiblesse étonnante. Son livre blanc sur le développement culturel a fait mourir d'ennui. Mais ce qui est plus grave encore, sa vision du monde est restée elle-même globalement provincialiste, alors qu'il demandait justement aux Québécois d'accepter de sortir de cette immaturité.'[30]

The Department of Cultural Affairs and the reflection on culture it has spawned over the past two decades have remained consistently weak. Under no government has culture received the support or attention that matches the importance given to economic affairs. Economic development has brought in its wake an acceleration of the processes described in chapters 2 and 3. The working classes in the 1950s were increasingly living their lives outside the institutions of the church and of traditional French-Canadian society. They were becoming a French-speaking section of North American mass-consumer society. The Department of Cultural Affairs represented a possible basis for the spawning of new institutions that would reflect the spiritual and communal roots of French-Canadian culture and perhaps arrest these trends. Its opportunity to play this role has now passed.

International relations

It is not accidental that as the church was declining in influence and the provincial government was embarking on its program of economic development, there was a rise in interest in the topic of relations with France. The institutional basis was partially established in the 1950s. In 1950, the Association France-Canada had been founded, and a new series of exchanges involving students in particular was begun. In the late 1950s, the Société Radio-Canada began participating in the ORTF, the international organization for French-language broadcasting. Intellectual interest also increased. In 1952, the French journal L'Esprit published a special edition on French Canada. Writing in Cité libre in October 1954, François Hertel called for a renewal of ties with France in order to prevent the decline of French-Canadian culture and its eventual Americanization.[31] The most tireless proponent of such ties was Jean-Marc Léger, a journalist and frequent contributor to L'Action nationale.

He saw such ties to be necessary for a defence and renewal of the culture of French Canada.[32]

When Charles de Gaulle visited Quebec in April 1960, the stage was set for a change in relations between Quebec and France. De Gaulle showed a keen interest in Quebec and its future. In a speech, he said: 'Vous pouvez compter sur la France, Canadiens, Canadiens français, vous pouvez compter sur elle dans le débat qui va s'engager. Elle compte sur vous pour penser à elle pour la suivre et pour l'appuyer, par tous les moyens, directs ou indirects que les hommes libres ont aujourd'hui de faire connaître ce qu'ils pensent.'[33] The desire to increase cultural, economic, and social relations with France became a standard demand of nationalist societies, the newly formed RIN, and, eventually, prominent politicians. The feeling among these groups was that the francophone community in Quebec needed to draw from France if its culture were to flourish. With the new economic direction being pursued by the provincial government, it was more and more evident that new pressures were building up on that culture, that traditional sources could no longer be tapped, and that new roots had to be found.

In October 1961, the government of Quebec opened a new Maison du Québec in Paris under the supervision of Lapalme in Cultural Affairs. In January 1964, after a series of negotiations involving Ottawa and France, the Ministry of Youth established an External Cooperation Service to implement the ASTEF program (Association pour l'organisation de stages en France) which provided training for Quebec officials and citizens in France. In June 1964, Gérin-Lajoie initiated negotiations for a program of exchange and co-operation with France in the field of education. On 27 February 1965, an agreement was signed in Paris between France and Quebec, with an exchange of letters taking place in Ottawa the same day ratifying the agreement. In November 1965, another exchange of letters between France and Ottawa established an accord cadre which provided a framework within which agreements could be reached between the province and France. Quebec signed a cultural agreement with France on 24 November.

The Union nationale government enthusiastically pursued the initiatives of its predecessor, and France was more than willing to go along. A new seventeen-point agreement on education and culture was signed in 1967. The basis for an Office franco-québécois pour la jeunesse was created; joint committees on investment, on technical education, on research, and on co-operation in geology and mining were mapped out.[34]

Relations began to be pursued with other French-speaking countries as well. There was developing a desire in several of these countries that a kind of francophone commonwealth of nations be established to foster support for French-language-based cultures around the world.

The pursuit of closer relations between Quebec and France brought to the political stage a new issue for dispute between the federal government and the government of Quebec. When Quebec and France signed an agreement to initiate the new program of co-operation in education in 1965, Gérin Lajoie, the minister of education of Quebec, stated that Quebec would pursue similar relations on its own in the future. He argued that Quebec should be able to act alone on the international stage in those areas that come under provincial jurisdiction in the Canadian constitution. Such a demand was not new to politics in Quebec. As early as 1949, in its brief to the Massey Commission, the Ligue d'Action nationale had suggested that provinces be able to deal on their own with UNESCO on educational matters. Similarly, the CTCC had asked for a more important role for the provinces in the International Labour Organisation in the 1950s.[35]

The Union nationale government in the late 1960s continued to push for the powers demanded by Gérin-Lajoie. In 1967, the Department of Federal-Provincial Relations was renamed the Department of Intergovernmental Affairs. The government also received the support of France in its quest for more power. In 1968, at French insistence, Gabon invited Quebec to an educational conference without consulting Ottawa. When the minister of education of Quebec attended and was treated similarly to other heads of state, Ottawa severed diplomatic relations with Gabon. The issue that lay at the heart of these disputes for the government of Quebec was cultural survival. Marcel Masse, during a visit to France while minister of intergovernmental affairs, stated this clearly:[36] 'Si le Québec a choisi d'exercer ces pouvoirs, c'est qu'il a compris, un peu tard certes, qu'il ne pouvait remettre son destin au gouvernement central du Canada dont les préoccupations et les aspirations sont souvent différentes des siennes et dont les décisions antérieures n'ont pas toujours été favorables, loin de là, à l'épanouissement de la culture française au Québec et encore moins dans le Canada tout entier.'

The federal government was just as firm in rejecting Gérin-Lajoie's original demand. Prime Minister Pearson stated that Canada could have only one international personality and that the responsibility for this personality rested with the federal level.[37] In documents released soon after, this position was reinforced.[38] The federal government rejected Quebec's claim that international dealings could be divided into technical subjects (which in certain areas could be carried on by provinces) and foreign policy. Larger considerations of foreign policy lay at the heart of all international relations. The members of federal states should have no independent capacities to make treaties, to become members of international organizations, or to accredit diplomats.

However, the federal government did move to change some of its practices. It suggested that Canadian delegations meeting with French-speaking countries on topics of provincial concern should be headed by a Quebec minister.[39] More systematic consultation was promised with the provinces on matters touching provincial jurisdiction. The federal government also moved to give full recognition to the Canadian francophone community within the Department of External Affairs. In 1969, a division for Relations among French-Speaking States was established. Canada participated in the creation of the Agency for Technical and Cultural Cooperation in 1970 and arranged for Quebec's admittance to the agency as a participating government in 1971. It also gave annual subsidies to the Association of Wholly or Partially Francophone Universities, the International Council of the French Language, and the French Language International Law Institute.

Throughout the 1970s, the federal Department of External Affairs asserted itself over Quebec as the main interlocutor with the international francophone community. The old disputes were not repeated again until 1980 under the government of the Parti québécois. The idea of a French-speaking commonwealth was resuscitated in the late 1970s by Léopold Senghor, president of Senegal, and a conference to discuss its possibility was called for December 1980. The issue that arose as the conference neared was the composition of the Canadian delegation. Mark MacGuigan, then secretary of state for external affairs, stated that the delegation would be headed by him and that Quebec could be represented in the Canadian delegation by a high-ranking public servant. He argued that the conference was on political and economic matters that were the responsibility of the federal government. Claude Morin, minister of intergovernmental affairs, retorted that Quebec should be represented by a minister, as it was in the Agence de coopération culturelle et technique des pays francophones. Quebec being the homeland of Canadian francophones, it was normal that it be represented by the highest levels in any new international body grouping francophones. France declared that it would not participate in the conference unless the demands of Quebec were met. Ottawa remained firm, and the conference was cancelled.

In reviewing the development of these conventions and disputes, one might be tempted to see only conflicts over power between two governments and between groups of francophones within both governments. To see them thus, however, would be too simplistic. The desire among certain members of Quebec's francophone community to strengthen ties with France and with other French-speaking countries is another aspect of the cultural search of that community that began in earnest in the early 1960s. Political leaders in Quebec wanted to establish new cultural foundations that were consistent with industrial capitalism and that would help make that capitalism acceptable to the petite bourgeoisie. Nationalist elements among that petite bourgeoisie saw reinforced relations with France as both a counter to American influence and a source of support for the pursuit of sovereignty. The coincidence of interests enabled the government to pursue relations with France and to reach for power needed to pursue those relations on its own terms.

The desire for stronger relations with France reflected also the increasing importance of language in attempts to redevelop a distinct culture in Quebec. To engage in interchange with countries that spoke French, however different their histories and their levels of economic development, would bring Quebec into contact with fundamental cultural roots. This desire reflected an idealism carried over from Quebec's ideological past.

It is almost impossible to assess whether the stronger ties with France that developed in the early 1960s have affected the culture of francophones in Quebec. At the mass level, it seems unlikely. Whether France is a likely counter to the Americanization of the French-Canadian working class is questionable. However, even if these questions are answered in Quebec's favour, one must still acknowledge that the government has not been as successful as it might have been. The primary initiative in international dealings remains with Ottawa. Quebec, in 1980, simply added a stronger voice to the chorus shaping that initiative in dealings with France and other French-speaking countries.

Control over immigration

The culture of French Canada has been erected upon a social base that is ethnically homogeneous, a fact that seems remarkable given that Canada has absorbed millions of immigrants since the early nineteenth century. The quite conscious strategy of French-Canadian élites had been to minimize contacts with other cultural groups and to promote child-bearing in the hope that a high birth rate could maintain French Canada's demographic strength at a constant proportion of the Canadian population. This strategy was largely successful until after the Second World War. Successive censuses show a decline in the percentage of citizens whose mother tongue is French from 29.2 in 1941 to 25.5 in 1976. In the period of 1951–66, Quebec experienced a net immigration of 270,000 people.[40] This influx was to raise important questions about the character of the 'new culture' for French Canada and in combination with other demographic trends was to provide the basis for several crises in the late 1960s and early 1970s.

The first response of élites in Quebec to the influx was typical and consistent with traditional cultural norms. Pius XII had called upon North Americans to accept as many war refugees as was possible.[41] The Catholic hierarchy in Quebec supported the pope. Typical was the statement of the archbishop of Quebec in 1951 calling upon French Canadians to welcome immigrants in the name of Christian charity.[42] The Feast of the Epiphany, 6 January, was designated in many dioceses the jour de l'immigration. The semaines sociales in 1954 devoted sessions to établissement rural and immigration. A number of sociétés d'assistance aux immigrants were established under the church's supervision to minister to the special needs of the newcomers. Similarly a Service des Néo Canadiens was established under the auspices of the Montreal Catholic School Commission.

Yet some nationalists and some members of the francophone business community favoured first francophone and second Catholic immigrants.[43] Some in these groups speculated openly that federal immigration officials were seeking to undermine *la nation* by directing non-francophones and non-Catholics to Quebec. Figures aggregated for the period 1946–61 by the Commission of Inquiry on the Position of the French Language and on Language Rights (Gendron Commission) show that 18.41 per cent of immigrants were Italian, 18.01 per cent were British, 10.41 per cent were German, and only 7.6 per cent were French. The pattern shifts in the following decade, 1962–71, with Italians accounting for 14.65 per cent, French for 14.1 per cent, British for 11.65 per cent, and Germans only 3.5 per cent.[44] By the mid-1970s the largest national block migrating to Quebec was made up of Haitians.

After the initial concern over immigration in the late 1940s and early 1950s, immigration receded in importance on the public agenda. Traditional patterns were continued, with all non-French-speaking immigrants gravitating to the anglophone community in Quebec. This behaviour was consistent with the distribution of economic power in the province and with the institutional behaviour of the francophone community. Thus a secret report submitted to the superintendent of Roman Catholic schools on 11 April 1957 revealed that French Catholic school commissioners were in the habit of sending all non-French, non-British children to English-language schools.[45] Immigrants were simply not a part of the community in many ways. The Gendron Commission found those belonging to the immigrant community were under-represented in Montreal's civic government and in both the Montreal and provincial civil services.[46] The consequences of this policy in the educational system are illustrated well by the figures shown in Table 5. By 1971, only 10.8 per cent of third-party immigrant children were attending French-language schools.

As we have seen in many instances in this study, the traditional response to problems based on established cultural norms in the francophone community was inadequate in the context of an urbanized, industrial society. In the case of immigration one of the key components of the traditional response, a high birth rate, was not maintained as Quebec industrialized. Beginning in 1958, the Quebec birth rate began a dizzying decline from 28.8 live births per thousand,

TABLE 5
Proportional distribution of pupils of an origin other than French or British in French and English classes

Year	French classes (percentage)	English classes (percentage)
1930–1	52.2	46.8
1935–6	49.0	52.8
1940–1	40.9	59.1
1945–6	35.8	65.2
1950–1	34.3	65.7
1955–6	30.7	69.3
1959–60	26.5	73.5
1961–2	25.5	74.5
1966–7	15.9	84.1
1971–2	10.8	89.2

SOURCE: Figures adapted from Gendron Report II 485

well above the national average, to 14.2 per thousand in 1973, the second-lowest birth rate of Canadian provinces. Without the traditional high birth rate and with immigrants predisposed to integrate with the anglophone community, the proportion of francophones in the population of Canada and more importantly in the population of Quebec was poised, it appeared, for a decline. The alarm among nationalists arose gradually during the 1960s, becoming close to hysterical after the publication in 1969 of a study by three respected demographers that indicated that francophones might account for only 71.6 per cent of the population of Quebec and 52.7 per cent of the population of Montreal by the year 2000.[47] The concern voiced about these figures must be placed in context. The figures were published at a time when nationalist movements and parties were more and more conscious of the cultural consequences of the policies of economic development. They feared a serious erosion in French Quebec's capacity to maintain itself as a distinct people. These fears became all the more salient in the face of predictions that this people was about to be weakened relative to other groups in Canada and Quebec because of demographic factors.

The usual pattern in other policy arenas when traditional institutions have not been able to cope with a problem has been to turn to the state. In this case as well, the organized groups most concerned with immigration – nationalist societies based in the francophone middle classes – began to look to the province for help. As early as 1956, Jean-Marc Léger had called for the creation of a department for new Canadians which would oversee services for recruitment, welcome, and assistance to newcomers.[48] Léger's concerns were not echoed among his peers, and it was not until the mid-1960s that demands for state action became more pressing. Pierre Laporte in his unpublished white paper had suggested the creation of a Direction générale de l'Immigration within the Department of Cultural Affairs. In March 1965, an immigration service was set up in the department, and this was expanded to a full branch in August 1966. By this time, however, both the nationalist ssjBM and organized labour were calling for the creation of a separate department of immigration.[49] This department, it was hoped, would oversee the integration of immigrants into the francophone community. The notion of integrating immigrants into French Quebec was a significant departure from the traditional nationalist position noted above. Certainly it would have been a recipe for cultural disaster in the eyes of the Tremblay Commission. The Department of Immigration was created in November 1968 and began to operate an advisory service for immigrants in London and a more complete recruiting office in Paris. Using funds from the federal Department of Employment and Immigration, it also began to oversees the Centres d'orientation et de formation des immigrants (COFI). These centres had been set up to facilitate the integration of immigrants into Canadian society by giving them intensive language courses and other courses for orientation to Canadian and Quebec society.

In 1972, upon the release of its report, the Gendron Commission reviewed the performance of the new department, and its conclusions were not unlike those drawn by Georges-Émile Lapalme in 1964 for the Department of Cultural Affairs. The commission reported that restrictions in personnel, funds, and other facilities had led to a decidedly ineffective department.[50] Several proposed structures had not been created, and others had fallen into disuse. It appeared that like the Department of Cultural Affairs, the new department had been created partly for symbolic reasons to pacify nationalist sentiment. Aside from a lack of will among political leaders, the department was constrained also by the division of powers in Canadian federalism. Section 95 of the BNA Act had given the federal government primacy in immigration while granting the provinces concurrent jurisdiction. If the new provincial department was to meet the objective set out for it, certain powers would need to be devolved to it by the federal government.

In 1971, the first in a series of discussions between Quebec and Ottawa bore fruit when Quebec obtained the power to have its own immigration officers in federal immigration offices. By 1973, it had officers in Paris, Milan, London, Rome, Athens, and Beirut, with additional offices to be added soon in Port-au-Prince (Haiti) and in South America. In a second agreement, signed in October 1975, Quebec was given leave to associate itself closely with federal officials in the process of recruitment, evaluation, and selection of immigrants. Quebec immigration officers were given the power to take the initiative in recruitment, provided they consulted with federal officials. As a result of this agreement, the Quebec authorities foresaw an increase in immigration officers from seven to twenty-four.

By 1975, the province had negotiated a significant voice for itself on the first seven of the following eight tasks: 1 / informing immigrants about the nature of Quebec before departure; 2 / contributing supporting funds to francophone welcoming centres; 3 / establishing francophone welcoming centres; 4 / providing the education necessary for integration into the francophone milieu; 5 / providing French-language training; 6 / placing immigrants in jobs; 7 / recruiting immigrants; and 8 / defining the criteria and their weights for entry. In 1978, the process of devolution was completed when a new series of negotiations led to Quebec obtaining powers to perform the eighth task above.

In reviewing this series of developments in immigration policy, it is important to note that the movement to define a policy for integration into the francophone community occurred just as that community was seeking to redefine its own culture. The boundaries of the community were being expanded to include all those who lived in Quebec. The minimum condition for becoming a member of that community was that an individual or group be able to conduct itself in the French language. If this condition were satisfied, then other cultural particularities would be respected. The new community of reference was therefore to be culturally pluralist, with the use of French as the integrating force.

Ironically, perhaps, the very instability of the value system of francophone Québécois hindered integration on the cultural plane. This problem is illustrated in a study of the relationships between immigrants and French Canadians in the mining town of Noranda.[51] Immigrants found it difficult to interact with French Canadians because they could not grasp their scheme of reference. French-Canadian values were so much in flux and so unstable that immigrants found it easier to gravitate toward the anglophone community. They were not able to build institutional bridges to the French-Canadian group.

The government's commitments to constructing the missing institutional links were actualized, it will be argued in the two chapters to follow, only in the fields of education and language, However, the new institutions put in place in these fields will be shown not to reflect a renewed sense of culture but the government's own commitments to economic development and integration. Hence the institutions facilitate the adoption by both francophones and new immigrants of the value system of mass consumer–oriented North America. As a final note, the provincial government gained increased powers over immigration into Quebec just as it was placing new emphasis on the private sector for economic development. The changes thus gave the government an increased capacity for tailoring the labour force to the needs of the private sector. The economic facet of these powers over immigration may be as important as the cultural-linguistic facet.

Control over mass communications

Control over broadcast communications is important to any group concerned with cultural protection or development. The struggle that developed between Quebec and Ottawa over this power is important because its result was perceived as a defeat and rejection of Quebec's aims. It thus presented to many nationalists further evidence that Quebec would never be able to define its new culture freely under the existing federal régime. Our attention will be confined to radio and television programming, cable distribution, and telecommunications.

After 1945, the technology for cable distribution was not sufficiently developed to be an issue of public policy; in the other three areas, the government of Quebec had little control and apparently little interest. The dominant telecommunications corporations – Bell Canada, Canadian National, and Canadian Pacific – were regulated by the federal government. Radio broadcasting was in both private hands and in those of La Société Radio-Canada, the French-language part of the Canadian Broadcasting Corporation (CBC). Television in French Canada was completely dominated by Radio-Canada. The CBC served as a broadcaster and as the federal agency regulating broadcasting and was thus the dominant force in Canadian broadcasting. Radio-Canada, unlike many other federal institutions, was a vibrant and dynamic voice for French Quebec. After the report of the Royal Commission on Broadcasting in the late 1950s, the CBC was relieved of its regulatory role. Government action on the commission's recommendations opened up the possibility for private groups to set up broadcasting networks. In Quebec, the Télémedia (TVA) network, a counterpart to the private Canadian Television network (CTV), began to grow, beginning in 1962.

We have seen that nationalists drawn from the traditional francophone middle class had come to view the government of Quebec as the national government, and we would expect that they would oppose federal predominance in broadcasting. A reading of briefs submitted to the Massey Commission provides evidence for such an opposition. The Ligue d'Action nationale in its brief called upon the federal government to withdraw from any involvement in determining the content of broadcasts and to restrict its attention to technical questions such as those involving installation and the quality of reception. This position was supported by the chambres de commerce from Montreal and Quebec City and by the Union catholique des cultivateurs. These groups were particularly concerned that the federal government might use its position to interfere in education. In its brief to the Tremblay Commission in 1954, the SSJBM called upon the provincial government to study the possibility of creating its own broadcasting network. Subsequently, it made its demand more direct by calling upon the government to set up such a network immediately.[52] It was supported in this quest by other conservative nationalist groups, the Alliance laurentienne, the Ligue d'Action nationale, and the pre-1963 RIN.[53] In short, the established and traditional nationalist societies, consistent with their ideology, had placed on the table by the early 1960s proposals for a radical shift in powers over broadcasting.

Beginning in 1963, the newer, more left-wing nationalist groups made similar proposals for different reasons. The Parti socialiste du Québec, a nationalist group that had broken away from the NDP in Quebec, argued that the government of Quebec should have full control over all communications media: radio and television, telephone, telegraph, and communications satellites. Similarly, the new Parti québécois called for a rigorous penetration by the provincial government into all areas of mass communications to ensure that the media did not harm efforts at a national recovery (redressement).[54] It added that the media must be converted into an instrument of popular education and used to instil in the population a spirit of 'collective responsibility and the constant desire for progress.'[55] Those nationalist groups which enjoyed more support from the new middle class saw control of the media to be necessary if a new culture were to replace the traditional one. Unlike the established nationalist groups, they were not satisfied with simply having control over broadcasting. They wanted the government to intervene actively and shape the content of the material transmitted.

In February 1968 the Union nationale government began to breath life into Radio-Québec, an institution created on paper by Duplessis in the late 1940s. Radio-Québec was given the mandate to create an educational broadcasting network and to develop audio-visual resources of an educational sort. By 1975, it had begun regular broadcasting using UHF channels in Montreal and Quebec City and has continued to expand into other centres under the Parti québécois. Its relative success provoked discontent among some private broadcasters in Quebec who felt that private networks could have been subsidized to carry out the same tasks.[56]

A concerted attempt to expand provincial powers in the field began when Jean-Paul L'Allier became minister of communications in the Liberal government of the early 1970s. In May 1971 he released a green paper on communications.[57] In it he suggested that the government of Quebec should elaborate a global communications policy. It had a duty to guarantee Québécois 'the inalienable right' to communicate according to their cultural, social, economic, and political needs.[58] Accordingly, L'Allier demanded that cable broadcasting come under its authority.[59] In December 1972, Bill 35 was passed giving the Public Service Board the authority to regulate cable (now classified as a 'public service'). The board immediately undertook a survey of all cable distribution companies in the province. L'Allier helped forge a common front of all the provinces to press for concessions from the federal government.

In a white paper published in 1973, Quebec amplified its demands in the communications field.[60] The minister demanded control over all communication media and the capacity to set up communications networks.[61] Full control of land, subsoil, and airspace would be needed, he added, to ensure a right of veto over any communications system. Further, such control implied the legal capacity to extend activity to the international plane through work with other countries and international organizations.[62] The minister suggested the creation of an interprovincial body with federal representation which would be given control over the distribution of frequencies in areas outside federal jurisdiction. At an interprovincial conference in 1974, these demands received some additional support when all the provinces agreed to ask for control over all intraprovincial communications services.

In general, Ottawa resisted the provincial demands. The federal minister of communications, Gérard Pelletier, reacted vigorously against the granting of powers over cable to the Public Service Board in Quebec. By 1974, the dispute had reached the courts in the form of a quarrel over the power to distribute cable licences. In 1973 and again in 1975, Pelletier proposed the creation of a single national telecommunications agency responsible for the supervision of broadcasting, with provisions built in for consultation with the provinces.[63] He resisted any formal transfers of legislative authority to the provinces but did agree that they should be able to control intraprovincial aspects of telecommunications and suggested various advisory bodies as a means to give the provinces input in deciding communications policy.[64] At a federal-provincial conference in July 1975 he rejected provincial demands for control over broadcasting, arguing that their satisfaction would only shatter an important force for unifying Canada on the cultural plane, thus repeating the traditional federal arguments in this area.[65] He also repulsed arguments that cable distribution was a public service and hence did not fall under federal control of broadcasting. Dismayed, L'Allier walked out of the conference after only the first day's proceedings.

In 1977, the federal position was reinforced by two decisions of the Supreme Court of Canada. In *Capital Cities Communication v. Canadian Radio Television Commission* and *Public Service Board v. Dionne,* cases that had originated in the mid-1970s, the court upheld federal claims to jurisdiction over cable television undertakings. The Parti québécois, however, continued throughout its first government to push the program outlined by L'Allier, not really departing from his proposals.[66]

It is tempting in reviewing these events to conclude that the government of Quebec's initiatives in broadcasting were the results of the personal energy and ideology of Jean-Paul L'Allier. There is no doubt that L'Allier brought a certain ability and determination to his portfolios. But was there any reason beyond his personality that caused the government of Quebec to move on communications in the early 1970s? It could, of course, have been responding to the demands of the radical nationalists and of the Parti québécois. It could have been anticipating the rapid expansion of cable television, pay television, and related technologies. It might have hoped that these projects would be developed by local entrepreneurs and was seeking to obtain the powers to provide them with a protective umbrella while they were starting up. Perhaps it saw these technologies as a new threat to French-Canadian culture (though it had little idea what were the unique constituents of that culture). Perhaps it wished further control of these media in order to direct more strongly the process of legitimating its own economic policy. Whatever the government's motives, it did emerge from the fracas with its hands virtually as empty as when it had begun. The federal government, it was argued, had imposed its will, and Quebec was denied again the possibility to control an important instrument of cultural development.

Conclusion

This chapter has been devoted to the analysis of an apparent paradox. The economic policies that the government of Quebec began to pursue in the early 1960s were directed at engaging the francophone community fully in the advanced industrial economy of North America, including in particular some participation in the direction of that economy. At the same time, the Quebec government moved in cultural areas in a way that suggested it wished to separate Quebec from the rest of Canada. It is now evident that this latter activity was only apparently drawing Quebec out of mainstream North American society.

The partially successful struggle with the federal government over control and fiscal support of social policy broke down some cultural barriers between francophone Quebec and the rest of Canada. Quebec used its new authority in this area to dismantle the traditional system for the delivery of social services and to replace it with a more integrated and rationalized system under its own control. This new system was more similar to others in Canada than was its predecessor. The federal government, however, retained control over those social programs it deemed important for maintaining an integrated national economy. Quebec was thus prevented from differing too much from the national norm. The government of Quebec made only limited gains in its attempts to secure a more powerful voice on the international stage. Its major accomplishments here were several agreements with France in education and support for the arts. The agreements led to greater interchange between the two countries on the level of specialized professional education, and this accomplishment complemented the thrust of educational reform. The latter will be shown in the next chapter to be complementary to the new economic policies. Quebec's success in increasing control over immigration did not promise to make it different from other provinces but did give it an additional tool for putting its economic policies into effect.

Despite its creation of the Department of Cultural Affairs in 1961, the government of Quebec was not actively involved in fostering cultural development during the 1960s. The department had virtually no impact on the mass of the population. In the early 1970s it began to develop some presence in various regions and obtained more funds to support the fine and performing arts. A similar pattern characterizes government activity in broadcasting. The government was uninterested during the 1960s when the economic policies were being put in place. In the early 1970s, it developed a presence in the field with the growth in the educational network of Radio-Québec. Neither in support for the arts by the Department of Cultural Affairs nor in fostering Radio-Québec was the government contradicting the thrust of its economic policies.

In fact, an argument can be made that it was indirectly supporting these economic policies through these latter two activities. In Quebec in the 1960s there was an explosion of cultural activity. Poetry, novels, theatre, music, fine arts, and literary criticism were developed to new heights, breaking older patterns and styles. Many of the works were political statements and implicitly critical of the government's economic policies. Many were separatist in that they represented attempts to define and elaborate what it meant to be a Québécois and what the culture of French Quebec entailed. They were often anti-capitalist and borrowed freely from the symbolism and thinking of world-wide critiques of imperialism and of Third World national liberation movements. They thus were opposed to the greater integration of Quebec's francophone community into the mainstream of capitalist North America. They rejected clearly the consumerism, hucksterism, and materialism of capitalism. Many of the artists involved were active in the RIN and were prominent in the Parti québécois in its early days as well. Intervention by the province into the arts in the early 1970s was one means of putting a cap on some of this dissent. The artistic community was gradually made more dependent on support from the state and experienced the constraints on its expression that normally comes from this dependence. By the late 1970s, artists in Quebec were no longer a political force of note and either withdrew into themselves or were absorbed into the government and PQ bureaucracy. Their disappearance helps explain as well the rather empty reflections on cultural issues noted at the outset of this chapter.

In cultural policy, then, the Quiet Revolution itself was a revolution of symbols. The increase of symbolic activity – the Maison du Québec in Paris, the Service de Canada français d'outre frontières, the Department of Cultural Affairs – probably functioned here much as theorists of symbolism such as Edelman and Offe suggest.[67] An increase in symbolic activity usually occurs in order to foster acquiescence, acceptance, or even support for policies that are against the better interests of the population. The symbols we have presented often provide images that are misleading about the economic policies of the government, that suggest policies are nationalist when they are integrationist, for example. In chapter 7, it will be shown that important parts of language policy played the same kind of distracting or legitimating role in Quebec during the 1970s. Before that argument is made, however, we must consider how the most important institutional change of the 1960s, the reform of education, related to the policy of economic development and the impact of that change on French-Canadian culture.

6

Educational reform

If one were to show a group of students things that have been important in the life of the new Quebec, one might think of the minutes of the Conseil d'Orientation économique du Québec, the new steel complex at Contrecoeur, the Manicouagan hydro-electric project, the offices of the Department of Cultural Affairs, or the Maison du Québec in Paris. One should also stop at the grave of Mgr Alphonse-Marie Parent, deep in the crypt of the old Séminaire de Québec; he headed a royal commission the recommendations of which have transformed education in Quebec. If one asks: What was the Quiet Revolution?, the answer often refers to the Royal Commission of Inquiry on Education, the Parent Commission. The major change of the 1960s was the implementation of a program of educational reform based upon the recommendations of this commission.

Changes in its system of education will be important for any community, but such a change in the francophone community in Quebec was perhaps even more significant. As we have seen in chapter 2, its educational system was developed within the traditional culture of the French-Canadian nation. Drawing their inspiration from the Catholic faith and tracing their roots to New France and the classical structures of the ancien régime, those institutions were for many the hallmark and protector of French-Canadian civilization. Traditional nationalists felt that if the education system were to be changed, it should be done with delicacy and with the knowledge that the distinctiveness of the French-Canadian nation hung in the balance.

Aside from being a cultural legacy, the educational system also had a political property that other areas of Quebec's culture often did not possess. Education was primarily a provincial responsibility under the Canadian constitution and somewhat sheltered from federal-provincial acrimony. The shelter was not perfect, as we saw in chapter 3, but it was far superior to those of social welfare and culture. If members of the francophone community wished to pursue a program of cultural regeneration and invention with minimal outside interference, education was perhaps the best field available for such an attempt. If the program failed the blame could be attached to federal authorities only under special circumstances.

As educational reform began to be seriously contemplated in Quebec in the late 1950s, three avenues were open. A preliminary discussion of these possibilities took place at the Université de Montréal in February 1958 at a Provincial Conference on Education, convened jointly by the Chambre de Commerce de la Province de Québec and the Fédération des Sociétés Saint-Jean-Baptiste du Québec. It was attended by individuals from these groups as well as by representatives of the labour movement and by intellectuals. The forces that gave the conference its life and its prominence constituted the same coalition that came together to push for economic reform and that was discussed in chapter 4. The conference was chaired by Esdras Minville, who had just completed his duties as a member of the Tremblay Commission. In his opening address, he presented the first of the three views on educational reform, and it was a derivative of the reasoning of the Tremblay Report itself.

Minville readily agreed that change was needed, that room had to be found in the existing system of education for instruction in the science-based, technological knowledge that was more and more central to the life of modern society. However, the process whereby room was created for this knowledge had to be based upon and respectful of the precepts of French-Canadian culture. Any other process was unacceptable: 'Toute réforme et toute politique nouvelle de l'enseignement qui s'éloignerait de l'esprit de notre culture traditionnelle et en ignorerait les valeurs, devrait être tenue pour téméraire et aventureuse.'[1] For Minville, educational reform was a matter of integrating the advances of science and the power of the industrial economy with the existing value system and national culture. If this approach were not adopted the consequences would be dire. Reform would be based upon foreign values imposed from without: 'Cette revision des grandes structures sociales, nous l'accomplirons nous mêmes selon notre esprit ou elle nous sera imposée de l'extérieur selon un esprit différent, ruinant ainsi nos chances de rétablir l'accord entre la vie sociale et la vie nationale, et de redonner à notre milieu sa pleine homogénéité.'[2] The traditional French-Canadian élite would need to fashion such a response imminently, or else the population of Quebec would call upon outside forces to accomplish the task.

The second avenue for reform might be labelled pragmatic. Individuals sharing in this view felt that Quebec's educational system was ill-adapted to industrial society and technology. They argued that the system had to be adapted as quickly and as efficiently as possible to compensate for this weakness. Without such action, the francophone community was destined to become even more of an economic backwater than it already was. Concerns about the cultural consequences of educational reform were virtually absent from this point of view.

A third approach developed in the 1950s would reform the educational system to fit the modern age but as part of a larger project of developing a new culture, a new 'humanism' to replace the traditional culture cherished by Minville. Proponents of this view were to be found in intellectual circles outside the traditional intelligentsia. Prominent among these were Arthur Tremblay, a specialist in education at Laval, and Jean-Charles Falardeau, a sociologist at Laval.[3]

Given the approach to economic development pursued by the government of Quebec after 1960, one would expect that the avenue of reform suggested by Minville would not be followed. In rejecting the Tremblay Commission's position on economic change, the government was rejecting the notion that economic policy had to be based upon traditional French-Canadian values. The government saw education policy to be intimately related to its economic policy and was more likely to base the former on principles that were consistent with the latter. Given also the government's lack of interest in a global project to define a new culture for Quebec (see chapter 5), it would probably not be disposed toward following the third path. This would leave the second, pragmatic path to educational reform as the likeliest.

In this chapter I will trace the pragmatic reform of the educational system from the early 1960s. The government passed up the opportunity to follow the third, more global and more innovative route to change. The failure to seize this opportunity had important political consequences. The educational system has been wracked by a series of crises that are the result of inconsistencies and political compromises that crept into its reform. Several of the key structures in the new system seem ill adapted to the society of which they are a part. In chapter 7, they will be shown to be inconsistent with aspects of the language policy promulgated in the 1970s. The tendency of the new educational system to promote the materialism of advanced capitalism rather than new distinctive values will help foster alienation and disillusion among the key social groups that are most predisposed to supporting the political independence of Quebec.

These several points will be established by studying three issues that were central to the debate on education in Quebec: 1/ Which institutions should have overall responsibility for education? 2/ How should pedagogical structures be changed to accommodate the advance of technology and industrial capitalism? 3/ How should administrative structures be changed to match changes in overall responsibility and pedagogical structures?

The emergence of these three issues was not surprising, given the questions about education raised during the previous decade. First, in the 1950s, the debate over the relationship between the collèges classiques and the public écoles primaires supérieures noted in chapter 2 became public and more widely discussed. Part of this debate centred around the advisability of giving the latter public schools a status more equal to the colleges and making them into a viable public secondary school system. Another part of the debate focused upon the development of a science-based program option for inclusion in the college curriculum, which would be a marked departure from practice. Both these issues point to growing dissatisfaction with the classical college–based approach to higher education and to uncertainty over whether it would remain workable in an advanced industrial society.

Second, questions arose about the method of funding education in Quebec. Duplessis preferred to give grants to educational institutions on a discretionary rather than a statutory basis. Institutions were forced to come begging year after year. In this way, Duplessis was able to squeeze maximum political returns from the funds he had available. This policy, however, had disastrous effects on educational institutions, because they were unable to plan more than a year ahead. For example, during the 1950s, Université Laval experienced a 109 per cent growth in its registrations and a constant dollar grant in its annual subsidies.[4] It was difficult for educational institutions to welcome many new students without creating grave financial problems for themselves. They also increasingly lacked adequate physical plants because demands on their facilities were rising rapidly. There was an increasing shortage of teachers. Class sizes were increased, and in many institutions run by religious orders unqualified lay persons were hired to teach.[5] By responding to increased demand by lowering standards of instruction, the educational system became even more a magnet for dissatisfaction.

Third, there was a change in the demands placed upon the system. If one surveys the concerns of the coalition of forces that pushed for a change in economic policy – the French-Canadian business class, the nationalist societies, and organized labour – one is struck by the increased importance they gave to technical and scientific education. In its annual brief to the premier in 1958, the Chambre de Commerce de la Province de Québec called upon the government to take whatever steps were needed to increase the number of engineers educated in Quebec.[6] It noted the increasing importance of engineers in industry and regretted that French Canadians accounted for only 8.1 per cent of the engineers in Canada. Worries of a similar nature were expressed by the Société Saint-Jean-Baptiste de Montréal (SSJBM) and the voice of the nationalist societies on economic matters, the Conseil d'expansion économique.[7] The conservative independence group, the Alliance laurentienne, thought the matter sufficiently important that it suggested as an incentive that all students in commerce, business, and engineering be paid salaries.[8] The CTCC for its part had noted the need for revision and expansion of professional and technical education beginning with its 1956 convention. These same needs came to be voiced by leading members of the Liberal government shortly after its election to power in June 1960.[9] The perceived need for an increase in the capacity to educate citizens in technical areas was consistent with demands for greater participation of francophones in the direction of the economy and for more 'modern' business approaches voiced by these same groups.

These various frustrations gradually placed more and more pressure on the government. Many were first aired in the wide-ranging discussions that occurred during the public hearings of the Tremblay Commission. They received additional impetus in the report of the Commission du programme de la Faculté des Arts au Conseil universitaire submitted to Université Laval in 1957, which was highly critical of the operations of the classical colleges.[10] In 1958, they were raised again at the Provincial Conference on Education. By 1960, a host of organized groups and individuals had taken up the recommendation of the Tremblay Commission that there be a wide-ranging and intensive study of the educational system sponsored by the government.[11] On 28 February 1961, the Legislative Assembly passed an act to establish a Royal Commission of Inquiry on Education. The commission was to be presided over by Mgr Parent, vice-rector of Université Laval, with Gérard Filion, later head of the SGF, as its vice-president. Important among its members were Arthur Tremblay and Guy Rocher, a sociologist well educated in European and American sociological theory.[12]

Overall societal responsibility for education

It will be recalled from chapter 2 that during the first decade after the Second World War, responsibility for education was shared in Quebec's francophone community between the Roman Catholic church and the provincial government. The former controlled all education save that of a specialized technical or vocational kind. The church's widespread control was justified in Catholic social thought by referring to the church's duty to ensure that temporal institutions were infused with the Christian spirit necessary for personal salvation. Further, as we have seen in the discussion of the traditional approach to culture exemplified in the Tremblay Report, religious precepts and values are seen to infuse the whole of culture and its institutional articulation. In this view, no institution can be neutral. Society has a form and structures that are either

Christian or anti-Christian. The duty of Catholics was clear, as *Relations* reminded its readers in 1961: 'Il serait à souhaiter que tous nos catholiques qui poussent actuellement à la neutralité des institutions se souviennent qu'ils ont aussi, *à titre de catholiques,* le devoir de donner à la société une forme et une structure chrétienne, et d'opérer ainsi *la consecratio mundi* dont le Christ les a chargés.'[13] This position, that religion and society cannot be separated, meant that any attempt to separate one from the other would be considered a frontal assault on the bases of French-Canadian civilization.

Opposition to this long-dominant ideology flourished with a new vigour in the early 1960s. Perhaps the definitive shot in this debate was delivered by Pierre Charbonneau in a virulent article published in *Cité libre* in December 1960. Charbonneau called for a complete laïcization of Quebec society and particularly of education. He wrote, 'Les clercs ont eu deux siècles pour faire leurs preuves; la bâtardise de notre société et la faillite de notre culture démontrent amplement la nullité de leurs efforts.'[14]

In April 1961, the Mouvement laïque de la langue française (MLF) was formed, with Maurice Blain as its president.[15] Blain had written several articles critical of the church during the 1950s.[16] The Mouvement laïque in its publications attacked the traditional ideology directly along lines similar to those of Charbonneau. Its supporters argued that the traditional view which called for the Christianization of all social institutions had the effect of isolating and making suspect those who did not share in the belief in church doctrine. The rights of these dissidents were being denied when they were forced to function in institutions built on principles foreign to their beliefs. In order to avoid these injustices, society should not be linked to any particular set of religious beliefs. Rather it should be neutral and non-confessional.[17] This neutrality should be guaranteed by the state, which should act as a neutral arbiter among religious communities and yet above all of them.[18]

The MLF was probably the first organization to speak for elements of the middle class that were nationalist without being clerical. Although it is difficult to gauge accurately, the MLF probably drew most heavily from what might be termed a new middle class. It included professors in the social sciences, authors of less established rank, and journalists. Many of these would later support the RIN or the Parti québécois. We shall also see that groups drawing from this base tended to replace traditional nationalists in the coalition with organized labour and the francophone business class in the drive for educational reform. However, the lines are not clear, and probably some traditional nationalists supported educational change as well.

The attacks by the MLF on the church's ideology and on church-controlled institutions helped lift the debate over the issues involved into a wider public forum. They also elicited a vigorous response from the church and from traditional nationalists, who interpreted them as attacks on the foundations of French-Canadian civilization. The debate that ensued was by no means temperate, as the following quotation from *Relations* illustrates:[19] 'Une laïcité qui signifierait le mépris et la négation de Dieu, l'hostilité ou même l'indifférence devant le fait religieux serait tout à fait inadmissible. Plusieurs néo-Canadiens venus de France, aidés de quelques autochtones d'esprit colonial, voudraient nous imposer les frais de la Révolution française ... Bien peu d'authentiques Canadiens français sont prêts à saboter les institutions originales bâties par deux siècles de luttes pour le respect de droits légitimes réciproques.' None the less the traditionalists were placed clearly on the defensive, especially in the field of education.

The question for these groups was how to reform the Conseil de l'instruction publique (CIP) in order to maintain church control and yet meet the crescendo of criticism directed toward it. The CIP, which decided educational policy in Quebec, drew from the Catholic and Protestant communities. The Catholic Committee of the CIP was controlled by the bishops, thus ensuring that the episcopate gave the educational system in French Canada its form and direction. The most elaborate reform proposal came from the Fédération des collèges classiques (FCC) in its voluminous brief to the Parent Commission submitted in June 1962.[20] The FCC called for an end to the twin involvement of the church and the province in education by transferring all educational institutions run by the provincial government and its departments to the responsibility of the Conseil de l'instruction publique. It suggested that the council be purged and be composed of pedagogical experts named by religious bodies interested in education and approved by the bishops. It suggested also the inclusion of associate members who would represent non-confessional bodies and be given a right to vote on matters of 'general interest.' Essentially, the FCC wanted to gather the growing number of public institutions dispensing technical education back under the wings of the church and to provide the bishops with more channels to receive expert advice and hear from a wider portion of the community.

The opposing position called for the replacement of the CIP by a department of education headed by a minister sitting in cabinet. This position was supported by most of the social coalition behind other Quiet Revolution reforms. It enjoyed the support of the CSN and the FTQ, of the CCPQ, and of more progressive nationalists such as those found in the RIN and the student wing of the Parti libéral, as well, of course, as the MLF. Traditional nationalists such as those in the SSJBM tended to lean more toward a position like that of the FCC. The government had already tipped its hand in favour of the creation of a department of education when Lesage in 1960 gave the Department of Youth under Paul Gérin-Lajoie responsibility for all provincial-government educational institutions.[21] In 1961 Gérin-Lajoie presented a Grande Charte de l'éducation which, among other things, relieved the superintendent of public instruction of powers to administer grants to educational institutions, placing them in his own hands.[22]

In April 1963, the Parent Commission delivered the first volume of its report and gave this process a push that was to be irreversible.[23] Its first recommendation was that a minister of education be appointed and given the function of promoting and co-ordinating all systems of education in the province. Its fourth recommendation was that this minister be given a department of education formed by the fusion of the Department of Youth and the administrative offices of the CIP supervised by the superintendent of public instruction. It justified these recommendations by pointing to four major problems confronting the province's educational system and asking which institutions in society would be best able to address these problems: 1/ the explosion in the number of students at all levels of the system; 2/ the need to assimilate the scientific and technological revolution under way in Western societies; 3/ the profound changes in living conditions brought on by this revolution; and 4/ the rapid evolution of ideas found in modern society.

The minimal response to these problems, the commission argued, had to be, first, planning of education on a rational and global basis. Second, there had to be a massive allocation of funds for the necessary reorientation of the system. Such responsibilities could only be given to the state: 'Cette tâche d'organisation et de financement appartient en propre au pouvoir politique responsable du bien commun.'[24] The proposals of the FCC and others like them were, in the commission's view, inappropriate in a democratic society. The spending of such large amounts of taxpayers' money and such global planning were responsibilities that could be conferred only on a minister and department that were ultimately responsible to the electorate.

The Parent Commission also felt that some voice had to be given to the diverse range of organized social groups with a stake in education in the province. The normal electoral bodies had to be supplemented by 'corps intermédiaires' that would provide these groups with an opportunity to participate in the planning of education. This idea was related to the concept of organic democracy which was popular in established intellectual circles at this time.[25] In an organic democracy, intermediary institutions were to be created for bringing together organized groups and democratic representative bodies. The notion is derived from earlier ideas of corporatism and was given a sharp push in John XXIII's encyclical *Mater et Magistra*, published in 1961.

Accordingly, the commission recommended that an intermediary body of this type, to be called the Superior Council of Education, be created in order to represent social groups and to advise the minister of education. The new council bore some resemblance to the old CIP but, unlike that body, was not to have a bicameral structure. The commission here was taking as its reference point all the people of Quebec. This political community it described as pluralist, and it was the task of the state to give that diversity some semblance of unity: 'Le pluralisme de la province de Québec, qui doit s'exprimer au niveau des écoles par la variété des institutions et des programmes, rend plus nécessaire encore ce travail en commun au niveau supérieur des structures scolaires.'[26] The underlying presupposition was that there were no longer two kinds of Québécois but one. Such an argument was used later by Paul Gérin-Lajoie, the first minister of education, to justify creation of the council.[27] The council was to divide into religious committees only in order to define programs of religious instruction in the schools and to oversee the religious character of the schools.

The ensuing career of the commission's recommendations was far from smooth. They were presented to the legislature as Bill 60 in June 1963, but had to be withdrawn after intense pressure, particularly from the bishops. The debate that followed was intense and has been carefully analysed elsewhere.[28] In January 1964, a revised version of the bill was passed with a new preamble, suggested by the bishops, consecrating the right of parents to choose the institutions in which their children would be educated.[29] It also strengthened somewhat the Superior Council of Education and the bishops' power over the committee of the council responsible for Catholic religious instruction. In the end, however, the bill was quite true to the recommendations of the royal commission. Gérin-Lajoie became Quebec's first minister of education, and the church's power had been narrowed to control over religious instruction in the schools.

The public debate between the Assembly of Bishops and the provincial government was a sign, Léon Dion has argued in his magistral study of Bill 60, that the old clerical conservatism had finally lost its hold on Quebec.[30] The bishops' appearance on a public stage like any other interest group rather than using the traditional mechanism of private negotiations in itself symbolized the decline in their power. As a result of the new legislation, the provincial government had been established in an ascendant and neutral position not unlike that demanded by the Mouvement laïque. In adjusting its view from these new heights, the government saw itself overseeing not two communities with two faiths, but a pluralistic community with diverse beliefs. As we shall see, the concept of pluralisme occupies a pre-eminent place in the discourse of the Parent Commission. The Tremblay Commission spoke not only of two societies in Quebec but of two societies founded on opposing principles. The task of the governing of Quebec, in its view, could never be one of integrating these societies; rather it had to be one of cementing the barriers between the two. The thrust of the Parent Commission could hardly have differed more.

One might be struck by the almost complete absence of concern on the part of members of the commission over the cultural consequences for the francophone community of the dismantling of the traditional educational framework. The arguments made by the commission are based on such values as rationality, efficiency, and efficacy. No concern is displayed that implementation of changes based on these values might be done at the expense of a cultural heritage. However, the espousal of these values is quite consistent with the policy of engaging the francophone community fully into the advanced capitalist economy of North America. The revamped educational system is seen by members of the commission as a necessary condition for the pursuit of such a policy. This point will become more clear as this chapter proceeds. Even at this juncture, however, it would be unfair to describe the commission's values as 'tout à fait anglo-saxon et par conséquent étranger et même hostile aux traditions religieuses et humanistes des Canadiens français,' as F.-A. Angers was wont to do.[31] The suggestion by the commission that the superior council be created as a democratic institution that would bring local community perceptions to the ears of the minister was founded on a concept of 'organic democracy' derived from Catholic social thought, as we have seen.[32] The presumption in favour of local organization and expression was quite consistent with French-Canadian tradition and signalled an attempt by the commission to subsume the values of rationality and efficiency under a new kind of humanism. This attempt at cultural renewal will be outlined more fully in the sections that follow.

Internal structural reform

Upon shifting from the question of who should have overall responsibility for education in the province to that of what form educational institutions should assume, the problem at hand becomes more specific. In the early 1960s the dominant problem being examined was how to make technical education available at higher levels to members of the francophone community in Quebec. Raising this question immediately led to a critical examination of the classical college system. First, the élites of the French-Canadian community had been trained in these institutions and were left singularly unacquainted with economics, science, and technology because of the restricted focus of the college curriculum. Second, because the colleges were private, access was limited and the colleges acted as a kind of barrier for many to higher education. The baccalauréat from a college remained the main ticket to entry into university. Third, the existence of the colleges and their specialized program drew resources away from public secondary schools, which remained an 'afterthought.' The weakness of the latter lowered the quality of students entering technical schools from the secondary schools.

As we saw in chapter 2, in the 1950s, individuals such as Arthur Tremblay and groups representing organized labour had called for an expansion and upgrading of the public secondary schools. They wished these schools to be an equal alternative to the colleges and their graduates to have full access to university education. In the early 1960s, the Chambre de Commerce de la Province de Québec complemented these suggestions by calling for the creation of a series of intermediate professional schools or collegial institutions that would follow the secondary level and prepare students for university education.[33] In particular, it wanted institutions that would graduate technicians in engineering. The Quebec division of the Canadian Manufacturers' Association (CMA) strongly supported this idea.[34] Both the CMA and the CCPQ wished the government to create a Conseil supérieur de l'enseignement technique to co-ordinate and elaborate the new programs of study in the technical field.

Conservative nationalists such as were found in the Ligue d'Action nationale and the Société Saint-Jean-Baptiste de Montréal, along with the administrators of the colleges, viewed these proposals with alarm. They saw them as representing a move toward Anglo-American models of education.[35] They thought that the classical colleges helped to develop the *esprit* and to promote thinking and reflection, while the Anglo-American models sought to maximize knowledge of technique and foster development of technical aptitudes. If reforms were to be made, the SSJBM argued, they should be based upon a return to sources françaises.[36] Unfortunately it did not elaborate. These groups were completely opposed to the reforms proposed by the CCPQ, the CMA, organized labour, and others. A statement in the editorial pages of *Relations* ten years earlier summarizes their feelings well: We need, it said, 'un système d'enseignement qui, organisé comme un tout, se fixe pour objectif non pas l'acquisition des connaissances propices à l'apprentissage professionnel, mais le développement intellectuel du collégien, en égard à ses propres exigences, c'est à dire à l'épanouissement de sa vie dans la pleine liberté et l'infallible lumière de la sagesse chrétienne.'[37]

The second part of the Parent Report, released in late 1964 and early 1965, articulated a point of view completely opposed to these conservative groups and to the spirit of the Tremblay Commission and consonant with that of the CCPQ and its allies. The key statement, from the first chapter, was as follows: 'Most of our educational problems may be stated in the same basic terms here as elsewhere.'[33] The commissioners approached their study by placing Quebec in a world context and, based upon this exercise, concluded that the social changes buffeting Quebec were common to all industrializing societies. All these societies had experienced a technological revolution, which had uprooted traditional ways of living and thinking. Workers were becoming technicians more and manual labourers less. In order to continue to earn a living they needed more education at a higher intellectual level. The modern societies in which these workers lived were becoming more and more pluralistic on the cultural plane. The commission identified four distinct cultures, each separated from the other by barriers: the humanist, the scientific, the technological, and the mass.

When this analysis is placed in the context of Quebec, several implications can be drawn. The spirit of the analysis is not unlike that behind the economic reforms developed at the same time. The emphasis is on seeing similarities between Quebec and other industrialized societies and of asking how Québécois might participate fully with maximum benefits from industrialization. 'Quebec has now started along the road of industrial and scientific civilization,' the commissioners wrote. It can become a part of that civilization 'only if it raises its level of education and makes it accessible to all who can and will devote themselves to study.'[39] In the commission's view, education was to serve to integrate Quebec into a wider world, much as the economic policy described in chapter 5 was designed to do. This concern with universal values and supranational civilization was an outright rejection of the traditional nationalist viewpoint.

The 'new humanism' that the commission wished to see develop drew together the various cultures of the modern world. The renovation of educational structures was to facilitate this development. The commission summarized its position as follows:[40]

Knowledge of Greek and Latin seems a luxury compared to the knowledge – today essential – of these new means of expression and of perceiving the world. For many people, continuing education now begins on the day when they realize that they must learn something about statistics, reading graphs, using a computer, about the meaning of the arts and understanding other men and other nations. From now on the school must provide everyone with a certain number of these channels of access, which will allow him to understand the world in which he lives and to adapt himself to it; it must also supply future technologists and men of science with a general notion of a humanism in which their special disciplines henceforth constitute a major element.

It is beyond the scope of my project to summarize all the reforms that the Parent Commission recommended on the basis of these principles. We shall consider the two that are the most relevant to my argument, the change in secondary schooling and the change in the first stage beyond secondary education.

The commission recommended first that there be a single stream of secondary education and the abolition of both the existing classical colleges and the public secondary schools. The new secondary school was to extend five years beyond the six years of elementary school. It was to provide a 'general' education for all students and was to include a series of streams ranging from the academic, for those planning to go to university, to the commercial and vocational. The same type of school and program was to serve all religious and linguistic communities in the province. The new schools were referred to as polyvalentes, because they combined the various sides or cultures existing in modern industrial society. They were to be of the smallest possible size in order to concentrate the resources needed for the vairous streams. The polyvalentes were, in effect, no different from most public high schools in anglophone North America.

A second and perhaps more innovative recommendation was the creation of a series of institutes which would provide pre-university and advanced technical instruction to graduates of secondary schools. These converged quite well with those recommended by the CCPQ and discussed above. With larger campuses of at least 2,000 students, they could give students going on to technical fields general education in the humanities. They could develop training in the specialized areas necessary for an industrial economy. Students planning to attend university would be able to obtain an introduction to technical fields of study in addition to a general education in the humanities and social sciences. Bringing together on one plane students planning to go to university and students completing advanced technical training would increase all students' awareness of the various cultures present in the modern world. Most importantly, the institutes would increase training in technical and professional careers which was Quebec's most urgent need, in the view of the commission.[41]

In March 1966, the cabinet passed an order-in-council that led to the opening of such institutes or, as they have been called, collèges d'enseignement général et professionnel (CEGEPs). The CEGEPs had two streams – a two-year general stream leading to university and giving students a basic introduction to the liberal arts and sciences, and a vocational stream that would produce skilled workers for the labour market. This latter function was emphasized when advisory groups linking industry to the CEGEPs were formed to co-ordinate their programs with the needs of the labour market.

With the expected demise of the classical colleges, the secondary school system was revamped as advised, so that it would feed directly into the CEGEPs. Hence academic, vocational, and technical schools were regrouped into the recommended large new polyvalentes which had streams corresponding to those in the CEGEPs.

A further effect of these reforms was the concentration of higher education in the universities and the elimination of the quasi-university level of education provided in the colleges. The universities were left free to move toward a degree structure and programs that approximated the North American model.

They were gradually given increased financial support, particularly for library enrichment.[42] French-Canadian universities had been characterized by significantly lower library usage than their other Canadian counterparts.[43] This period showed a vast increase in public library holdings, another area in which Quebec lagged behind. Finally, in December 1968, the authorities created the Université du Québec, which was to expand the opportunities for university-level education by creating campuses in the outlying regions – La Mauricie, the Saguenay, the Gaspé, Outaouais, Abitibi, and so on. These campuses were established on the foundations of the collèges that had operated in these regions. As a result of these changes, Quebec had a much more unified system of education than before. Catholics and Protestants followed the same sequence through the same types of institutions studying the same programs. The new system assumed that the population of the province could be treated as a single community, much as the Parent Commission had conceived it.

Both labour and business, in briefs to the Parent Commission, had urged that the authorities undertake a general expansion of adult education in order to improve the competence of workers. In each volume of its report, the commission broached this theme, emphasizing that such an expansion was necessary for immediate economic development and that Quebec could not afford to wait for a future generation. In 1964, the province set up a Service de l'éducation permanente, which was expanded in March 1966 to become a Directorate of Continuing Education within the Ministry of Education. Several innovative programs involving electronic communciations media – Sésame, Tévec, Multi-média – were developed in the late 1960s.

In short, the reforms marked the acceptance of the principle that education was essentially a tool for economic advancement and conformed to an ideology that suggested that francophones, by educating themselves and reforming their business practices, could gain greater control of the economy. In the opening pages of the final volume of its report, the Parent Commission re-emphasized the role of the educational system in producting a specialized labour force, in developing scientific and technical knowledge, and in giving to all the socialization necessary for more rational behaviour.[44] As we have seen in previous discussions, this view was enthusiastically supported by the French-Canadian business class. In the late 1960s it also was generally accepted, for different reasons, by nationalists drawn more from the new middle class. The leaders of the Mouvement Souveraineté-Association (MSA), one of the founding groups of the Parti québécois and a break-away group from the Parti libéral, subscribed to the vision of the educational system developed by the Parent Commission. For them as well, there was an evident complementarity between science and technique on the one hand and culture on the other:[45]

L'essor de l'éducation permanente et le développement de l'enseignement technique, particulièrement de l'enseignement technique supérieur, représentent sans doute la plus haute priorité pour le futur État québécois. C'est par là seulement que le peuple québécois aura une chance de contrôler son propre développement et d'entrer dans le concert des nations progressistes ... Jamais il ne fut aussi vrai que l'éducation est libératrice: elle l'est non seulement de la crainte mais aussi de la pauvreté et de toutes les formes de domination. De même, il ne fut jamais aussi évident qu'entre la science et la technique d'une part, la culture de l'autre, il n'y a pas opposition mais complémentarité essentielle: ce sont le progrès technologique et l'expansion économique qui, en libérant le travailleur, font de la culture, un bien également partagé.

The evidence for workers supporting the reforms is less clear. However, one study of metal workers in Montreal showed that they shared to a degree the vision of education propounded in the Parent Report.[46] In short, by the time the commission's report was completed and the initial institutional reforms were implemented, they appeared to have the support of the three social groups who gave impetus to the reforms – the business class, the new middle class, and organized labour.

The old principle generally rejected by the commission and expressed eloquently in the brief of the ssjвm to it was that the educational system should dedicate itself primarily to ensuring ethnic survival by forming a strong national consciousness and sense of identity.[47] The rejection of this old principle did not pass without critical response from traditional nationalists. Canon Lionel Groulx, often called the father of French-Canadian nationalism, in one of his last articles before his death in 1967, described the commission's report as a call to shift the axis of French-Canadian civilization from its old Mediterranean roots to Anglo-American sources.[48] Several years later, Jacques Poisson, writing in *Maintenant,* elaborated the same theme. He saw the commission's report as infused with American culture: 'Or, le drame du Québec, c'est justement que l'école instaurée par la Commission Parent propose à notre jeunesse une réprésentation de la société largement empruntée à une culture étrangère, qui, par surcroît, est négatrice de la nôtre et hostile à nos solidarités naturelles. La pédagogie américaine incite le jeune Québécois à s'identifier à une image qui n'est pas sienne.'[49] Père Richard Arès, a member of the Tremblay Commission, gave the response one might have expected, given that commission's perspective. He wondered why all the old values had to be placed aside. He speculated that the institutes recommended by the commission would 'se transformer en énormes usines automatisées d'où sortirent en série des citoyens de formation planétaire, mais déracinés et interchangeables.'[50] In 1969, Arès continued his analysis.[51] He wrote that the commission had relied almost exclusively on a sociological analysis of the current problems in education, and in so doing it had neglected to develop a philosophy of man and society as the Tremblay Commission had done. Even more important, the commission had considered individuals as producers, consumers, and citizens but not as members of the nation canadienne-française. Thus, he implied, the commission had failed to take account of the collective interests of the French-Canadian nation.

The support for the educational reforms by the modified coalition of three groups was not sustained for long. Just as with economic policy, a division developed between the business class on the one hand and organized labour and nationalists from the new middle class on the other. The former continued to support the reforms, while the latter groups became increasingly critical. The roots of the dissatisfaction of the working class will be discussed in a more appropriate place later in this chapter. The concerns of the new middle class are by now rather familiar. There was a growing fear among its leaders that the bases of a distinctive culture in Quebec had been dangerously eroded. French-Canadian civilization was being reduced to a mass, consumption-oriented Americanized culture.

In the mid-1960s, the radical left had warned about this possibility. In an editorial written in March 1965, the journal *Parti pris* described the proposals of the commission as converging with the interests of the rising 'néo-bourgeoisie industrielle et d'affaires.'[52] It added that the proposals reflected a bias in favour of the Canadian federal system: the commission accepted that Quebec should remain part of the Canadian union and in doing so neglected considering the possibility that the problems that it was seeking to address were the consequence of the 'débilitation culturelle' that came with belonging to Canada. The problems would not go away if the educational system was reformed.

The Centrale de l'enseignement du Québec (CEQ), formerly the Corporation des instituteurs et institutrices du Québec, extended this kind of critique in the early 1970s. The CEQ partook of the radicalization of the labour movement in Quebec that occurred between the late 1960s and 1972. In 1971, it published its first manifesto, *Phase 1* in which it reflected at length upon the status of the teaching profession.[53] It concluded that teachers in Quebec could not pretend to be professionals because they did not control the quality, content, and purpose of their work. Rather they were proletarians of a special kind, 'ideological workers.' The reforms of the 1960s had reduced teachers to anonymity by placing them in factories for the mass production of ideology. The humanist component of education recommended by the Parent Commission had been forgotten and only the technical aspect retained. Teachers had seen their role reduced to one of producing skilled manpower for the capitalist economy.

Guy Rocher, a member of the Parent Commission, and Fernand Dumont, a celebrated sociologist and ardent supporter of the Parti québécois, reached similar conclusions after examining the new CEGEPs.[54] They found that the education being given there was diverging significantly from the recommendations of the commission. Students were tending to specialize in one stream only, and cross-fertilization between the humanities and the technical sciences was not taking place. They were not being introduced to what Dumont and Rocher called une culture fondamentale, that is, one that would permit them to feel at home in the various cultures of modern society and that would help them to reflect upon and criticize elements from each. They called upon the provincial government to establish a new inquiry into post-secondary education. These two men wrote, the white paper A Cultural Development Policy for Quebec, published by the Ministry of State for Cultural Development in 1978, which expanded upon this critique. It argued that the cultural influence of the school had been taken too much for granted and that education had been considered in too utilitarian a fashion. 'The school was viewed as the road to social advancement and mobility, education as a condition of personal success, the school system as a requirement for the adaption of society to the industrial and technological world.'[55] The paper concluded that this perspective was too narrow. Québécois had to remember that education was the only active agent of cultural development almost entirely under their own control. Such a conclusion was remarkably similar to the argument being put forth by traditional nationalists a decade earlier.

During the later 1970s, a series of new inquiries of the educational system were commissioned. These included studies of the universities, the CEGEPs, and primary and secondary education. The study of the latter was the most extensive, including a green paper in 1977, a round of discussions and consultations centred on the green paper, and an orange paper of statement on policy in 1979.[56] The orange paper began with a statement that reflected the critiques described above. The school had always to be considered as part of a particular socio-cultural context: 'Ce nécessaire enracinement socio-culturel fait de l'école à la fois un lieu de développement de la culture d'un peuple et un foyer de reflexion où convergent les actions culturelles.'[57] Nevertheless, the orange paper did not propose a major restructuring of the educational system in order to reintroduce a cultural role for the school. It did suggest some changes in course selections that would make the study of history compulsory at certain levels, but these changes hardly promised to address the criticisms that had been made. In short, after the most recent inquiries and recommendations, there is no reason to conclude that the basic orientation of Quebec's secondary schools and CEGEPs – technical and relatively unconcerned with cultural questions specific to the *nation* – will change.

Confessionality and administrative reform

The preceding analysis suggests that the structures created in the late 1960s diverged significantly from those that had been erected upon the traditional values of French Canada. They were no longer even specifically tailored to the French-Canadian community but were expected to serve everyone in the province. Despite these changes, the schools have remained segregated along religious lines. Given the importance of religion for grounding the values of traditional French-Canadian culture, is it not possible that the schools might still serve to socialize French-Canadian youth into a culture with distinctive basic values? It is my contention that this possibility existed but that because of the particular way confessionality has been dealt with politically it has not been realized. In fact, the existing confessional properties of the school system serve to render the schools more technical and instrumentalist in orientation than they might have been. The opportunity for an alternative, more humanist school system based upon the recommendations of the Parent Commission was rejected.

The analysis in this chapter would imply that there were two basic positions on confessionality. The first was supported by the church establishment and by many traditional nationalists. In their view, religion was a part of the national culture of French Canadians and thus should colour demonstrably the national, that is, the public schools. The curriculum, the atmosphere, and the daily practices of the schools should reflect its presence. The second position was presented by organized labour, by some of the new nationalist groups such as the RIN and later the MSA/PQ, and by the Mouvement laïque. In their view, religion was a personal affair and could no longer serve as the foundation for national culture. Religion should not be an important part of the school and should enter the curriculum only as one of a number of possible subjects of study. The French-Canadian business class did not take a position that was sufficiently clear to place it on either side.

The Parent Commission did not take a firm position on these questions until the publication of the final volumes of its report in March 1966. In these last volumes, the commission presented a position on confessionality that was sensitive and eloquent. In these pages one senses a possible new direction for the culture of French Canada. Underlying the commission's position was the assumption that it was speaking for the whole of society in the province and thus was speaking about a society that was religiously and culturally diverse. In light of this assumption, the commissioners drew the following conclusion about their own role: 'Hence a commission of this kind would be betraying its civil trust if it were to define society, the state or education in terms of one particular faith, and it would be abusing the authority entrusted to it if it sought to impose on everyone the point of view of a single, specific church.'[58] Following from its own neutral role, the commission argued that the state had to be similarly neutral: 'Consequently in a pluralistic country, the state must grant equal treatment to all churches and all faiths as institutions and to believers and non-believers as free, responsible and equal citizens.'[59]

By beginning with these two postulates, the commission staked out a position almost diametrically opposed to that adopted by the Tremblay Commission a decade earlier. The earlier commission had written from the point of view of the francophone community in Quebec only. Its basic philosophy suggested that no neutral position could be adopted on matters related to culture. Further, it had argued that the state in Quebec had to be French Canadian and to reflect in its institutions and its policies the culture and therefore the religious values of the nation canadienne française.

In formulating its two postulates, the Parent Commission was by no means denying that schools might have a confessional orientation. It was simply stating that such an orientation should not be imposed by the state. In a pluralist society such as Quebec, schools might be expected to organize themselves in a number of ways in order to achieve the common good. Confessionality might be one of these orientations, and it was perfectly acceptable in the commission's view, provided that two further principles of a pluralist society are respected. First, the adoption of a confessional orientation by a school should not result in infringement of a person's freedom of conscience. Second, confessionality could not take precedence over the duty of the state to guarantee each citizen an education of the best quality extending to the highest levels. If having confessional schools meant either that the education system would be so fragmented or that schools were so small that the state could not make such a guarantee, confessionality would need to be restricted appropriately.

The commission concluded that a confessional orientation would be assumed only by individual schools. It would result from an agreement by the parents sending children to the school and the teachers and administrators of the school. It would arise from the quartier, the milieu in which the school was situated. Confessionality would not be a property of the public agencies – school boards, regional administrative offices, the Department of Education itself – that administered the educational system. These agencies were to share in the neutrality of the state. In those instances where the school declared itself to be confessional, two individual rights had to be respected. First, every child was to have the right to be exempted from religious instruction, and every teacher the right to be exempted from teaching the catechism. Second, and inferred from the postulate of freedom of conscience, the religious orientation of the school should be given expression primarily in religious subjects and not throughout the curriculum. Thus confessionality would be more restricted than had been the case.

For the Parent Commission, the culture of the French community in Quebec would arise and develop out of the local neighbourhoods. These neighbour-hoods would give their schools their own particular flavour and in so doing discover a solidarity with other localities as the common goal of a high-quality education was pursued. Participation at the local level would give individuals an understanding of the problems facing their wider national community and provide the basis for a mass culture rather than 'something more or less theoretical, entrusted to the care of a few small groups of intellectuals.'[60]

To these ends, the commission recommended a new administrative structure to be anchored by small committees of parents, teachers, and administrators attached to each school.[61] These school committees were to provide a means for parents to participate with teachers and administrators in improving the school at a pedagogical level. In turn, the committees were to form an electoral college for the election of commissions scolaires. Conseils de développement scolaire, elected by the Commissions, were to operate at the level of economic regions in order to ensure equal development of the system throughout the region. They were also to play a role in decentralizing the operations of the Department of Education. The whole system was to be linked to the basic school committees; schools could be either confessional or non-denominational, depending on the wishes of the parents; and commissions scolaires were to be neutral and able to administer schools of various orientations.

The system outlined by the commission has yet to be fully established. Education beyond secondary school is now completely secular, but few real changes have taken place in primary and secondary schools. Bills 62 and 28, which made some initial attempts in the direction of the commission's recommendations, were never passed. They received strong criticism from conservative elements in the church as well as from the Protestant school board. In 1972, the legislature passed Bill 71, which reduced the number of school boards but left them subdivided along confessional lines. Each of these three bills was directed at reform only of schools in the Montreal metropolitan area, where the problems posed by ethnic and religious diversity were most serious. Students were given the formal right to be exempted from religious instruction, provided they submitted a formal request for exemption. It was also apparently possible for a school to apply for the lifting of its confessional status, although subsequent events showed that such applications could be blocked. In 1971, school and parents' committees were created, but these were allocated strictly advisory powers and not the more extensive powers recommended in the Parent Report. In 1980, the government created conseils d'orientation which were to be attached to each school and to have more of the powers recommended in the Parent Report.[62]

The failure to follow through on the recommendations of the Parent Commis-sion has had major consequences in the francophone community in Quebec.

First, because the Catholic school system remains the main instrument for instruction in the French language and because the society has moved to have most children attend these schools (as we shall see in the next chapter, on language), the freedom of conscience of some children is not being respected. Second, the failure of the authorities to unify school boards has created an excess of bureaucracy with concomitant inefficiencies and lowering of the quality of education. Third, the confessional orientation of the schools remains in the hands of these same bureaucracies and not in the hands of the parents, as the commission had originally hoped. For Catholic schools in Montreal, these problems have caused continuing difficulties, perhaps best illustrated by the case of the École Notre-Dame-des-Neiges.

This school is an elementary school under the jurisdiction of the Commission des écoles catholiques de Montréal in the Côte-des-Neiges area of Montreal. It is located in a neighbourhood that is ethnically diverse and religiously pluralistic. In many cases, both parents of children at the school were working. A large number of children were exempted from religious instruction, and it seemed to the parents that, given the diversity of the school body, it was no longer appropriate that the school remain officially Catholic. The parents attempted to have it declared 'pluralist' and to have its designation as a confessional school dropped.

The parents' concept of a pluralist school was reminiscent of the 'neutral' schools in the Parent Report.[63] Students would have the option of formal instruction in the catechism or a program in formation morale. Neither option would be favoured over the other, unlike in a confessional school (where the catechism would be privileged) or in a 'neutral' school (where general moral education would be favoured). A chaplain or animateur pastoral would be involved in school activities only for those students being taught the catechism and for purposes related to that objective. Thus the pluralist school, unlike a neutral school, would be open to the religious dimension but would not have that dimension colouring its whole projet éducatif as in a confessional school. This conception was consistent with the principles elaborated by the Parent Commission. It sought to respect the right to freedom of conscience and to accommodate those who did not want religion to be completely absent from the schools. As might be expected, the parents' decision to seek pluralist status gave rise to considerable controversy.

Those who supported the parents tended to argue along the following lines.[64] Quebec is a pluralist society with a diversity of cultures and religions. It is also primarily a French society, where newcomers are asked to integrate themselves with the francophone community by sending their children to French schools. In seeking to establish French as the common language in Quebec society, it is unacceptable that these same immigrants be forced to accept the religion of the majority community and to have their children educated in schools imbued with the majority faith. The parents' concept of a pluralist school would allow the process of integration to take place without infringing upon the freedom of conscience of any individual.[65]

Those who were opposed, including a majority of the elected members of the CECM and the archbishop of Montreal, argued that a pluralist school was neutral. There was no intermediate status. A Catholic school had not only the catechism being taught but also a projet éducatif chrétien. The tenets of Christianity grounded all instruction and practice. It did not limit the animateur pastoral to catechism but allowed him a role in directing all activities in the school. The archbishop of Montreal wrote that it was the duty of all Catholic parents 'd'envoyer leurs enfants dans des écoles catholiques, de les inscrire dans les cours d'enseignement religieux prévus pour eux, de s'assurer qu'ils y auront les services d'une animation pastorale et de les aider personnellement à vivre le projet éducatif chrétien qui y sera promu.'[66] Others made an even more traditional argument by stating that confessional schools in Quebec were a major factor preventing that province from becoming part of anglophone North America.[67] In short, the restrictions on confessionality in the pluralist school were too severe and deprived those who wished a true Christian education for their children. The archbishop implied that sending children to a pluralist school would be against the tenets of the Catholic faith.

The attempt by the École Notre-Dame-des-Neiges to have itself declared pluralist has been unsuccessful. In May 1979, the Conseil supérieur de l'éducation granted the school's request to have its confessional status revoked. The following December, the CECM, which was dominated by the conservative Mouvement scolaire confessionel, overturned the decision of the CSE and declared the school to be confessional. In the months that followed, in a judgment rendered by Jules Deschênes, chief justice of the Supreme Court of Quebec, the decision of the CECM was upheld. The decision by the court threw the matter back into the hands of the politicians, where it now stands. If schools are to have the right to become pluralist or even neutral, laws will need to be changed in order to make this right explicit.

Should one conclude that confessionality remains an effective means for reinforcing traditional French-Canadian values and for inserting them into modern Quebec? There is little reason to accept such a conclusion. The defence of confessionality has preserved some of the educational bureaucracies developed under the old system and provided a smokescreen behind which these institutions could fight a rearguard action against the Parent Commission's proposals for rationalization. The defence of confessionality appears to be a last-ditch attempt by the Catholic church to hold on to a traditional base of power and influence. The doctrinaire defence of the Catholic school by the hierarchy appears out of step with the ecumenism of the post–Vatican II church. Traditional nationalists have supported the church because they tend to see the confessional school system as the last remaining bastion of the old culture. Ironically, perhaps, these groups have been joined in the struggle by several groups and many individuals from the anglophone community. These latter are not interested in confessionality per se. Rather they see the maintenance of the confessional system as important for guaranteeing the English-speaking community in Quebec control over its own schools. A full understanding of this struggle, however, must wait on the analysis of language policy in the next chapter.

The defence of confessionality has perhaps stifled the development of French-Canadian culture. By remaining an affair of the bureaucrats, the place of religion in the schools has not been given over to the parents and the local quartiers as the Parent Commission envisaged. Individuals have not been able to enter into a dialogue about their culture and how it should be expressed in the educational system. A logical place for French Canadians and néo-Québécois to come together, to find common ground, and to come to know each other has not come into being. Without this input of spirit and culture from the base, the schools will continue to accentuate the technical, to give prominence to the instrumental goals of education, and to instruct rather than educate. The proposals of the Parent Commission contained the germ of an alternative outcome. This germ is now virtually dead.

Conclusion

Several important points must be retained from the analysis in this chapter. Since 1961, the educational system in Quebec has been changed in order to meet the needs of a society committed to participation in an advanced capitalist economy. The system has been opened up beyond the elementary level, so that it is now possible for students in Quebec to receive free of charge an education appropriate for university studies or for employment in technical occupations. Secondary education is no longer private. Through the creation of the CEGEPs the province has rationalized and expanded the provision of education in advanced technological fields. Similarly, the creation of the Université du Québec with campuses throughout the province has given more individuals the opportunity to obtain an advanced education. The granting of degrees has been changed to conform to the established pattern in North America, and a bachelor of arts obtained in Quebec now means the same thing as one from British Columbia or Arizona. The new structures at the secondary and post-secondary levels are now basically comparable with those elsewhere on the continent. The secondary-level curriculum has been revised to play down the traditional classical emphasis and to give more importance to subjects relevant to the industrial world. By the mid-1970s, this system was producing engineers, MBAS, commerce graduates, social science graduates, and the like in numbers that were adequate for greater involvement of the francophone community in economic activity of a higher and advanced kind. In this sense, the reforms have been a success.

The movement in favour of these reforms drew its support from a modified version of the same social coalition that made the initial push for changes in economic policy in the early 1960s. Thus the changes were supported by the French-Canadian business class, organized labour, and nationalists drawn from the new middle class. As in economic policy, while a policy on educational change was being developed and implemented, divisions began to emerge within this coalition. Business groups tended to support the policy, while organized labour and nationalists became disenchanted. This disillusionment has become a component of the frustration that has fuelled the independence movement.

Organized labour has become more critical of educational policy because this policy has not altered the subordinate position and status of workers in Quebec society. In a review of the educational system in 1974, Marcel Pepin, president of the CNTU, noted that the hopes of labour in the 1950s that education would serve as a tool for vastly increasing the social mobility of workers had been thwarted.[68] He concluded that the educational system served only to reproduce the existing structure of classes. Studies tended to show that it served to advance middle- and upper-class children. Claude Escande, in a study of seven CEGEPs in the Montreal area, found the upper and middle classes over-represented and the working and farmer classes under-represented.[69] There was a decided trend for the latter two classes to follow the non-university 'professional' stream, while the upper and middle classes were found more commonly in the 'general' (university) sections. Similarly, a study of the social class of students at the new Université du Québec, which was supposed to provide higher education to lower classes, showed that the class background of the students was virtually identical to that of the 1962, pre-Parent Report, Université de Montréal.[70] A further study by the CEQ demonstrated that these trends were initiated by selection mechanisms operating as early as elementary school.[71]

The class divisions that have developed over educational policy are perhaps most evident around the issue of state support for a network of private schools and colleges. The reform of the educational system did not entail the elimination of private schools. Private institutions, usually with a distinct confessional character, dispensing instruction at all levels up to and including the CEGEP curriculum, are part of Quebec's system of education. The Parent

Commission, along with the CCPQ, the SSJBM, the bishops, the Union nationale, and the Parti libéral, demanded that public assistance be made available to these institutions.[72] These demands were satisfied in 1968 when the legislature passed Bill 56 providing almost complete subsidization of the private system.[73] Such assistance was opposed at the outset by the CEQ and later by the other labour centrals and the Parti québécois as well.[74] They argued that the private system was the preserve of the privileged, since most could not afford its fees, and that it drained resources that would normally go toward improving the public sector. Some preliminary studies comparing private colleges with CEGEPs indicated that the former tended to draw more heavily from the upper classes.[75] The private sector embraced approximately 10 per cent of the total number of students at the CEGEP level in the years 1970–1.[76] This campaign by labour and by the Parti québécois was effectively countered by a network of clerically controlled organizations that had grown out of earlier associations such as the FCC.[77] These associations received strong continuing support from business groups.[78]

As we have seen above, after the educational reforms were realized, there occurred among many middle-class intellectuals in Quebec a sense of loss. They began to sense that old cultural values had been discarded and that no new values unique to French-Canadian society and derived from its history had been put in their place. Instead, the materialistic, individualistic, and competitive values characteristic of North American capitalism appear to have become dominant. This sense of loss is not unlike that described in the previous chapter in other areas of cultural activity. In this instance, however, there is hardly anyone other than the community's own leaders to blame. The reforms were drawn up with minimal outside interference and on the basis of a report by a commission controlled by the francophone community. The *Angst* that has developed is largely self-induced.

The more progressive independence groups – the RIN, the MSA, and the Parti québécois – supported the reforms in education proposed and carried out in the 1960s. More than that, however, they supported the full implementation of the Parent Report, the parts relating to the welcoming of a pluralistic society and those sections designed to draw strength from the communalism of the nation canadienne-française. These latter wishes were not acted upon, and this failing probably contributes to the discontent of nationalists. The majority of PQ members have endorsed strongly the idea of a pluralistic Quebec society. In addition, they have dreamed of a dynamic and flourishing francophone community giving that society its lead and its verve. Indépendantistes today are unhappy that the francophone community still seems incapable of playing such a unique and leading role. The failure to act decisively on the vision of the Parent Commission may be responsible in part for that frustration.

This same frustration has led some of the middle classes to seek the semblance of a return to the old days when the Catholic religion provided the inspiration for French-Canadian culture. The actions of these groups appear to be most inappropriate in the pluralistic society one now finds in Quebec. Further, they are giving rise to serious splits in the nationalist forces. These splits are taking their own toll on the energy and creativity of the francophone community. However, they at least have forced further reflection on the nature of Quebec society by francophones and reaffirmed the prescience of the Parent Report.

The independence movement is no longer defending a unique and distinctive culture. It is seeking to preserve a community that is grasping to hold on to the skeleton of a value system and to a glimpse of its history. The universal pragmatism and materialism of capitalist societies have swept deep into the hearts of the Québécois. If the concern about the loss of a culture that was expressed widely in the late 1970s has some basis, the task of these independence supporters may be monumental. Rather than acting to protect a basis for a distinctive culture, in reaching for independance they may now be pursuing a vision of a distinctive culture. Visions tend to be much more ephemeral and fleeting than established foundations.

7

Language policy and cultural development

We are Québécois ... Being ourselves is essentially a matter of keeping and
developing a personality that has survived for three and a half centuries.

At the core of this personality is the fact that we speak French. Everything else
depends on this one essential element and follows from it or leads us infallibly
back to it.

René Lévesque *An Option for Quebec* (Toronto 1968) 17

By the late 1960, language had become for most élites in Quebec the cultural
hallmark of the French-Canadian nation. Formerly prominent features such as
the Catholic faith and spiritualism were no longer considered relevant, and the
main distinguishing characteristic of members of the Quebec community was
their French language. By 1978, this change in perceptions received official
recognition. In its white paper on cultural development, the Parti québécois
government designated Quebec's French tradition the cornerstone of its new
policy on culture. French culture, derived from the acts of speaking, thinking,
and living in the French language, was to be the focal point of Quebec society.

In retrospect, it would appear that the elevation of language to a primary
position in the definition of what it meant to be a Québécois had been an
objective of Quebec's political leaders since 1960. In 1961, the Office de la
langue française, an official caretaker for the French language, was created and
placed under the aegis of the Department of Culture Affairs. In 1969, this same
office was strengthened under the terms of the now infamous Bill 63, which
gave parents the right to choose the language of instruction for their children.
The same year saw also the passage of the federal Official Languages Act which
set in motion a series of processes designed to give French a status equal to that
of English in the workings and services of the federal government. By 1973, the
federal Treasury Board had apparently taken the further steps needed to ensure

French would become an operational language of work in the federal bureaucracy. In 1974, the Quebec legislature passed its own Official Language Act, more commonly known as Bill 22, which was the province's first attempt to develop a global policy on language use in the province. In 1977 it passed the Charte de la langue française, a revision of the previous policy. These latter laws touched upon language use in formal political institutions, the public service, the business world, and schools.

Chapters 4–6 have shown that the consequences of the economic development policies, social policies, and educational reforms implemented during the 1960s have been the systematic dismantling of a series of institutions and the discontinuation of several practices long considered essential components of French-Canadian culture. The analysis in these chapters suggests that the basis of a distinctive cultural community in Quebec has been seriously undermined by these changes. The attempt to formulate a global policy on language use thus is an event of singular importance to that community. If everything in the culture of the Québécois depends on the fact that they speak French, as René Lévesque has argued, policies designed to reinforce the use of that language might also strengthen a distinctive culture. In other words, language policy might help to counter the effects of the other policies we have studied thus far. Alternatively, of course, it might complement these other policies and do little to reverse their effects on the culture of French Canada. In this chapter I will demonstrate that of these two possibilities, the second is the more credible interpretation. Policies on language use are unlikely to stem the erosion of the cultural foundations of the once distinctive nation that has existed on the banks of the St Lawrence for three and a half centuries. Rather they will be shown to be adjuncts to the policies of economic development and thus as facilitating greater integration of Quebec's francophone community into the North American economy and culture. The formulation of this interpretation will begin with a brief consideration of the link between language and culture.

Language and culture

In *Languages in Contact,* a classic in sociolinguistics, Uriel Weinreich proposed the concept of language loyalty: 'A language, like a nationality, may be thought of as a set of behaviour norms; language loyalty, like nationalism, would designate the state of mind in which the language (like that nationality), as an intact entity, and in contrast to other languages, assumes a high position in a scale of values, a position in need of being "defended." '[1] In this sense, language loyalty has long been a component of nationalist ideologies in Quebec. In the more dominant ideologies existing today, it has become the core idea, the idée force.[2] As it becomes more central to nationalism, there may come to the fore a particular view of the relationship between language and culture, called in linguistics the Whorfian hypothesis or the 'linguistic relativity thesis.'

Although the theory may be traced back as far as the philosopher Herder,[3] it is most commonly associated with the work of Benjamin Lee Whorf.[4] Whorf has argued that language dictates the way that we cut perceptually into the flux of nature, the very way we organize cognitively our world. Language generates for us a 'physics of the cosmos'; through the basic relationships between words and through the kinds of words that exist for our use, a point of view is constructed and then projected on the universe. Whorf writes: 'And every language is a vast pattern system, different from others, in which are culturally ordained the forms and categories by which the personality not only communicates, but also analyzes nature, notices or neglects types of relationships and phenomena, channels his reasoning, and builds the house of his consciousness.'[5]

According to Whorf and his followers, language determines the categories of psychological experience and leads to different systems of meaning in different linguistic communities. Language has a single function, that of defining the world. This view is similar to that of many nationalists in Quebec. It is certainly not inconsistent with the statement by René Lévesque that heads this chapter or with the view presented in the 1978 white paper. To argue that French culture is the focal point in Quebec is to imply that the use of the French language gives that culture its distinctiveness and orientation.[6]

The contrasts drawn by Whorf were more drastic and pronounced than those existing in Quebec. He usually compared Indo-European languages as a group with other languages, particularly those of native cultures in the Americas. The conceptions of time and space found in French and English, their grammars (which tended to objectify the world), and other characteristics were sufficiently similar that Whorf placed them together in the Indo-European group and described the group as determinative of Western culture. However, when he generalized his conclusions, he argued that his hypothesis applied to every language individually and not just to major language groups.

Whorf's hypothesis has been widely studied and discussed by linguists and anthropologists and is more and more rejected as being too simplistic. Dell Hymes, an anthropologist and a pioneer in sociolinguistics, sees this tendency to oversimplify as the result of isolation between linguistics and the social sciences: 'The difficulty is that we have tried to relate language, described largely as a formal isolate, to culture, described largely without reference to speaking. We have tried to relate one selective abstraction to another, forgetting that much that is pertinent to the place of speech in behaviour and culture has not been taken into either analytic frame. The angle of vision has been in effect a bifurcated one, considering speech primarily as evidence either of a formal linguistic code or of the rest of culture.[7] A more useful approach, in his view, presupposes regular relationships between language usage and social structure, which would allow for the possibility of social structure conditioning language as well as vice versa. Such a presupposition would seem necessary in the face of empirical findings that languages have different functions and enjoy different intensities of use in different speech communities.

Even at this early stage in its development, sociolinguistics has cumulated evidence on several instances in which social structure might constrain language. Hymes has argued that one cannot restrict the notion of competence in communication to Chomsky's notion of ability to use grammatical rules.[8] There is also competence in the sense of knowing the rules for what form of speech is appropriate in a given situation. The learning rules defining appropriate linguistic behaviour in given situations results from membership in a society with particular customs, cultural norms, and attitudes that govern such matters.[9] Communication is a matter not simply of speaking French using correct grammatical forms but also of speaking French using words and expressions correctly in particular situations. These ways of using words and expressions are not derived from the language itself but from the social context in which the language is spoken. Basil Bernstein has shown how speech forms may vary significantly among speakers of English, depending on their social class.[10] Similarly, Labov's studies of different socio-economic groups and of the Black English Vernacular have demonstrated the impact of social structure and varying social situations and contexts on speech.[11]

Language is never the only means through which members of a society acquire their habits of thought. It is a resource that different societies allocate for different purposes, and its function may vary from society to society. This variation takes place in the individual speaker and in the society as a whole. Hymes writes that any speech act can be broken into a number of components such as sender, receiver, message form, channel, code, topic, and setting.[12] Depending on how these components are constituted, the function of language might vary. If the emphasis is on, for example, the form rather than the sender, the function might be poetic rather than expressive. In a society as a whole, the function of language will vary depending on the scope or range of its use. A dialect or folk language might facilitate person-to-person oral communication within a particular cultural group, while a 'standard language' such as High German or Parisian French might provide a common communicative form for scientific and technical discussion for a series of distinct communities. Such variations in the functions of speech are to be explained primarily by variations in social structure. Hymes further suggests that the constraints imposed by human needs and situations control the instruments through which those needs and the characteristics of those situations are expressed.[13] Social structure is ultimately determinative. Whorf is almost stood on his head.[14]

If one adopts Whorf's perspective, the establishment of policies to expand the use of French may be viewed as an attempt to reinforce and even expand a given culture. If one accepts the view that underlies sociolinguistics, one considers these policies to be responses to other kinds of changes in social structure and adjuncts to those changes. I shall argue for the latter view and seek to relate the policies on language to the other changes in social structure that have already been described.

The evidence for such a relationship exists. It is the thesis of this chapter that the various policies on language developed by the provincial and federal governments since 1960 may be interpreted as attempts to ensure that French could function as the language of all 'formal' and 'informal' communication in Quebec society and as one of two recognized languages for formal communication in Canada.[15] Policies with these objectives could be successful only if the domains of society where French could be used a formal means of communication were expanded. French, of course, is already an established standard language. None the less, even as a standard language, it has to change to absorb within its lexicon the words and concepts (mostly English) that have come with advancing technology and expanding industrialism. Within Quebec, where the use of French had been excluded systematically from important realms of economic and technical discourse, the need for such changes was even more pressing. Once introduced, these additions to French complemented and facilitated the process of inserting the economy of Quebec's francophone community fully into the advanced capitalist economy of North America. Furthermore, in the light of my rejection of Whorf's hypothesis, preserving the language does not guarantee a distinctive culture for Quebec's francophone community. A full assessment of the likely impact of language policy must be done in the context of the economic, social, and educational policies that preceded and accompanied it.

The construction of the argument from which this conclusion follows requires the introduction of two additional sociolinguistic concepts, that of a speech community and that of language planning. Gumperz defines a speech community as 'any human aggregate characterized by regular and frequent interaction by means of a shared body of verbal signs and set off from similar aggregates by significant differences in language usage.'[16] A speech community may embrace several language groups, provided that it itself is a recognizable social group. Both Canada and Quebec may be defined as speech communities because each is a recognizable political community – a set of individuals sharing in a given division of political labour. Such co-operation creates a boundary that constrains communication and regularizes interaction within those boundaries.[17] Social change or political intervention may serve to strengthen or dismember a speech community. The study of language policies developed by Quebec will reveal such dynamism because these policies have been aimed at clarifying and strengthening the boundaries of the French-language speech community.

The process through which these boundaries have been strengthened may be described as language planning, i.e. planning to maintain a standard language,[18] a codified form of language that is accepted by and serves as a model to the larger speech community. Gumperz writes that within a given speech community one can speak of 'superposed variation' in language usage.[19] Within a single social group, different kinds of activities may be carried on in different languages. The language of everyday discourse may differ from that of religious ritual or technical discussion. Such superposed variation is minimized the more domains a standard language conquers. Such a language is distinguished by four properties. First, it is stabilized through an appropriate codification.[20] Formal grammars and dictionaries exist; norms are enforced through rules of orthography and orthoëpy; a codifying agency may watch over the construction of the language; the various norms may be inculcated and enforced through the school system. Second, a standard language is intellectualized. Havránek, who helped as a member of the Prague School of Linguistics to develop the concept of a standard language, described this property as the language's 'adaption to the goal of making precise and rigorous, if necessary, abstract statements, capable of expressing the continuity and complexity of thought, that is, to reinforce the intellectual side of speech.'[21] Such a property is associated with a lexicon that is suitable for increased terminological precision and that possesses a range of abstract and generic terms. Third, the structure of a standard language permits the construction of elaborate, tightly knit compound sentences which can be used in technical and philosophical discussions. Fourth, a standard language can expand its lexicon in a rapid and flexible way to absorb new concepts and terms emerging because of technological change or scientific progress.

Possessed of these properties, a standard language can fulfil several functions. It serves as the medium of formal and official communication and thereby creates a unifying link among speakers of different dialects and vernaculars. It is generally the language of workday technical communication and of scientific communication. It is also the foundation of poetic language. Mukarovský of the Prague School writes: 'For poetry, the standard language is the background against which is reflected the esthetically intentional distortion of the linguistic components of the work, in other words, the intentional violation of the norm of the standard.'[22]

A standard language is not established in a community simply by having the requisite properties; it must also be accepted as such by the members of the community.[23] To this end, a certain degree of loyalty toward the standard language must exist among members of the community. They must take pride in it and must be aware that the language is a standard with specified norms and codes. Without these attitudes and this acceptance, a language, whatever its properties, will remain the vernacular of a particular group and not function generally throughout a wider community.

French is one of the great standard languages in the world. However, it does not function as a standard language in all areas of Canada. It was not used very much in several areas of essential activity, notably business and the institutions and offices of the federal government. Being absent from these areas, it possessed a lower social status and its speakers were barred from certain avenues of power.[24] The lexicon of the language in economics, technology, and science was less well developed as a result of lack of use. From the late 1950s, as we have seen, the business class in francophone Quebec, supported by organized labour and middle-class nationalists, sought to reverse its inferior position in the economy of the province. A series of economic policies was developed to facilitate such a push for power, and the educational system was reformed to provide the cadres and skilled workers needed.

These changes coincided with attempts at 'status language planning' (government attempts to alter the status of the language) and at 'corpus language planning' (attempts to develop the language).[25] Status planning would include the policies designed to expand the use of French in the private and public sectors in Quebec and in the federal public service and those policies designed to encourage supportive attitudes toward the expanded use of French and to create a situation where acceptance of French as the standard for all formal communication became more and more necessary. Corpus planning would refer to those policies designed to stabilize a standard-language norm and to develop new lexicons and includes the establishment of the Office de la langue française and the restriction of English-language schooling to anglophones originating from Quebec. Each of these groups of policies is described in fuller detail below.

Status language planning: Expanding the scope of French

The private sector

It has already been established that the primary goal of Quebec's economic policy after 1960 was the establishment of economic institutions controlled by francophones that were competitive with the dominant capitalist institutions of North America. This policy was pursued both by relying upon state enterprises and by pushing for greater francophone participation in the dominant corporations in the province. These policies were to have the effect of creating a viable francophone capitalist class. The reforms in education begun in the 1960s and completed in the early 1970s helped to ensure that the cadres required for this expansion were available and that the francophone working class would have the skills necessary for such economic growth. The policy of establishing French as the primary standard language in Quebec complements these other policies in that it removed linguistic barriers in the private sector to their pursuit. Previously, two areas of economic activity of importance to these economic policies supported only a restricted use of French: the shop floor of larger industrial factories and establishments and the middle and executive levels of management in these same enterprises.

It had, of course, long been part of the mythology in Quebec that one spoke French at home and with one's fellow workers and English with the boss. During the 1960s, as the reality that gave rise to this mythology became more and more a source of discontent, systematic information was compiled describing it.

A survey conducted by the CNTU in 1965 showed that the workplace, especially in enterprises owned by non-francophones, was not ideally suited to francophones' advancement.[26] In the latter kind of enterprise, only 50 per cent of workers used French in speaking to their bosses (56 per cent in the case of superintendents), despite the fact that 90 per cent of the workers were francophone. While company regulations were usually published in French, only 70 per cent of the companies permitted negotiations in French and only 52.4 per cent had a French-only collective agreement. English was the official language of the collective agreement in 61.4 per cent of cases. Only a minority saw the situation in the enterprise as evolving toward greater use of French. Another survey, conducted by the CMA, found that only 54 per cent of workers could reach a supervisory position without knowing English.[27] Conditions were better in francophone-owned firms, but these tended to be smaller and less important in the economy.[28]

A series of studies beginning in the early 1940s showed the dominance of the use of English as well at the management levels of the larger corporations in the province.[29] The first comprehensive assessment of the extent of this dominance was made by the Royal Commission on Bilingualism and Biculturalism in volume III of its report, published in 1969. Its work was expanded upon considerably by the Quebec government's Commission of Inquiry on the Position of the French Language and on Language Rights in Quebec (Gendron Commission), which reported in 1972. This commission sponsored a series of studies on the use of French in the workplace with perhaps the most important being one written by Serge Carlos.[30] The commission, using his work, reported that in the secondary sector labourers used French 95 per cent of the time.[31] However, among themselves, in reading and writing in secondary industry, activities more characteristic of management, the use of French was 37 per cent and 42 per cent respectively.[32] Francophone administrators or professionals could use French in communicating with anglophone superiors only 22 and 23 per cent of the time respectively.[33] In contrast, anglophones in the same categories used English with French superiors 83 per cent and 72 per cent of the time.[34] Thus French was not the principal language of use in two areas essential to an advanced capitalist economy: it was not used by management, and it was not used on the factory floor in communications with management or in dealing with technical details of production and the maintenance of equipment. The commission's concluding statement described a situation of superposed variation where French was not used in critical areas of the economy: 'We have defined a socio-linguistic structure which proves beyond question that the domain of the French language is particularly characterized by inferior duties, small enterprises, low incomes and low levels of education. The domain of the English language is the exact opposite, that of superior duties involving initiative and command, and large enterprises, and high levels of education and income.'[35]

The Gendron report included the most comprehensive study of the position of the French language in Quebec and set the stage for the first attempt by the government to formulate a global linguistic policy. The Liberal government of Robert Bourassa introduced and had passed into law in 1974 Bill 22, the Official Language Act. It sought to regulate language use in the public administration, both provincial and local, in para-public institutions such as public utilities and professional associations, in labour relations, in affichage, in education, and in the internal operations of private enterprises. It came after the economic policies of the 1960s had been revised to give greater support to francophone businessmen and after educational reforms had begun to yield graduates with skills more appropriate to an industrial economy.[36] The bill was brought in by an avowedly federalist party that enjoyed the support of the business community, both francophone and anglophone, and received the support of this same business community. It was opposed by many middle-class anglophones and by a formalized coalition of organized labour and the new and traditional middle classes, the same coalition that in a less organized fashion came to oppose both the economic and educational policies developed in the 1960s.[37]

After it came to power in 1976, the Parti québécois, which drew much of its support from these same social groups, moved to revise the language legislation to conform more to the wishes of these groups. The Liberal legislation had been directed at increasing the use of French not on the factory floor but only on the level of management. The three social groups supporting the Parti québécois advocated a more rigorous and comprehensive attempt at standardization than the business class, which preferred the government to use a gentler persuasive approach. The government presented a white paper on language in March 1977 and followed it with the introduction of Bill 1, the first version of the Charte de la langue française. Bill 1 was in many respects a radical departure from Bill 22 and enjoyed the strong support of labour and the middle classes and incurred the wrath of the business community, both francophone and anglophone. After public hearings, the bill was withdrawn and presented to the legislature as Bill 101. It had been changed so as to move it closer in some areas to the Official Language Act of the previous government.[38] Although still departing from it in several key aspects, Bill 101 can be seen as a continuation of the Liberal law. Accordingly, the discussion that follows will be mainly confined to Bill 101.

Bill 101 sought first to establish French as the primary language used in all communications on the shop floor. It did so by seeking to guarantee that workers could perform their jobs and could interact with their employers in their native language of French. Article 4 declared that workers had this assurance as a fundamental right. Subsequent articles stated that employers had to communicate with their workers in French in all industrial relations. Employers were forbidden from firing, laying off, or changing the job of a worker for the sole reason that he or she spoke only French. Other parts of the law required companies to use French-language repair manuals, instruction manuals, and other technical documents. Even trade unions were required to communicate with their members in French unless an individual had initially communicated with the union in a language other than French. These articles effectively ensured that French would be the main language used on the shop floor. Bill 101 went considerably beyond Bill 22 and probably reflected the more favourable attitude of the Parti québécois toward labour.

Second, Bill 101 followed Bill 22 in ensuring that members of the professions in Quebec used French. Professional associations (ordres in Quebec law) were to function in French. Similarly, their members were to ensure that their services were available in French. Entry into a profession was to be granted only after demonstration of competence in French in a test administered by the OLF.[39] Both professional associations and members of professions had to communicate ith the government and with other 'moral persons' in French.[40] When they received a communication in a language other than French, they were permitted to respond to that individual in that other language. The emphasis on the use of French in all formal communications is exactly what one would expect in status language planning.

Third, Bill 101 used the approach developed in Bill 22 to work toward the francization of activity at the management level of the private sector. Firms were required to register with the OLF to obtain a temporary francization certificate. Under the supervision of the OLF, the firms were to carry out a comprehensive and systematic analysis of the language used in all communication, written and oral, including all documents from memoranda to instruction manuals. They were then to draw up a program for changing their communication practices so that French would become the operational language of work in all phases of activity. They were given a deadline for accomplishing these changes. If they succeeded in meeting the deadline, they were to be awarded a permanent francization certificate; if they failed, they could be fined and denied access to government contracts. Head offices of firms having dealings outside the province, private research institutes, smaller firms, and enterprises in the business of producing cultural goods involving language were exempted from these provisions.[41] Head offices could be exempted only if they were able to negotiate a suitable agreement with the OLF that took into account their special needs.[42] The possibility of such exemptions means that although French will be the language of work in middle management, it may not be so in senior management in the larger corporations headquartered in the province. Nevertheless, and recent reports by the OLF indicate some success, French has clearly entered a sphere of use previously denied to it.[43]

To summarize, Bill 101 guaranteed that French would be the language used for all communication from the shop floor to the boardroom. These guarantees were developed just as the government adjusted its economic policy to favour the private sector and the development of an indigenous entrepreneurial class. They also coincided with the provision of more graduates from the reformed educational system capable of filling the management positions being opened.

The federal government

If a language is to function as a standard language in an advanced industrial society, it will need to be the language used by government. Much governmental activity is economic, whether it be building railroads, subsidizing firms, engaging in research and development, developing product standards, regulating waste disposal, or exploring and processing natural resources. Under the terms of the Canadian constitution, the level most involved in these kinds of activities is the federal government. Accordingly, if French is to function as a standard language for the people of Quebec, it will have to have a position of status with the federal government. If it were to lack such status it would be excluded from a range of activity essential to industrial society. In the 1950s, French did not have much status at the federal level of government. English was the language of work throughout the public service. Francophones were absent from the middle and upper levels of the service, particularly in those departments dealing primarily with economic questions. It was difficult and in many instances impossible for francophones to communicate with the federal government in French. In short, this area of society excluded French to as high a degree as the private sector in Quebec.

Federal statutes continued to be drafted in English with inadequate French translations.[44] Subordinate legislation and regulations tended to be in English only, with French versions sometimes available, usually only in Quebec.[45] Federal quasi-judicial boards tended to operate in English.[46] There was no simultaneous translation in the House of Commons, government cheques were issued in English only, and bilingual signs on government buildings were a rare sight. In a survey of federal buildings in 1960, the Conseil de la vie française (CVF), a language pressure group, found that 13.2 per cent had bilingual signs, 36.8 per cent had a little French and 50 per cent had no French at all.[47] The Canadian military was an overwhelmingly English institution. In 1951, only 7.9 per cent of officers with a rank of lieutenant-colonel or higher were francophones.[48] When a bilingual military college was opened in St-Jean, Quebec, in the early 1950s, it provided only the first two years of the officer's course. The final two had to be taken at the Royal Military College in Kingston, where all classes were in English. The Montreal Chambre de Commerce, in a brief submitted to the federal government in 1949, noted that only 3 of 18 deputy ministers and 4 of 23 associate deputy ministers were francophones. There was a paucity of francophones at the Bank of Canada, as was pointed out with regret by the SSJBM: 'Cette situation contribue à perpétuer dans l'esprit de beaucoup de gens cette légende tenace et nuisible que nous sommes tout à fait inaptes aux grandes affaires, qu'au surplus nous ne nous intéressons guère à la vie économique de notre pays.'[49] Not even the customs officers working at the Quebec–United States border were bilingual, the FSSJBQ pointed out in 1951.[50]

The low status of French in the affairs of the federal government was a particularly sore point for nationalists in Quebec, because it contradicted the ideal of a bilingual and bicultural Canada, developed in particular by Henri Bourassa. They felt that the spirit of the BNA Act, as reflected in section 133 which made the House of Commons and its legislation bilingual, had not been followed as the federal government had grown in size. To demand bilingualism is to ask that French be given the status of a standard language in the federal government. Demands for it had been made since Bourassa's time and throughout the 1950s were articulated by all major organized groups in French-speaking Quebec. Action on these demands finally came after an editorial by André Laurendeau in *Le Devoir* on 20 January 1962 in which he called for the creation of a royal commission to study the state of bilingualism and biculturalism in Canada.

After the Liberals regained power in Ottawa in 1963, the Royal Commission on Bilingualism and Biculturalism (RCBB) was created, with Laurendeau and Davidson Dunton, a former president of the CBC, as its co-chairmen. When the commission published the first volume of its report in 1967 calling for the establishment of an equal partnership between French and English in Canada, it began to lay the basis for giving French the status of a standard language.[51] Such a partnership, it argued, involved two aspects. First, equality meant access for the individual to the various benefits of a society without hindrance by cultural identity. Second, a culture can be experienced only within its own complete society. Its members had to have a position equal to those of other societies co-operating in an economic and political community. In the political community equal partnership had to be realized through a 'bilingual State.'[52] Such a state could either work toward providing special language rights for its national minorities or could attempt to place two or more national languages on an equal footing before the law. It was a régime built upon a community composed of two or more unilingual nuclei, and it was not expected to promote individual bilingualism.

In seeking to apply these concepts to Canada, the commission rejected the use of a territorial principle to define linguistic rights. Such a principle involves the separation of one language group geographically from another (except in a capital area) and is apposite where a country is composed of unilingual regions. The presence of a significant English minority in Quebec and of close to one million francophones outside Quebec made such a principle inappropriate. Instead, the commissioners demanded that both official languages be recognized in law and in practice wherever the minority was numerous enough to constitute a viable community. This implied that along with the federal government, the governments of Quebec, Ontario, and New Brunswick should become officially bilingual. Further, the commission suggested the formation of 'bilingual districts' throughout Canada wherever official minority communities existed and could benefit from services administered in their mother tongue. Finally, the commission proposed that a commissioner of official languages be appointed to be the active conscience and protector of the Canadian public wherever the official languages were at issue.

In response to these suggestions, in June 1969 Parliament passed the Official Languages Act. Section 2 confirmed the government's intention to give French a status equal to English in its operations: 'The English and French languages are the official languages of Canada for all purposes of the Parliament and Government of Canada, and possess and enjoy equality of status and equal rights and privileges as to their use in all the institutions of the Parliament and Government of Canada.'[53] The remaining sections spelled out the specifics of this statement for federal institutions, gave the federal authorities the right to proclaim bilingual districts and to form an advisory board to investigate where the districts should be located, and created the post of commissioner of official languages.

Can one say that French has achieved a status equal to that of English in the federal government? The answer to this question is mixed. There are certainly more francophones in the federal public service than before, and at higher levels. The numbers of francophones in the higher categories of Administrative and Foreign Service, of Scientific and Professional, and of Executive have steadily increased. The government appears bilingual in its signs, its literature, and many of its services. Virtually all government services are now available in French in Quebec and in the National Capital Region. The level of services available to francophones outside Quebec is improved but not as complete.

On the use of French as a working language the evidence is more sketchy and less positive. The annual reports of the commissioner of official languages indicate that French has made only slow progress toward becoming a viable language of work in the public service. The RCBB had recommended the creation of French-language units, which would work completely in French and communicate with other units in French, as a means for making French a language of work. Very few of these units have been created. It appears also that French has not gained acceptance as a language suitable for scientific and technical communication. In his sixth annual report in 1976, the commissioner cited the use of English for scientific and technical communication as a persistent problem.[54] He noted that French-speaking scientists and technicians were still rare in the public service.

The struggle still to be fought for such acceptance is illustrated by the dispute over air traffic control that flared in the summer of 1976. At the heart of this dispute was the demand by French-speaking pilots flying in Quebec that they be able to communicate with air traffic control in their own language. English-speaking pilots and controllers who did not understand French argued that such a practice would be unsafe. They exerted pressure on the federal government to change its support for bilingual air traffic control and had some success. While the details of this dispute and its resolution are beyond the scope of this study, suffice it to say that after extensive tests it was shown that bilingual air traffic control systems under visual flight rules or instrument flight rules were safe. Gradually, French-speaking pilots and controllers have begun using their own language in Quebec airspace. Still, if French functioned as a standard language in Canada as suggested by the RCBB, such a dispute would not have occurred.

The struggle for recognition of the French language in the federal government was very much linked to the development of economic policy in Quebec. Further participation in the direction of the economy in Quebec entailed access to the federal government and a government able to work and communicate in French. As the francophone entrepreneurial class grew and its ambitions rose to take in markets involving the whole province and beyond, it became concerned directly with federal economic policy and with influencing that policy. Further, the more it looked beyond Quebec and created operating units outside the province, the more it became interested in having federal services available in French outside Quebec. It was thus able to add both its voice and its economic arguments to the long-standing demands for recognition made by the francophone minorities. Finally, if the federal government failed to give French the recognition required for functioning as a formal language in its offices, the political consequences were severe. Each transgression, each act of insensitivity to the claims for equal status, appears to have been taken as a personal insult by thousands of francophones in Quebec. Not only are these acts interpreted as attempts to deny them control over their own economic destiny, but they are also holes shot through the federal government's claim to be the legitimate government of both the English and the French in Canada. The severity of the political consequences of such acts is again exemplified by the struggle over the language of the air in 1976. Thousands of francophones felt humiliation and despair over this incident. It serves to illustrate well the symbolic dimension that overlies the struggle for language recognition at the federal level of government.

Local political institutions

The previous two sections of this chapter focused on two aspects of status planning – its promotion of the language for technical communication and for formal communication in and between major institutions in the society. Formal communication, written and oral, takes place between individuals in official capacities or between formal institutions in the society. The range of communication likely to be seen as formal will depend on how the society defines itself and its boundaries. In the past three chapters we have seen that there has been a gradual shift in the definition of the boundaries of the francophone community in Quebec, from one based on ethnic criteria to one based on political and territorial criteria. The francophone community in Quebec is more and more seen to include all the people living within Quebec's borders. With this shift in definition, the francophone community has changed from one that was ethnically homogeneous to one that is ethnically pluralistic.

This change in boundaries increased the number of institutions engaging in formal communications in society. It implied that the formal governmental institutions in society should function in French. For the francophone middle classes this meant that society could not suffer institutional bilingualism, above all in the provincial public service. These classes staffed that public service or were often directly dependent on it. If French were to be the language of work in the private sector and one of two languages of work in the federal government, then the provincial public service need hardly remain bilingual. Bills 22 and 101 sanctified this logic by defining the provincial public service as unilingual.

The change in the community's boundaries also brought into language policy a set of institutions that had long been outside – the local public institutions serving the non-francophone communities, particularly the anglophone community. Within the francophone community there was a division of opinion over the extent to which these institutions should be integrated within the formally French communications grid.[55] For the middle-class nationalists they represented a threat to the expansion of the use of French. Backed by the economic power of the anglophone corporations, they helped constitute a separate society within Quebec, which acted as a magnet for non-francophone immigrants and had sufficient power to bilingualize the parts of the provincial public service that dealt with it regularly. However, the francophone business class saw such a community's existence as less threatening to the status and use of French. Further, it saw the community as the logical adjunct to the anglophone economic presence in Quebec and its stability as a factor aiding the growing co-operation between itself and the anglophone corporate class. Bill 22, which was more attuned to the views of the francophone business class, accordingly treated these local institutions much differently than did Bill 101, which had strong support from the francophone middle classes.

Bill 22 changed relatively few of the operations of local institutions. Municipal or school bodies with at least 10 per cent of their clients anglophone were to draw up official documents in both English and French. Formerly, most had drawn these up in English only. Those municipal and school bodies that administered a group that was in the majority anglophone were permitted to use either French or English for internal communications and for communicating with 'moral persons' and governments. Hospitals and other social welfare institutions were to ensure that their services were available in French and were to use French in communicating with the provincial government. Official notices, forms, and other communications were to be in French but could be accompanied by an English version. Even these changes had a relatively minor effect on the practices of these institutions.

Changes were much more substantial under the legislation of the Parti québécois. Under the terms of the Charte de la langue française, all local public institutions (municipalities, school boards, hospitals, and social service institutions) were to draw up their official documents in French. All their written communications with 'moral persons' and governments were to be in French. Before an individual could be hired, promoted, or transferred, it had to be established that he or she had an appropriate knowledge of French. French was to be the language of internal communication for all municipalities. School boards, hospitals, and social service institutions with clienteles in the majority anglophone could use both French and English for internal communications. All these local public institutions were also to apply for and obtain a francization certificate under a similar program to that described above for the private sector. That is, they were to undertake a systematic analysis of all communication taking place within their organization and then formulate a program for francizing all the operations involved. In short, even within institutions serving the anglophone community on the local level, French was to become the language of formal communication.

By 1980, significant progress had been made in establishing French as the primary language in the private sector and in all provincial and local governmental bodies. Advances had also been made in establishing it as a working language of the federal government. French was thus in a position of increased status: it was used for formal communication by all important sections of Quebec society.

Corpus language planning: Stabilizing the language

An important question considered in language planning is the extent of agreement on how the language is to be used and how it is to absorb new terms. A standard language has been codified and its grammar formalized and there are agencies existing that oversee its continued stabilization and that ensure that members of society are introduced to it correctly. The policies on language use developed in Quebec after 1945 contained some corpus planning measures that had the effect of stabilizing the use of French. The two measures of primary importance here were the creation and expansion of a codifying agency, the Office de la langue française (OLF), and the attempts to widen the scope of the French-language school system.

   The life of the OLF may be divided into three distinct phases. It was created in 1960 as one of several agencies under the Department of Cultural Affairs, where it remained until 1969 (phase 1), when it was transferred to the Department of Education as part of the linguistic reform contained in Bill 63. Phase 2 covers the five years it was part of the Department of Education, before it was formally abolished in 1974 and replaced under the terms of the Official Language Act by the Régie de la langue française (RLF) (phase 3). When Bill 101 was passed in August 1977, the Régie was replaced by a body again named the Office de la langue française. However this new OLF is the continuation with some new tasks of the former Régie. In short, despite the changes in name and department, the present OLF is an expanded version of the agency established in 1960.

In phase 1, the OLF mainly concerned itself with codifying and stabilizing language usage and with bringing technical and economic lexicons into the language. It began publication of a bulletin entitled *Mieux dire* and inaugurated a series of 'Cahiers' dealing with anglicisms and canadianisms. It conducted a series of studies of language use in various fields including labour relations, sylviculture, social insurance, hydraulics, eating, and the language of administration and later developed lexicons for these fields. It entered into permanent liaisons with organizations in France concerned with stabilizing and codifying the French language. These included: the Haut Comité pour la défense française, the Association francophone de normalisation, the Comité d'étude des termes techniques français, and the Fédération du français universel.[56] In phase 2, it expanded its activities in these areas because more resources were available. It also became involved in an additional aspect of stabilization, that of orthoëpy. It collaborated with the Department of Education in devising a program for instructing children in the oral language, which was to be administered in the primary schools beginning in grade 1.

In phase 3, the RLF/OLF continued its previous activities and added a series of regulatory and enforcement functions. Thus, according to its charge as defined in the Charte de la langue française, it still has responsibility for standardizing and diffusing proper forms of language usage. It was given the power to create terminology committees in fields of social and economic activity where language development was seen to be necessary. Once new terms were established in these fields, it could publish them in the *Gazette officielle du Québec,* thereby making their use mandatory in the public service, on public notices, and in educational texts. In addition to these established activities, it was given new powers that allowed it to intervene in wider areas of economic and political life, establishing where French was to be used and what correct usage was. As we have seen, the OLF directed the extensive francization programs required of the private sector and the public service at the local and provincial levels. It was also responsible for deciding what level of knowledge of French was necessary for the practice of the various professions and for devising and administering tests for those entering these professions. A Commission de surveillance was added to the OLF to investigate all alleged infractions of the law and to bring offenders to court if it found such action necessary. A Commission de toponymie was also created under the auspices of the OLF to review place names in the province to assess their suitability and to give names to those settlements or geographical features lacking the same. By 1980, the OLF had become a formidable organization with widespread powers for diffusing standard language forms, for adapting the language to advanced industrial society, and for enforcing the use of French in those areas of society where English had previously been used.

In addition to the creation of a special agency such as the OLF, another means for stabilizing and diffusing standard language usage is the school system. Careful instruction in the language facilitates the standardization of its use among those who have it as a mother tongue. Schools can also be used for introducing the language to those who have a language other than the proposed standard for a mother tongue. A number of changes in Quebec's various school systems since 1960 have involved their assumption of these kinds of functions.

From the early 1960s, when demands for unilingualism were becoming more widespread, pressure was first placed on the English-language school system. The radical early independence group, the Action socialiste pour l'indépendance du Québec, thus argued that anglophones had to learn to communicate in French. Accordingly, it demanded that English-language schools be required to provide their students with a functional knowledge of French.[57] Similarly to many other cases, these early cries in the desert by the indépendantistes were heard and later adopted by the nationalist societies. As the movement in favour of unilingualism gained force, the anglophone community saw the writing on the wall and made haste to indicate its willingness to have its children learn French as a second language.[58] The Protestant School Board of Greater Montreal (PSBGM) increased the number of French specialists in its elementary schools from 1 in 1958–9 to 107 a decade later.[59] French immersion programs were developed in elementary schools, and Quebec universities became leading centres for research on second-language instruction. These pressures for instruction in French were given legal form in section 44 of the Official Language Act, which stated that those receiving their instruction in English must acquire a knowledge of spoken and written French. Bill 101 added teeth to this provision by providing in article 84 that no certificate for completion of secondary school could be awarded without a student demonstrating competence orally and in writing in the French language.

Nevertheless, in the eyes of many who favoured unilingualism in Quebec, these adjustments within the English-language schools were insufficient. These schools included the children of parents whose mother tongue was neither English nor French and even an increasing number of children of French Canadians. The dominance of English in North America gave that language an irresistible strength, which undermined policies designed to increase the use of French. As early as 1963, leaders in the established nationalist societies demanded that English-language schools be reserved for those whose mother tongue was English and that all other children attend French-language schools.[60] By the end of the decade, this had become a standard demand of organized labour and the Parti québécois as well. As one might now expect, such a proposal was rejected by the francophone business class, which argued that parents should be free to choose the language in which their children were to be educated.[61] Opposition came as well from the linguistic communities that were neither English nor French.[62] The following statement by a citizen whose mother tongue was Italian illustrates well this opposition: 'We have left our friends and family and our country behind. We have come all the way to Canada in order to better ourselves and provide for the future of our children. It just simply wouldn't make sense for us to limit the range of jobs open to our children by educating them in French, for French is only spoken in the province of Quebec. English is the language of North America.'[63]

Various attempts to restrict access to English-language schools were to shake Quebec society to its roots. The first round in the struggle was fought out in the Montreal suburb of St-Léonard beginning in 1967.[64] Approximately 40 per cent of the population of this municipality was immigrant in character, mainly of Italian origin. Before 1967, 36 per cent of the students in the area, mainly non-francophones, went to bilingual schools, that is, schools which taught 60 per cent of the time in French and 40 per cent in English. In September 1967, five school commissioners passed a resolution stating that such schools should become unilingual French schools. Associations were quickly formed on both sides – the St-Léonard English Catholic Association of Parents, which wanted English-only schools, and the Mouvement pour l'intégration scolaire (MIS), which demanded French schools. The former received the support of the anglophone establishment, and the latter that of the nationalist societies.

The matter was strictly a bread-and-butter one for the immigrants.[65] Social mobility in North America, including Quebec, was impossible without knowledge of English. The fissure that developed between Italian and francophone as a result of this dispute was ironic and unfortunate, because the former had been the group that had mixed best with the majority. Intermarriages and friendly contacts between Italians and francophones were much more frequent than between Italians and anglophones, with religion being the integrative factor.[66] More Italians attended the St-Jean-Baptiste day celebrations than the Italian Day festivities.[67] However, 82 per cent of Italians said that French Canadians were the ethnic group that discriminated against them most.[68]

In a preliminary attempt to resolve the dispute and to pacify the Italian community and its supporters, the Union nationale government introduced Bill 85 to the legislature in December 1968. It gave parents the right to choose the language in which their children were to be educated. The government set up the Gendron Commission to investigate the position of the French language in Quebec and to recommend measures whereby the language rights of the minority and majority could be protected while the use of French was expanded. After concerted opposition from nationalists, the bill was withdrawn, only to be submitted in revised form as Bill 63 in October 1969. This bill again granted freedom of choice and added several measures to promote the expansion of French.

Bill 63 was to become a rallying point, the bullfighter's cape, for the nationalists. Not only did it mean that immigrants could continue to send their children to English schools, but it also meant that francophones could do the same. This point is often passed over in studying this dispute but is essential to understanding the fervour with which Bill 63 was opposed. With the breakdown of the confessional barriers and the erosion of religion as a cultural component, language had become, as we have seen, the defining characteristic of Quebec's francophones. The attempt to solidify the new basis of the culture by making Quebec a unilingual French society was increasingly floundering, in the view of the nationalists, because of open access to English-language schools. The bill also was a watershed in terms of trust and confidence in the government. To this point, the Union nationale government, through its energetic activity in international relations and its attempts to recast the symbols of the Quebec régime, had garnered significant goodwill from cultural nationalists. A rapid decline in such supportive attitudes among groups such as the FSSJBQ became evident after introduction of the bill.[69]

The BNA Act defined minority rights in education in terms of religion. While Protestants and Catholics were guaranteed their own schools in Quebec, the constitution said nothing about schools for 'anglophones' and 'francophones.' However, since the Protestant system in Quebec was virtually synonymous with education in the English language, representatives of the English-speaking community began to argue that they possessed 'acquired' or 'vested' rights to an education in English. Bill 63, in their view, simply reconfirmed those rights. This explains their support for Bill 63. Those who opposed freedom of choice, in particular nationalist societies such as the SSJBM (since 1969 headed by F.-A. Angers), rejected all arguments to the effect that anglophones had 'rights' to an education in English. Instead they spoke of 'privileges' granted to the 'minority' by the 'majority.'

On the initiative of Angers, the Front du Québec français (FQF) was formed to fight the bill. It gave institutional form to a coalition of forces that we have seen several times in this study, grouping together the nationalist societies, representatives of the trade unions, francophone teachers' unions and associations, and student organizations. Although at one stage it managed to mobilize 50,000 demonstrators to assemble on the lawns of the legislature demanding the withdrawal of the bill, the FQF ultimately failed. The supporters of the bill were simply too powerful. These included the newly formed Conseil du Patronat, the Centre des dirigeants d'entreprise (CDE), the CMA(Q), and the

Canada Committee. In short, the anglophone corporate sector, which controlled financial resources needed by the régime, with some support from the francophone business class, opposed the legislation.

The Liberal government of Robert Bourassa made a third attempt at resolving this problem in 1974 with its Official Language Act. The act allowed for instruction in both English and French. To receive instruction in English, one needed to demonstrate possession of a 'sufficient knowledge' of the language. If this 'sufficient knowledge' could not be demonstrated, then the pupil automatically was to be enrolled in the French-language school system. The act also gave the government the power to set quotas for total registrants in the English-language system and to draw up tests to determine whether a 'sufficient knowledge' existed. The essentially compromise character of the provisions upset to some degree large portions of the political community.

The SSJBM, the Mouvement Québec français (MQF) (the successor to the FQF), the CEQ, and the Association québécoise des professeurs de français (AQPF) rejected these provisions. For the law to acknowledge that instruction could be given in English constituted for these nationalists the recognition of a new right for anglophones and another step toward the legitimation of a bilingual Quebec. The nationalists were also upset by the fact that francophones could attend English schools if they possessed 'sufficient knowledge.'[70] They saw the bill as hastening a decline in the proportions of francophones within Quebec. The Parti québécois suggested unsuccessfully a compromise (which was to be seen again three years hence) allowing only Québécois with English as their mother tongue to attend English schools.[71]

On the other side, organizations such as the CPQ, the Montreal Board of Trade (MBT), the CCPQ, and Alcan felt that the bill did not provide sufficient guarantees for the use of English as a language of instruction in Quebec.[72] They reiterated their usual demands for freedom of choice in the area of language of instruction. Representatives of the immigrant groups such as the Fédération des associations italiennes du Québec and the Conseil des Fédérations ethniques suggested that freedom of choice come only after a period of one to three years of immersion in French instruction.[73]

As early as 1972, both the Gendron Commission and Léon Dion, an influential political scientist at Laval, had cautioned the authorities against using coercive measures to promote the integration of immigrants into the francophone community.[74] In introducing tests and quotas, the government failed to follow this advice. Injustices were soon perpetrated, and a crisis followed when schools opened in the fall of 1975. Many immigrant parents withheld their children from French schools, sending them to clandestine English schools. The tests proved to be quite traumatic for four- and

Vong - 45017   Oct 26

five-year-old children, a fact emblazoned regularly on the front pages of the anglophone newspapers. The situation became more intense when a local Montreal anglophone radio station undertook an intensive campaign urging withdrawal of Bill 22. Despite comparing the government to the Nazis, and playing martial and patriotic music, the station's campaign was not successful.

Bill 22 remained in force until the election to power of the Parti québécois and the passage of the Charte de la langue française. With the Charte came another attempt to resolve the education question. The basis of the new policy was to restrict freedom of choice in language of instruction as much as possible to anglophones having their historical roots in Quebec. This was accomplished by giving access to English-language instruction to four groups: 1/ children whose mother or father had received their primary schooling in Quebec in English; 2/ children whose father or mother lived in Quebec at the time of the promulgation of the law and who had received their primary instruction in English outside Quebec; 3/ children who in the previous school year had received legally instruction in English in the public school system; and 4/ younger brothers and sisters of the latter. A regulation proclaimed at the same time as the Charte gave the option to those persons or their children staying in Quebec temporarily to apply for authorization to receive instruction in English. The authorization would last for three years, with renewal possible for an additional three years. The provisions of the Charte applied as well to all private schools receiving subsidies from the province.

The new legislation thus ended the tests that were such an emotional issue under Bill 22. In the first four years of its existence, the school question was quieter than it had been for a decade. The new provisions have apparently been successful in directing the children of recent immigrants into French-language schools. For the first time, the majority of parents whose mother tongue was neither English nor French and who had children entering kindergarten were enrolling them in French-language schools.[75] Demographic studies suggested that the proportion of Quebec's population enrolled in the French sector would increase.[76] The educational system under this policy became better adapted to providing stability to the French language. An increasing proportion of the population was to be introduced to the language in the same system of schools following the same curriculum. English-language schools were required by law to give their pupils a working ability in French. The capacity to develop uniform language practice among the various communities making up the province's population was much improved. However, these changes had not been achieved without a social cost. Many members of the English-speaking community were bitter about the changes to the school system and received some support from members of other non-francophone communities. This bitterness and the divisions it rested upon made it more difficult for the province's leaders to develop the acceptance of the French language, the language loyalty, that status language planning has as an objective.

The cultivation of acceptance

A standard language, I suggested in the introduction to this chapter, is established only when it is accepted as such by all members of the speech community. Most of the academic literature on the process of standardization has not spoken very much, if at all, of the politics in this process. The literature has been developed mainly on the basis of examining standardization from below, so to speak. The presumption is that society almost unconsciously moves toward standardizing a language, using it for formal and technical communication, and reflecting upon its beauty, thereby strengthening attachment and loyalty to it. In the case of Quebec, there were two languages, French and English, both of which were standard languages elsewhere in the world. However, in Quebec, there was a division of labour whereby English was the dominant language in the economy and related technical communication and French was the language of everyday communication outside the industrial workplace and the federal government. The forces 'from below' were continually pressing upon French and probably diminishing the range of social situations in which it was used. In order to support its economic policy and in order not to give the lie to its policy on education, the government was gradually pressed to act to end this division of labour and to force Quebec society to adopt French as its standard language. This action represented a more direct political involvement in the process of standardization than the theory normally gives room for. The development of language loyalty took a particular form in Quebec. In part, it was a matter of support for the policy of a legitimately elected government, and thus the expression of disloyalty was constrained somewhat by the customs of what oppositions to legitimate governments allow. Further the government was able to take a larger advocacy role, which it used to create the feeling that the expansion of the use of French was inevitable and might as well be accepted, if only wearily.

The government created this sense of inevitability in two ways. First, to a degree with Bill 22 and much more with Bill 101, it took pains to ensure that Quebec society looked French. The provincial government dropped its previous bilingualism and advertised its programs, named its departments and agencies, published its documents, and communicated with citizens in French only. The same requirements were placed on local governments and local public agencies. The business world too was compelled to present itself in French only. All firms operating in the province were to call themselves with a

French name. All products were to be labelled in French (or in French and another language provided French was displayed at least as prominently as the other language). Catalogues, flyers, brochures, application forms, order forms, bills, and receipts were to be in French only. All public notices, including commercial printed advertising, were to be in French only. Even small enterprises owned by anglophones, serving anglophones in the midst of an English-speaking community, had to advertise their products on their premises in French only. The only parties exempted from this provision were businesses employing less than four persons and certain cultural activities of ethnic groups. In 1979, for example, new regulations were passed that allowed cultural and educational products such as books to be advertised in French and in another language. Second, the government complemented this creation of a society that was French in virtually all outward appearances by several intensive advertising campaigns. The first was sponsored by the Régie de la langue française, using the slogan 'De plus en plus, au Québec, c'est en français que ça se passe.' Similar campaigns were conducted by the OLF using all media, print, radio, and television, again stressing the inevitability of francization. The Régie found that francophones were somewhat surprised by the campaigns but liked them very much.[77] Italian-speakers also were quite receptive but anglophones negative in the face of these campaigns.

These two approaches have had some success. Surveys conducted by the OLF showed that Bill 101 was viewed positively by 80.6 per cent of francophones and almost half, 44.4 per cent, of anglophones.[78] They showed that the policies were having an impact even at the most entrenched local levels. In English-speaking municipalities, only 9.3 per cent of the respondents reported that they received public documents in English only, the long-standing past practice.[79] The government has apparently been successful in creating a sense of inevitability about the process. The OLF survey showed that 70.4 per cent of francophones and 74.3 per cent of anglophones thought the process of the francization of Quebec society was irreversible.[80] These findings match the apparent mood of the society in the early 1980s. The process of making French the prevalent language in Quebec appears to be well under way. The question that remains for our consideration is the impact of this process.

Conclusion

The analysis in this chapter has demonstrated that the various policies on language set up by governments in Quebec during the 1970s can be understood as an attempt to establish French as the official language for all formal communication within the speech community defined by the province's political borders. Similarly, the thrust of federal language policy was to establish French as one of two such languages in the country as a whole. To a certain degree, the success of these attempts is still not clearly evident, but it does appear to be more and more probable. In introducing this chapter, I argued that the success of efforts to increase the status and prevalence of French in Quebec would not necessarily strengthen the capacity of the French language to function as a cultural protector of French-Canadian civilization. The justifications for this assertion should now be more clear.

First, the movement toward the status of primary formal language has facilitated several of the policies that have helped created a cultural crisis in French Quebec. The policies on language have had the effect of opening up 'space' for a francophone capitalist class. In doing so they have facilitated the economic policies that began with the election of the Parti libéral in 1960 and were designed to integrate the francophone community in Quebec effectively into the advanced capitalist economy of North America and to give it a role in the direction of that economy. They have also aided the new graduates from the reformed educational system to take places in the private sector that draw upon their new skills. To a lesser degree perhaps, the federal policy has brought French Canadians into a position where they can exercise influence at the federal level and thus gain access to political power they were previously denied.

Second, as the francophone capitalist class has moved more and more toward integration into the North American economic milieu, the policies on language have served to homogenize the capitalist class in Quebec. Previously, class divisions in Quebec society often matched language divisions so that the class struggle could be fought on the plane of ethnic and national survival, giving it added emotion and intensity. The language laws of the 1970s, however, gave all of private enterprise a French face and forced it to speak with its workers in the French language. These changes lowered somewhat the visibility of foreign enterprises in Quebec.[81] By making these enterprises appear to be more a part of Quebec society, the policies may have also taken part of the emotional nationalist sting out of the critique of Quebec's economic dependence. The changes also served to draw the national dimension out of conflicts between workers and employers, thus making it less likely that organized labour and the nationalist middle classes could find themselves on a common platform during these conflicts. Any weakening of this coalition could only retard the political challenge being mounted by it.

Third, these same language policies, by their thrust toward standardization, have furthered the social and cultural integration of francophones and non-francophones in Quebec. They have been bringing these groups together in ways they never were before. They now more and more go to the same schools, can live in each others' communities, and can be served by the same institutions, whether these be hospitals, municipal governments, or welfare agencies. Given the existing confusion in the francophone community over its own values and culture, these developments can only further this confusion and weaken the distinctiveness of French-Canadian culture.

Corpus language planning has changed the French language itself as it is used in Quebec. It has brought the keepers of the French language in Quebec into more direct and regular contact with the keepers of the language in France. This had led to a movement to 'raise' the French spoken in Quebec to international standards. Perhaps even more important, the expansion of French into the economic and industrial sectors has been carried out by translating thousands of terms from English into French and distributing the resulting lexicons to private firms. The result of this process has been the addition of thousands of new and foreign words to the language. French, in becoming an improved medium for technological and scientific discussion, is also moving away more and more from its traditional roots and becoming more like the language of advanced capitalism in North American, English.

The public formal language therefore is diverging more and more from the older informal language. At the same time, this expanded formal language cannot fail to have an impact on the informal language used in daily communication. This language will gradually absorb some of the new vocabulary and become better adapted to the new industrial world. In doing so, it will move away from its traditional forms and expressions. The meaning of concepts long preserved through the language may be lost. The process of standardization may diminish its ability to play a role in preserving certain distinctive traits in French-Canadian culture.

This is not to say in conclusion that the policies on language have not helped those who are struggling to preserve and develop a distinctive community in Quebec. While they have facilitated the integration of Quebec into North America in the economic plane, they have also served to demarcate Quebec as a political community. When one crosses the border into Quebec, if you can read and bother to listen, you know something has changed. McDonald's restaurants may still be there, people may still drink Coca-Cola and buy washing machines from Eaton's, but there is a difference. It may be on the order of putting up a fence to mark off a circular piece of land in the middle of a large pasture: the grass may look no different inside the fence than outside, but in the encircled piece of land something new and different could be tried that would have been difficult before the fence was there. Nationalists in Quebec believe the differences are already more real between Quebec and the rest of North America than our analogy suggests, and they continue to seek the political power they feel they need to build on this belief. If this aspect of nationalist thinking can be understood, it clarifies why, somewhat to the surprise of English Canadians,

Bill 101 has not marked the end of the nationalist movement in Quebec. For the nationalists, the language law is only the beginning, the putting in place of a fence, the minimal first step in their quest for a new state and new society in Quebec. We turn finally to examine the character of this quest in our concluding chapter.

8

The movement for political independence

A question that remained unstated through most of this study is why has there arisen in Quebec since the late 1950s a significant political movement in favour of Quebec becoming a sovereign nation-state. The analysis in the preceding chapters has been carried out with the aim of finally being able to address this question. In my view, the independence movement was not the instigator of the Quiet Revolution or even part of that revolution. Rather it was a consequence, a product of the series of changes that began to be realized in Quebec late in the 1950s. It is a reaction to changes that have fundamentally shaken the culture of French Canada, that have left the traditional bases of that culture almost in ruins, and that hold no promise, not even a conception, of putting anything in their place.

This movement is based upon more than the frustration of the francophone middle classes arising from their inability to hold economic power, more than the anger of intellectuals who find it increasingly difficult to find values sufficiently shared to constitute a community, and more than the despair of workers who know only of the instability of economic recession. It is also a cry of fright from the people of which these groups are a part, a people that remembers having some sense of self and of being a community and that feels that both are now virtually gone. However much some might like to deny the facts, the emotions expressed by nationalists are real and deep-felt, the songs relay a truth, the poetry an anger and a love, and all are touched by their message and sense a danger that French Canada may not survive.

This conclusion, I feel, follows logically from the analysis found in the previous chapters. This study began by suggesting that existing theories and descriptions of the changes that have swept Quebec since 1945 were incomplete. Each, it was said, was capturing a part of the reality and yet was apparently contradicting the others. The existing, inadequate conceptions could not be accepted because they led to a less than complete understanding of political events in Quebec. Poor understanding begets not only unfortunate public policies but also raw feelings and broken lines of communication. It is my aim in this concluding chapter to draw from the preceding analysis in order to reflect upon why the independence movement has risen to a place of almost overriding importance in Quebec's political life.

The Quiet Revolution

The concept of a quiet revolution does not refer to changes in policy per se; rather it describes the spirit or atmosphere in Quebec society in the early 1960s. This was a spirit of collective strength, of co-operation, of a general will to move forward together. It was a spirit of elation, of joyful outbursts, and of hope. There was a sense that the divisions in the community that had become more and more acute after 1945 could be breached. There was a belief that soon a global vision of a new society would be constructed and that all would have an important role in that society. For a short period, there was a feeling among most major social groups that French Canada had come together in a new form as a rejuvenated nation and that the future of that nation was one of immense promise. This spirit of hope and confidence was short-lived. When it disappeared, many felt its loss keenly, and their disillusionment helped fuel the independence movement. In seeking to understand this movement, it is important to understand the particular social malaise out of which the Quiet Revolution emerged.

Toward the end of the 1950s, socio-economic conditions were such that three social groups in Quebec's francophone community were voicing discontent with their respective situations. The industrial working class, which was growing quickly as Quebec's regions lost their young people to the attractions of Montreal, found the educational system blocking its social advancement and not capable of providing the training it needed for the industrial workplace. The institutions that ministered to its social needs were stretched to the limit and run by a clergy rooted in rural Quebec and unable to understand the problems of the urban worker. The economy was unstable, making secure employment and a steady income difficult to achieve and allowing employers considerable room to fight the organization of the working class.

The localized francophone small bourgeoisie was finding itself pushed more and more into marginal areas of the economy. As the concentration of enterprises grew in North America, the need for large pools of capital became more intense if one were to have any hope of participating in the direction of that economy. In order to resist its marginalization, this small bourgeoisie was looking for a means to pull together the capital required for new competitive ventures.

Some individuals and groups based mainly in the organizations of the traditional middle class become increasingly concerned about the discontent of both the industrial working class and the small capitalist class. The inability of the traditional institutions of French Canada to respond to the needs of the working class brought these institutions into question. The critique of these institutions was implicitly a critique of the traditional professionals who directed them and of the values upon which the institutions had been built. Further, the inability of the traditional institutions to influence the working class meant that its members were quickly developing values more attuned to the consumerism and materialism of anglophone North America than to those of the traditional middle class. The desires too of the francophone capitalist class to participate more fully in the North American economy threatened to increase further the influence of value systems different from those of the established culture of French Canada. The traditional middle class saw the bases of French-Canadian civilization to be eroding and threatened with ever more rapid decline.

In seeking solutions to these problems, the organizations of labour and of the francophone business class arrived at rather similar positions. The traditional middle class was split, with part of it inclined to follow the recommendations of the Tremblay Commission and other parts articulating a position not unlike that of the working and business classes. The elements of the solutions proposed by what we have called the Quiet Revolution coalition – organized labour, francophone business class, and elements from the traditional middle class – were as follows. A stronger and more viable capitalist class had to be formed within the francophone community. It was to be built by using the economic base provided by the province's natural resources. Most of these resources, it was observed, were being exported in brute form, and it was suggested that there was room for curtailing this practice in favour of manufacturing and processing these resources in Quebec. The co-operation needed for realizing such a project was to be achieved by bringing these major social groups and the government together in an organization that would have responsibility for planning economic development. It was also generally conceded that the provincial government would have the primary responsibility for bringing the scattered collections of capital existing in the francophone community together into larger and more accessible pools. Together, these policies would help develop capitalist enterprises controlled by francophones that would compete effectively in the North American market and ultimately give francophones a significant voice in the direction of the provincial economy.

These elements of an economic policy that would satisfy these three groups were brought together as specific proposals in the program of the Parti libéral du Québec in the 1960 election and began to be implemented shortly after that party came to power. They were accepted by organized labour because they contained the promise of a more balanced, autocentric economy which would bring more stable employment and enhanced job security. The francophone business class saw the policies as creating a significant opportunity for reversing its marginalization and for finding the capital needed for expansion. The sympathetic elements of the traditional middle class saw increased control over economic development by francophones as a base upon which the distinctive aspects of French-Canadian culture could be rejuvenated. This policy was received more cautiously by the dominant, mainly non-francophone, fractions of the capitalist class in Quebec. The outright commitment to expanded capitalist development that it entailed was obviously welcome. Yet if this development were largely to aid francophone capitalists through the use of state intervention, the policy would be viewed as unfair. It was greeted with even more concern by traditional nationalists sympathetic to the point of view found in the Tremblay Commission's report.

Once the principles of the economic policy were accepted and began to be implemented, a series of other reforms and changes were countenanced. The Quebec government entered into a series of struggles with the federal government over control of fiscal resources. It sought to retain and control in Quebec all pension contributions, seeing these funds as a potentially large capital pool that could be used to further its economic objectives. It wished also to have control over all taxes that were to be used for the funding of educational and social programs in the province, because far-reaching changes were being planned for these. The educational system was being completely withdrawn from ecclesiastical control and being placed in the hands of the provincial government. Educational programs and structures were being revised in order to give greater emphasis to technical instruction and to ensure greater access to higher levels of education. The system of delivery for social services was also being withdrawn from clerical control and being rationalized and expanded under government control. The Office de la langue française began to develop the lexicons that were needed by francophones, whether workers or cadres, for functioning in the new industrial worlds being sought after.

Again, as well, there was acceptance of these changes by the groups in the coalition. The educational reforms held out the promise to workers of better technical training and of greater access to higher education. The social changes appeared to be geared to providing a wider range of social services at a superior level. The new lexicons, when learned, would allow workers to labour more completely in their own language and to avoid developing a pidgin for use in workplace communication. The francophone business class saw the educational reforms as eventually yielding a more skilled labour force and the social changes as a means to ensure that the workforce was adequately serviced in the area of health care. The language policies were expected to be useful for penetrating new areas of the economy without the disadvantage of having to use English. The traditional-middle-class elements that supported the economic reforms saw the changes in educational and social policy as a means to bring the working class back under institutions that could potentially be new building blocks for French-Canadian culture. They saw the changes as creating the conditions needed for reunifying the French-Canadian community.

The atmosphere in Quebec's francophone community in the early 1960s, the feeling that a Quiet Revolution was taking place, rested on a consensus on how to proceed in economic, educational, social, and cultural policy. This consensus was reached by three social groups of importance in the community. When this consensus began to founder, so did the revolutionary spirit. When the consensus was replaced by confrontation among the three original groups, the idea of independence emerged as a tool in the battle.

Why did the consensus fail to last? The economic program that was agreed upon in the early 1960s was never fully implemented, and those aspects that were put into place did not have the expected impact. After the original activity of the COEQ, no systematic planning of the economy was carried out. The COEQ faded into oblivion, and the harmony among social groups that it fostered disappeared with it. Similarly, after the nationalization of hydro-electric power companies in 1962, no systematic attempts were made to gain majority control over other resources, and the practice of shipping resources out of the province in brute form was not discontinued. A series of state institutions was created that was designed to be developed jointly with the francophone business class. These institutions started slowly, providing some growth and expansion of the business class but no significant economic benefits for the community as a whole. They failed miserably to compete with the established corporations in the province. In the early 1970s, the strategy was revised in two ways. Direct participation of the provincial government was de-emphasized, and the private sector was saluted as the prime motor of economic development. Co-operation with established corporations replaced the goal of competing with them.

Until the early 1970s, then, the economic policy was essentially one of fostering capitalist expansion without directing that expansion. The educational reforms ended up being of a similar nature. Changes were made in structures and programs on an instrumentalist basis; they were designed to further as rapidly as possible the graduation of a more technically skilled labour force. Cultural aspects of education received little attention, and no large advances were made in opening up higher, specifically university-level education, to workers.

The demands of organized labour were not satisfied in the area of economic planning. No extensive planning was instituted, and minimal control over natural resources was achieved. As the instability and insecurity of their economic situation did not change, workers became disenchanted with the government and with its economic policy. This disenchantement was given additional force when, after the organization of public-sector workers in the mid-1960s, that government became a much more visible 'boss' as well. Organized labour increased the strength of its organizations and moved sharply to the left, becoming more and more critical of the *fondements* of the economic system itself. The strengthening of labour's organizations was matched by an increased visibility of organizations representing capitalists' interests and by an increase in their strength. New organizations were created, such as the Conseil du Patronat du Québec and the General Council of Industry, to speak for the capitalist class as a whole. The lines between the labour and the employer components of the old coalition were sharply drawn.

The promise of the heyday of the Quiet Revolution was not realized for the traditional middle class either. The capitalistic thrust of the economic policy (without the salve of greater economic control) and the instrumentalist character of educational reform tended to increase the materialism and consumerism of society rather than decrease it. The movement toward the idea of a pluralist Quebec with single bureaucracies to serve all the cultural communities broke down further some barriers between French Quebec and the rest of the continent. The replacement of traditional institutions with distinctive properties by institutions apparently less rooted in French-Canadian culture was also viewed with more and more concern. The hope of those elements of the traditional middle class that the Quiet Revolution would create the conditions for the reunification of the French-Canadian community and the rejuvenation of its culture was not realized.

The economic, educational, and social changes of the early 1960s added a significant number of individuals to the social category titled the new middle class. The expanded state bureaucracies included numbers of white-collar personnel and middle managers. These were added to the journalists, academics, teachers, and technical professionals who also increased during the 1960s. These individuals in their jobs were constantly reminded of the economic and political weaknesses of the francophone community. On economic matters, they found themselves treating with English-speaking corporations in English or with a largely English-speaking federal government. Within Quebec, on educational and social matters, they found themselves forced to work in English when it came to dealing with the Protestant school system, or with municipalities in western Montreal, or with hospitals in English-speaking communities. Everywhere, it appeared, the routes to advancement for francophones were blocked. What is more, the economic and educational reforms were also apparently injecting further the anglophones' culture and values into the lives of Québécois.

In short, for many in the middle classes, particularly those predisposed to be nationalistic, the lack of a culture and a sense of direction in the cultural sphere that accompanied the changes of the early 1960s led to a questioning of state policy and of the constitution. The economic reforms and educational changes were simply too pragmatic and too devoid of a sensitivity to the culture of the francophone community to be accepted without question. The movement toward creating institutions that would serve a single, albeit pluralistic, society in Quebec added to this anxiety. In inviting the anglophone community to participate in a single educational system with a single curriculum, the openness to that community was leading to an unquestioning acceptance of its values. These worries, when joined with demographic statistics indicating a decline in the proportionate strength of francophones in Quebec, led to great political tension. Important parts of the middle classes thus also went into opposition against both the provincial government and the francophone business class that continued to support that government.

This disaffection of the middle classes and the working class was to be channelled into the political movement in favour of the independence of Quebec. This point will be demonstrated first by looking at the origins of the modern-day independence movement and showing that its orientation would be attractive to the above-discussed social groups as they came to reject the consequences of the Quiet Revolution reforms. I shall next discuss why the concept of independence holds sufficient promise to have attracted significant sustained support from these social groups over the past fifteen years.

The rise of the independence parties

The modern-day independence movement in Quebec began on a small scale in the late 1950s. Two small groups proposing that Quebec become politically sovereign were formed, both heavily critical of the road to capitalist expansion being taken in Quebec. At the very beginning of the independence movement, a prime point of criticism and of concern was the likely effect of uncontrolled capitalist growth in Quebec. Nevertheless, the criticisms by the two groups differed sharply. The first was a conservative Catholic organization inspired by an unreformed Groulx-type nationalism. In January 1957, the Alliance laurentienne organized itself to promote the political independence of Quebec. It cited the brutality of the conquest of 1759 and the threat of assimilation as the reasons underlying its proposal.[1] It envisaged a radical change – the erection of a Catholic corporatist régime – and saw itself as the movement that would prepare the way for Quebec's Salazar or Bolivar![2] 'Rien n'est jugé en histoire.

Pas plus notre défaite militaire que notre infériorité économique. La volonté populaire, la décision d'un Chef, l'union sacrée des forces vives de la Nation, le combat incessant, discipliné, auront raison, un jour prochain, de nos conquérants. Nous préparons la voie à notre Salazar, à notre Bolivar, au libérateur que notre peuple attend depuis une siècle.'

In the spring of 1959, on the other end of the ideological spectrum, a second independence group entered the scene. The Action socialiste pour l'indépendance du Québec (ASIQ) also expressed a sharp opposition to the existing economic order in Quebec. Socialist in character, it used the concepts of colonialism and imperialism much discussed in Algeria and the Third World in justifying its proposal: 'Les Canadiens (français) forment un peuple opprimé ... Le Québec est occupé économiquement par une grande bourgeoisie colonialiste de langue et de culture étrangère qui se sert d'un mercenariat politique, prostitué à ses intérêts élitistes, pour asservir la majorité de la population.'[3]

In September of the following year, the independence movement, still very small, took a step toward the centre with the formation of the Rassemblement pour l'indépendance nationale (RIN). Formed jointly by individuals frustrated by English-Canadian domination of the federal civil service and by moderates from the Alliance fearful of its corporatism, the RIN was to become the leading independence group of its day. Its symbol was a stylized ram, an obvious rejection of the traditional lamb in the arms of John the Baptist, long the symbol of French Canada. The RIN, as it grew, developed a vision of a new Quebec that would be independent, secular, and social democratic. The new society would supersede the old Catholic province with its 'hewer of wood, drawer of water' economy. The RIN retained in its ideology the critique of undirected capitalist growth. It added to the indépendantiste ideology the rejection of traditional clerical institutions and practices, thereby echoing the sentiments of the Mouvement laïque de la langue française discussed in chapter 6.[4] The RIN was to become one of several forums where an attempt was made to define a new distinctive culture for Quebec.

At the same time as the small independence parties were first coming to public attention, there were developing elsewhere in the francophone community more intense feelings about the need for a strong autonomous Quebec. Nationalist societies and others stated, quietly at first, that French Canada constituted a nation; with each subsequent opportunity, they stated that idea more joyfully and assertively. Linked to this affirmation was the demand that the État du Quebec be granted the powers and status of a national state (État national), which would guarantee the flowering of the French-Canadian nation. The implication was that under existing political arrangements, and despite the Quiet Revolution, French Canada was still not free to be itself, free to be a distinctive national community.

These sentiments were translated into more specific political demands by the nationalist societies and by intellectuals and politicians who moved toward the indépendantiste position. In 1962, the nationalist societies began promoting the notion of 'associated states': virtually independent national states, headquartered in Ottawa and Quebec, with a new Confederal Parliament to treat a few matters of common concern. The most detailed proposals of this kind were made by Jacques-Yvan Morin, a profesor of international law and future PQ minister, and by the SSJBM.[5] The proposals of the latter group were most fully elaborated in its brief to a special committee on the constitution set up by the legislature in 1963 and were set in the context of a very pessimistic view of Confederation drawn, in the main, from the work of the historian Brunet. The theory was that any federation is formed out of two sorts of power – a federating power (pouvoir fédérant) and a federated power (pouvoir fédéré). The federation is established when the former imposes a union on the latter. The pouvoir fédéré in the Canadian case was seen to be, of course, the francophone community in Quebec. In 1964, this proposal received the tentative support of two members of the Lesage cabinet, René Lévesque and Pierre Laporte.[6]

A further indicator of the development of the idea of Quebec becoming a national state is the change in the terms used by nationalists to refer to the potential citizens of that state. The community was now the nation québécoise and the members of that nation were Québécois, thereby defining it by political rather than ethnic criteria. The term Canadien français, which embraced individuals throughout the continent, gradually disappeared from many vocabularies. Many of the nationalist societies began changing their names from Société Saint-Jean-Baptiste de ... to Société nationale des Québécois de ... . (The SSJBM, however, retained its traditional name.) The Fédération des Sociétés Saint-Jean-Baptiste du Québec became the Mouvement national des Québécois. Table 6, which lists themes chosen by the SSJBM for the celebration of French Canada's national day, Saint-Jean-Baptiste Day, 24 June, illustrates this shift in emphasis well, with the break coming between 1966 and 1967.

By the 1966 election in the province, the independence movement was an established though minor force. Split into various groups, it shared a concern for the establishment and maintenance of a distinctive national community in Quebec. The RIN, however, went beyond this objective by seeking to outline a vision of a new Quebec which would be secular and thus different from the old society, and socialist and thus economically restructured as well. This attempt to define a new culture for Quebec that drew from its history and yet superseded that history was complemented by intensive reflection in the artistic community. Here the journal *Parti pris* played a central role, publishing poetry, essays, and literature that were emotional and magnetizing. The mid-1960s saw feverish reflection and creation by poets, novelists, playwrights, musicians,

TABLE 6
Themes of Saint-Jean-Baptiste Day celebrations 1949–75

1949	La cité
1950	L'expansion française en Amérique
1951	Le folklore
1952	Notre héritage culturel
1953	Nos richesses économiques
1954	Fidélité mariale
1955	L'Acadie rayonnante
1956	Le visage du Canada français
1957	Sa majesté la langue française
1958	Champlain, Père de la Nouvelle France, et Québec, Capitale du Canada français
1959	Le Saint-Laurent ... 'la route qui marche'
1960	La présence canadienne française
1961	Hommage à la femme canadienne-française
1962	L'épanouissement du Canada français
1963	La joie de vivre au Canada français
1964	Le Canada français, réalité vivante
1965	Montréal, ville dynamique
1966	La présence canadienne-française dans le monde
1967	La vocation internationale du Québec
1968	Québec 68
1969	Québec, mon amour
1970	Faîtes la fête
1971	Chantons la Saint-Jean
1972	Québec français
1973	Un pays, un drapeau
1974	Le 24 juin, c'est ma fête
1975	Notre fête nationale, faut fêter ça!

and artists. The political and artistic communities interpenetrated and drew inspiration from each other. There was real hope in these admittedly restricted circles that the bases for a new, distinctive community could be established.

The RIN did not have the independence platform to itself in the mid-1960s. Two other groups were to share it. The Ralliement national (RN) was formed jointly by the Regroupement national and the Ralliement créditiste prior to the 1966 election. It was to a degree the heir of the Alliance laurentienne in that it was conservative, strongly Catholic and anti-socialist. It received less electoral support than the RIN, and its members tended to be older and more concentrated in rural areas. The third group was the Mouvement Souveraineté-Association (MSA) which was founded by René Lévesque after his departure from the Parti libéral in October 1967. Its platform suggested that it drew support from the new middle class in particular, because it strongly favoured economic growth, with the public sector as the catalyst. It drew from some of the earlier ideas, such as the associated states concept, in proposing that political independence be accompanied by an economic association with Canada under the guise of a customs and perhaps a monetary union.

In 1968, the MSA and the Ralliement national joined together to form the Parti québécois. The RIN did not formally become a partner because the leaders of the MSA and the RN would not agree to the RIN's position on language policy, a strict unilingualist position. Instead, the RIN dissolved itself, and most of its members joined the Parti québécois. At this point, it is fairly safe to say, the Parti québécois drew support from both the traditional and new middle classes. As these events were occurring, the CNTU was putting into place new comités d'action politique (CAPs) which were inspired by Marcel Pépin's call for the creation of a Second Front described in chapter 4. These were to be labour organizations that would represent and lobby for the labour point of view in various political arenas. Many of these CAPs became cornerstones of PQ riding organizations and thus brought a labour voice into the party. By the mid-1970s, it has been shown, the Parti québécois drew the support of a majority of professionals and semi-professionals in the francophone community.[7] Managers and top administrators tended to support the Parti libéral. The Parti québécois drew majority support from workers who were in favour of social change.[8] The militants in the party tended to be disproportionately frequently from the new middle class (public servants, teachers, professors, journalists), as is shown by the fact that 53.2 per cent of the party's candidates were drawn from this group.[9]

The Parti québécois and the independence movement grew in strength impressively after 1968, capturing 24 per cent of the vote in 1970, 30 per cent in 1973, 41 per cent in 1976, and 49 per cent in 1981. The movement increased in force after the reforms of the early 1960s had been put in place and some of their consequences had become known. In some ways, it was a more cautious movement than it had been in the early 1960s because it accepted the original goal of the Quiet Revolution – insertion of Quebec's francophone community fully into the continental economy, with an emphasis on the need to develop some powers of direction over that economy.

Admittedly, there was to be a struggle in the Parti québécois between the visionaries and the pure indépendantistes of the RIN and the pragmatic technocrats and 'associationists' formerly of the Parti libéral. In the end, however, as Vera Murray shows, the latter won and came to control the party.[10] One can, of course, view the PQ proposal for economic association as simply being 'realistic,' as recognizing the fact, as Jane Jacobs puts it, that the economic culture of Quebec is now the same as that of English Canada.[11] However, to what degree can one separate culture as a broad concept from economic culture? It was certainly the position of the Tremblay commissioners on the one side and the RIN on the other that the two could not be separated. The former argued that if traditional French-Canadian culture was to be preserved, then there would need to be major changes in the norms governing economic activity to make it complementary to that culture. If such changes were not made, the commissioners warned, the distinctive culture of French Canadians would be mortally wounded. The RIN and its supporters in the artistic community always argued that the redefinition of cultural practice in a new communal, secular Quebec was tied intimately to the reversal of economic underdevelopment. The fact that the writers, poets, and artists of *Parti pris* were simultaneously reflecting upon a new culture in their art and forming and promoting the socialist Mouvement de libération populaire also illustrates this assumption. The program of the Parti québécois was not built on this assumption, and the behaviour of the party in power bears this out. It did not reverse the economic policy of the Parti libéral and even confirmed in its economic policy document, *Bâtir le Québec,* that the private sector had to be the main source for economic growth and innovation in the province.

Conclusion

The movement in favour of the political independence of Quebec is a social coalition of several groups in the francophone community – portions of the working class, those in the middle classes who work outside the private sector, and the intelligentsia. These three groups, despite different interests, have come together in a single political movement because each perceives a need for the francophone community to have greater control over its own affairs. Each group was mobilized to join the movement after it had concluded that the possibility of such control was being seriously eroded by the package of policies that began to be implemented upon the death of Maurice Duplessis in September 1959. It is important to note the coincidence between the conception, and initial implementation of these reforms and the successful birth and early development of the independence movement. It is also useful to observe that the independence movement has grown in strength almost in step with the full implementation and experience of the consequences of these reforms.

Jane Jacobs, in her wise and perceptive book, *The Question of Separatism: Quebec and the Struggle over Sovereignty,* has described the independence movement as a political response to the decline of Montreal in Canadian economic affairs. She writes that since the beginning of the Second World War, the balance of economic strength has been shifting in Canada from Montreal to Toronto, with the latter becoming Canada's major economic centre. For the first time in post-Confederation Canada, a national economic centre has begun a decline toward the status of a regional city. The decline of Montreal has been relative to Toronto. The city itself has grown remarkably because of unprecedented rural out-migration. This migration has contributed significantly to the end of the rural-based culture of French Canada. In addition, according to Jacobs, the economic dislocation resulting from the decline of Montreal has put immense additional strains on Quebec's culture. The independence movement is seen then as a reaction to this dislocation and as a proposal for obtaining sufficient power to ensure that economic dislocation can be managed and eventually reversed. The proper use of this power is seen as essential if a distinctive cultural group is to remain in Quebec.

Such a view of the independence movement is in some respects similar to mine. The decline of Montreal as an economic centre is another side of the processes of concentration and centralization that caused concern among members of the francophone business class in the 1950s. I have described the end of the rural-based culture as a crisis affecting the traditional culture of French Canada and have shown how this crisis has been triggered largely by the growth of an urban proletariat. I have also discussed how these several changes have placed stress on the culture of the francophone community, almost to the breaking point in some respects. However Jacobs's treatment of the independence movement differs from the one proposed here in that she presents it as a more or less homogeneous group. In my view, it is a coalition of groups, each having a different interest in the attainment of political sovereignty. A failure to consider the economic orientations of these groups leads to an understatement of the class character of the movement. The discussion of both these points will help to clarify our understanding of the independence movement.

For those elements of the working class that support the goal of political independence, the reasons are mainly economic in character. In its initial support for the reforms of the early 1960s, organized labour saw these policies as a means to restore to the people of Quebec, particularly the francophone community, significant control over economic affairs. Such control, it was felt, was necessary to increase economic stability and job security. As the decade progressed, the workers' movement became less and less certain that its demands would be fully acted upon and that the desired effects would occur. At the end of the decade, Quebec was the subject of a renewed series of plant-shutdowns and layoffs. Many of the leaders of the workers' organizations attributed this continuation of disorder in the labour market to the fact that Quebec's economy remained underdeveloped and beyond the control of Québécois. Control over major natural resources remained sparse at best. Autocentric economic growth was a fiction. Many in the labour movement concluded that the control and will necessary for reversing the structure of underdevelopment would come only with political sovereignty. The capacity to formulate a global economic policy affecting external trade, capitalization, the restriction of foreign ownership, and the promotion of local initiatives would come only when full state powers were in the hands of Québécois.

The intelligentsia, which includes both academic intellectuals and members of the artistic communities, viewed the independence movement in different terms. Accustomed to setting the cultural norms and rules for the francophone community and accustomed to giving expression to the culture of the community in their works, these individuals experienced a decline in influence after 1945. The materialism and consumerism that came with the expansion of capitalism were built on values far different from those cherished by both conservative and radical wings of the intelligentsia. Its members sensed deeply this loss of control and felt that the increased gap it brought between them and the majority of the community would have nefarious consequences for the culture of the francophone community. The intelligentsia was also keenly aware that no new bases were being set in place for the culture of the community and that the community was therefore becoming less and less distinctive. It came to believe that only with sovereignty and the capacity to control communications and the diffusion of art that came with it could these trends be reversed.

Those in the middle classes – the traditional professions, public-sector white-collar workers, and teachers – also experienced a loss of control as the program of the 1960s developed. The social contexts in which they worked and the individuals and groups with which they dealt all seemed increasingly foreign to the values and heritage with which they had grown up. There was an ever-widening gap between their expectations about how community life in Quebec should be and how it actually was. With language reform, even words used became more antiseptic, technical, and less rooted in the old cultural values. Public-sector workers who had supervised the dismantling of the traditional institutions for education and for the delivery of social services saw themselves as having insufficient power for creating the institutions that would take their place. Continuing intervention by the federal government in higher education and manpower vocational training and the commitment by successive provincial governments to pursuit of the economic policies of the early 1960s placed constraints on the orientation and form the new educational institutions could assume. The capacity to influence matters at the federal level was not seen to be very significant. French was becoming a language of work in the federal public service only very slowly, and in many respects the federal bureaucracy continued to behave like the anglophone monolith it always had been. The ability to exercise complete power in the areas of educational, social, and cultural policy that would come with sovereignty appeared increasingly to those involved the only means for removing these constraints.

Each of these three groups therefore brought particular concerns and emphases to the demand for political independence. To be sure, each has had some influence over the other, so that the movement often behaves in a consistent way. The movement is given further unity by having an opponent in common – members of the business community, anglophone and francophone. The economic policies of the early 1960s and their subsequent amendments as described in chapter 4 did help foster a certain expansion in the number of francophones belonging to this class. The more successful these individuals became in their business dealings, the more they became interested in larger markets and ventures, the more they developed interests outside the province, and the less they were interested in a politically independent Quebec. Further, the more successful they became as capitalist, the more they found themselves supporting values held by other capitalists in North America. In becoming more open to the dominant economic values of North America, they became less likely to fear the cultural consequences of the policies of the Quiet Revolution period the way the other three social groups did.

Both francophones and anglophones in the capitalist class in Quebec have been overwhelmingly against independence. The CCPQ in particular has been consistently critical of the notion, commissioning special studies on its likely economic effects and dismissing it as 'sheer emotionalism.' Ironically, the growing ties between the francophone business community in Quebec and other business people in North America have been complemented by policies on language. The employer class now, whatever its ownership and whatever the mother tongue of its management, presents itself to consumers and workers in French. The language laws gave the capitalist class a certain homogeneity it did not have before and perhaps dampened the intensity of the critique of foreign control of the economy of Quebec. The linguistic homogeneity of the capitalist class is consistent with its unified and negative response to proposals for independence.

The debate over independence has often resolved itself into a struggle between economic classes, which gives it a particular intensity. The conflict over independence has been overdetermined, that is, economic, political, and ideological struggles have often been expressed in the context of this single issue. First, economic acts become by definition political acts, and vice versa. If workers strike a plant or protest a series of layoffs, these normally economic acts are often readily interpreted as political, as indicative of the need for independence. When independence comes, it is argued, the bosses will not be allowed to treat workers so badly. If Sun Life professes to make an economic decision to move its head offices or some of its personnel out of Quebec, it is at the same time attacking the nationalist PQ government. Any economic decision that may harm Quebec is interpreted as having political roots, as being taken to harm Quebec because its citizens are considering independence seriously. If a worker becomes active in the Parti québécois, he is affirming his opposition to his boss. If a business makes a donation to the Parti libéral or to a pro-federalist group, it is attacking the workers of Quebec. The political and the economic so interpenetrate each other that every area of social and economic life becomes a potential battleground for the struggle over independence.

Second, the class character of the struggle constrains the independence movement to be anti-capitalist. Because of the strong presence of the workers' movement in the independence coalition, this anti-capitalism has been expressed in the terminology of the left and not of the right. Since a socialist position aligns one against the capitalist class and the capitalist class is against independence, indépendantistes feel comfortable in espousing socialism. Even such traditionally conservative middle-class groups as the Mouvement national des Québécois and the SSJBM express themselves from time to time in a socialist idiom, using the language of imperialism developed by the left. Similarly, when for a short period in the mid-1970s the Jesuit journal *Relations* was espousing independence openly on its pages, it was doing so within a socialist perspective. Père Joseph-Papin Archambault must have shuddered in his grave. The overlaying of this ideological struggle on the independence movement gave it an added intensity. The one side views the struggle for independence as a struggle to end capitalist exploitation in Quebec, and the other sees it as an attempt to abolish free enterprise and to create Cuba north. Once in power, the Parti québécois had to work hard to convince business interests that its pursuit of sovereignty was not simultaneiously a struggle for socialism, so fixed together were the two notions in the eyes of the business class.

The class character of the independence issue has created particular problems for the Parti québécois as a government. I have shown in earlier chapters that the party continued the policies of previous governments by promoting continued integration into the North American economy and the growth of an indigenous capitalist class. As the governing party in a component of a capitalist state, it has felt pressures to pursue policies that benefit in the long run the capitalist class. The more successful the party is as a government in pursuing such policies, the more it strengthens groups fundamentally opposed to its primary objective. The party has worked quite well with the capitalist class in the province, much to the surprise of both. In doing so, it has created discontent within its own ranks and accentuated tensions between the leadership and the base of militants. At times, it appears to the membership that the Party as a government is working against its interests and objectives as a political movement. A certain degree of this tension may be derived from the class dimensions of the independence debate and the dominant position the capitalist class enjoys vis-à-vis the state.

You need not visit or live in Quebec for too long before one becomes aware of a certain distinctiveness and of a warm sense of community. After a little while, you can drive along the north shore of the St Lawrence and view its majesty with the perspective of four hundred years. You can marvel at the long and green splendour of the Île d'Orléans, and walking around this island from Sainte-Pétronille to Saint-Jean and on to Saint-Pierre the songs of Félix Leclerc ring in your mind and you can finally understand the anger he expresses when he senses it all might soon be gone. There are the rocking chairs as well – a slow, meandering drive through the Beauce on a Sunday afternoon in the summer shows you families gathered on front porches and older people quietly rocking in their chairs. In other environs, the cold brutality and the mills in Louiseville and in Magog call to mind the strikes and zeal of the CTCC during the 1950s. You can read the novels, reflect on the poetry, submerse yourself in the music. You can join the crowds on the Fête nationale, sing the songs, maybe even wave a flag. There is a culture, a way of life, a particular approach to doing things and viewing the world in Quebec. The 1978 white paper on cultural development captured it well when it spoke of the originality of Quebec as an 'inner quality,' something that can be sensed.

Nevertheless, inner qualities do not arise from nowhere and do not last forever if they are not supported by social institutions. They develop over time and are transferred from generation to generation in an infinite number of ways. In particular, they are fostered and supported by institutions that have themselves developed slowly and adapted in countless ways over many years. In the rather short period from 1945 to the mid-1970s, because of a whole series of pressures about which we have spoken, many of these long-established institutions in Quebec were changed in fundamental ways. The changes were made to integrate the economic activity of the francophone community fully into North American capitalism and to create an economic culture facilitative of that activity. To a significant degree, this integration has taken place and that economic culture has been formed. For certain groups of people in a variety of different settings, these changes are sensed to be contradicting that inner quality of what it means to be a Québécois and what the future might be for the Québécois. There is a gnawing fear that this feeling, this sense of self, might soon no longer be passed on to the young because the institutional framework within which the young live will contradict and undermine that inner spirit. It is, in my view, this fear, this sense of impending loss, that is uniting many in a struggle for independence. The hope is that with full political power, the offending institutions can be taken in hand and reordered. In this sense, there is a certain similarity between the proposals of the indépendantistes of today and those nationalists of the Tremblay Commission almost three decades ago.

One can also sense, however, that it is getting late. The leading proponent of independence, the Parti québécois, has increasingly weakened its demands for political independence without economic independence. It assumes that the common economic institutions now in place in Canada must be retained in the new nation-state and that a common economic culture with North America will be a foundation of that state. Jane Jacobs has asked whether such a policy is wise. She suggests that the future of the francophone nation in Quebec will depend upon its capacity to erect its own economic institutions on its own terms. Her advice today was long ago the advice of the Tremblay Commission and no so long ago that of the RIN. An independent and distinctive culture must rest upon an independent economy.

This study has demonstrated that there is a certain validity to this assumption. As Quebec's francophone community has come to participate more fully in the continental economy, its culture has become more similar to others active in that economy. In the view of many, this has led to a situation where that inner quality burning in the hearts of Québécois will soon be extinguished. If this does happen, then the nationalist movement in Quebec will have failed and may itself die.

Notes

Introduction

1 See Hubert Guindon 'The Social Evolution of Quebec Reconsidered' *Canadian Journal of Economics and Political Science* XXVI (November 1960) 553–61; 'Social Unrest, Social Class and Quebec's Bureaucratic Revolution' *Queen's Quarterly* LXXI (summer 1964) 150–62; 'Two Cultures: An Essay on Nationalism, Class and Ethnic Tensions' in R. Leach ed *Contemporary Canada* (Durham, NC, 1967); Charles Taylor 'Nationalism and the Political Intelligentsia: A Case Study' *Queen's Quarterly* LXXII (spring 1965) 150–68; Kenneth McRoberts and Dale Posgate *Quebec: Social Change and Political Crisis* (Toronto 1976). For a recent analysis of events based on this hypothesis by French-Canadian political scientists, see G. Bergeron and R. Pelletier ed *Le Québec en devenir* (Montreal 1980).

2 The provincial government administered a series of vocational schools and technical colleges. These were attached to different government departments, such as Agriculture, Lands and Forests, Mines, and the Provincial Secretary.

3 Thus the various classical colleges were not integrated systematically into any network. It was not until 1953 that the Fédération des collèges classiques was formed to represent their interests. It was set up to defend the collèges in the face of increasing criticism in the post-war period and to put more pressure on the provincial government to provide them with adequate grants. Duplessis had, to a certain degree, administered grants to individual collèges on a patronage basis.

4 Frère Untel was the pseudonym used by a teaching brother, Jean-Paul Desbiens, who wrote a scathing critique of the church's role in education in Quebec. The critique began with a letter to *Le Devoir* in 1959. André Laurendeau, then editor of the paper, invited Untel to elaborate on his letter. The series of criticisms was

then published in a book entitled *Les Insolences du Frère Untel* (Montreal 1960). The book became a best seller, with over one hundred thousand copies being sold. The book was not greeted warmly by the church hierarchy or by Untel's superiors. He was sent on a study trip to Europe shortly thereafter.

5   McRoberts and Posgate *Quebec* 102

6   Enrolment in the social sciences in francophone universities remained between 400 and 500 students throughout the 1950s. In 1958–9, 423 students were enrolled. After that year, the numbers began to increase steadily. By 1964, the figure had almost tripled, to 1,293; Canada, DBS, *Survey of Higher Education* Catalogues 81–402, 81–518, 81–211.

7   See Gérard Lapointe *Essais sur la fonction publique québécoise,* Documents of the Royal Commission on Bilingualism and Biculturalism, No. 12 (Ottawa 1970).

8   Jean-Louis Roy *La Marche des Québécois: le temps des ruptures 1945–1960* (Montreal 1976) 256

9   For example, Jean Marchand, secretary general of the CTCC during the 1950s and president 1961–5, and Marcel Pépin, Marchand's successor, were both educated at the Faculty of Social Sciences at Université Laval.

10   Roy *La Marche* 325

11   This is a point made by Dorval Brunelle. See his book *La Désillusion tranquille* (Montreal 1978) 79–80.

12   Guindon 'The Social Evolution'

13   See Jean-Louis Roy *Les Programmes électoraux du Quebec* II (Montreal 1971) 378–88.

14   François-Albert Angers 'Éditorial' *L'Action nationale* L no 1 (1960) 9–10

15   *Ibid*

16   This approach is most fully developed in a series of studies sponsored by the Comparative Politics Committee of the Social Science Research Council in the United States. Prominent contributors in this series were Leonard Binder, James S. Coleman, Joseph LaPalombara, Lucien Pye, Dankwart Rustow, Sidney Verba, Robert E. Ward, and Myron Weiner. Gabriel Almond was an important early inspiration to this group. The series was published by Princeton University Press.

17   See for example the studies by Horace Miner, *St.-Denis, A French Canadian Parish* (Chicago 1939), and Everett Hughes, *French Canada in Transition* (Chicago 1945).

18   These influences are particularly evident in the earlier works of Marcel Rioux and to a lesser extent those of Jean-Charles Falardeau. The use of the concept of a folk society was the subject of an academic debate in Quebec in the 1950s, with the chief protagonists being Marcel Rioux and Philippe Garigue, then dean of the Faculty of Social Sciences at the Université de Montréal. For a flavour of

this debate, see Marcel Rioux, 'Remarques sur les valeurs et les attitudes des adolescents d'une communauté agricole du Québec' *Contributions à l'étude des sciences de l'homme* no 3 (1956) 133–143; 'Kinship Recognition and Urbanization in French Canada' in Rioux and Y. Martin ed *French Canadian Society* (Toronto 1964); 'Remarks on the Socio-Cultural Development of French Canada' in ibid; Philippe Garigue 'Change and Continuity in French Canada' in ibid; 'Mythes et réalités dans l'étude du Canada français' *Contributions à l'étude des sciences de l'homme* no 3 (1956) 123–32.

19 Roy *La marche* part I

20 For a useful examination of the Chambre de Commerce de la Province de Québec, see Monique Odstricil 'La Chambre de Commerce de la Province de Québec, 1935–1970: Une étude d'un groupe de pression,' MA thesis, Carleton University, 1974.

21 The Rassemblement was a group founded in 1956 with the object of educating the people of Quebec about democracy. It sought to be above party politics, although its major goal was the end of the rule of Duplessis. Trudeau and Marchand were prominent figures in the group.

22 For example, the following quotation is drawn from the 1962 platform of the PLQ: 'Le peuple du Québec a confiance, comme ont confiance *toutes* les nations jeunes qui, un jour, ont résolu de s'affirmer ... Pour la première fois dans son histoire, le peuple du Québec peut devenir maître chez lui! L'époque du colonialisme économique est révolue. Nous marchons vers la libération! Maintenant ou jamais! MAÎTRES CHEZ NOUS!!!'

23 This hypothesis is developed in Brunelle *La Désillusion tranquille*.

24 Ibid 102

25 Gilles Bourque and Anne Legaré *Le Québec: La question nationale* (Paris 1979)

26 This class in terms of its definition is very similar to the entity that is at the centre of Brunelle's analysis.

27 Trudeau and Pelletier founded *Cité libre* in 1950 and in the early years of the journal wrote several articles critical of the church. Marchand, at this time, was general secretary of the CTCC and Pelletier, editor of the newspaper *Le Travail,* published weekly by the CTCC. Trudeau served some time as a researcher for another labour organization, the Fédération des unions industrielles du Québec, a fact that is less well known.

28 Quebec, Royal Commission of Inquiry on Constitutional Problems *Report* (Quebec 1956). The commission was headed by Judge Thomas Tremblay.

1 Underdevelopment in a dependent economy

1 See Michel Brunet *Les Canadiens après la conquête, 1759–1775* (Montreal 1969).

2   This usage is found in both Samir Amin *Accumulation on a World Scale: A Critique of the Theory of Underdevelopment* trans Brian Pearce (New York 1974) and in Arghiri Emmanuel *Unequal Exchange: A Study of the Imperialism of Trade* (New York 1975).

3   Glen Williams 'Canada: The Case of the Wealthiest Colony' *This Magazine* x No. 1 (1976) 28–32

4   Wallace Clement *Continental Corporate Power: Economic Linkages between Canada and the United States* (Toronto 1977)

5   Leo Panitch 'Dependency and Class in Canadian Political Economy' *Studies in Political Economy* No. 6 (autumn 1981) 7–33

6   *Ibid* 23

7   Susanne Bodenheimer 'Dependency and Imperialism: The Roots of Latin American Underdevelopment' *Politics and Society* I (May 1971) 327–58

8   Dale L. Johnson 'On Oppressed Classes' in James D. Cockcroft, André Gunder Frank, and Dale L. Johnson ed *Dependence and Underdevelopment: Latin American's Political Economy* (Garden City, NY, 1972) 283

9   Teotonio dos Santos writes that dependency is a 'situation in which the economy of a certain group of economies is conditioned by the development and expansion of another economy, to which their own (economy) is subjected; … an historical condition which shapes a certain structure of the world economy such that it favours some countries to the detriment of others, and limits the development possibilities of the (subordinate) economies'; cited in Bodenheimer 'Dependency and Imperialism' 331.

10 André Gunder Frank argues that development should not be equated with industrial growth but 'involves a structural transformation of the economy, society, polity and culture of the satellite that permits the self-generating and self-perpetuating use and development of the people's potential'; Frank 'Introduction' in *Dependence and Underdevelopment* xvi.

11 Amin *Accumulation* Introduction

12 Kent Trachte 'Unequal Exchange: A Mode of Global Exploitation?' paper prepared for presentation at the International Studies Association Convention, 22 March 1980, Los Angeles, 49ff

13 Amin *Accumulation* 15

14 Ibid 262–70

15 Ibid 15–16

16 The theory and practice of the staple concept were most extensively developed by Harold Innis in a series of works on fur, fish, and other Canadian staples. See his *The Fur Trade in Canada: An Introduction to Canadian Economic History* 2nd edn (Toronto 1956); *The Cod Fisheries: The History of an International Economy* 2nd edn (Toronto 1954); and *Essays in Canadian Economic History* ed Mary Q. Innis (Toronto 1957). A recent critique of the use of staple theory was made by David McNally 'Staple Theory as Commodity Fetishism: Marx,

Innis and Canadian Political Economy' *Studies in Political Economy* No. 6 (autumn 1981) 35–63.

17 This is precisely the issue that was debated in the late 1960s in connection with the wheat staple in Canada. Edward J. Chambers and Donald F. Gordon argued that the production of wheat in the years 1900–11, the supposed boom period for the resource, was not sufficiently important to count wheat as a staple. See their article 'Primary Products and Economic Growth: An Empirical Measurement' *Journal of Political Economy* LXXIV (August 1966) 315–32. Their argument was attacked on two fronts. First, on theoretical grounds, see John H. Dales, John C. McManus, and Melville H. Watkins 'Primary Products and Economic Growth: A Comment' ibid LXXV (December 1967) 876–80. Second, on empirical grounds, see Dwight Grant 'The Staple Theory and Its Empirical Measurement' ibid LXXXII (December 1974) 1249–53.

18 Innis *The Fur Trade* 384

19 Melville H. Watkins 'A Staple Theory of Economic Growth' in W.T. Easterbrook and Watkins ed *Approaches to Canadian Economic History* (Toronto 1967) 33–57

20 *Ibid* 53

21 Innis points out that Canadian politicians have tended to overcome depressions by shifting export bases. He shows that each time a crisis occurred their capital imports served to tap fresh natural resources. Further they have 'extended the life' of staples by improving such infrastructure as transportation systems. See his essay, 'Government Ownership and the Canadian Scene' *Essays in Canadian Economic History* 78–96.

22 Ibid 94–6

23 Richard J. Barnet and Ronald E. Muller *Global Reach: The Power of Multinational Corporations* (New York 1974) 14

24 'The central thesis of our argument is that the subsidiaries and branch plants of large American-based multinational corporations have replaced the operations of the earlier European-based mercantile venture companies in extracting the staple and organizing the supply of manufactured goods ... It [the corporation] organizes the collection or extraction of the raw material staple required in the metropolis and supplies the hinterland with manufactured goods, whether produced at home or "on site" in the host country'; Kari Levitt *Silent Surrender* (Toronto 1970) 23–4.

25 For example, of the 1,851 top managerial positions in American companies having large foreign operations, only 1.6 per cent were held by non-Americans. Most major multinational corporations still have their major assets and sales in the home market; Canada *Foreign Direct Investment in Canada* (Ottawa 1972) 57. For an opposing argument, see J.K. Galbraith *Economics and the Public Purpose* (New York 1973) chap 17.

26 'Rigidity in prices tends to be strengthened by increasing dependence on the

United States in eastern Canada ... Producers of staple exports subject to wide fluctuations are penalized by the increasing rigidities which accompany the increasing importance of the United States. Unorganized groups of labour in the industrial areas are squeezed between the depressed income of exporters of raw materials and rigidity of prices, as the evidence of unemployment and sweated labour has shown'; 'Labour in Canadian Economic History' *Essays in Canadian Economic History,* 297.

27   Barnet and Muller *Global Reach* chap 2.

28   The Orion Bank is an international consortium organized by the following institutions: the Chase Manhattan Bank, National Westminster Bank, Royal Bank of Canada, Westdeutsche Landesbank Girozentral, Credite Italiana, and Nikho Securities (Japan).

29   Canada *Foreign Direct Investment* 47–50

30   André Raynauld *La Propriété des entreprises au Québec* (Montreal 1974) 44ff

31   Canada, Dominion Bureau of Statistics (DBS) *Iron Ore* Catalogue #26–005, 1960

32   Canada, DBS, Asbestos *Catalogue* #25–004, 1955

33   André Raynauld *Croissance et structures économiques de la Province de Québec* (Quebec 1961) Table 40

34   Canada, DBS *Canada Year Book* for 1955

35   Amin *Accumulation* 287

36   Raynauld *Croissance* Table 40

37   Ibid

38   Figures are based on calculations from Table 12 *Canada Year Book* for 1953, 944–5.

39   M.A. MacNaughton, J.M. Mann, and M.B. Blackwood *Farm Family Living in Nicolet County, 1947–48* (Ottawa 1950)

40   W.E. Haviland 'The Family Farm in Quebec – An Economic or Sociological Unit' *Canadian Journal of Agricultural Economics* v No. 2 (1957) 82

41   These are collected together in Gerald Fortin *La Fin d'un règne* (Montreal 1971).

42   For evidence of this orientation, see M.-Adélard Tremblay and Gérald Fortin 'Enquête sur les conditions de vie de la famille canadienne française: l'univers des besoins' *Recherches sociographiques* IV no. 1 (1963) 9–116; 'Enquête sur les conditions de vie de la famille canadienne française: l'univers des aspirations' ibid IV no. 3 (1963); and *Les Comportements économiques de la famille salariée du Québec* (Quebec 1964).

43   Tremblay and Fortin *Les Comportements économiques* chap 12

2 Catholic social thought and traditional French-Canadian culture

1   The themes chosen for sessions of the semaines sociales also enjoyed the approval of the ecclesiastical hierarchy. At most sessions, one finds Paul-Émile Cardinal

Léger, archbishop of Montreal, Maurice Cardinal Roy, archbishop of Quebec, a majority of the province's bishops, the provincials of the Jesuit, Dominican, and Oblate orders, and so on.

2 The ISP ceased actively publishing in 1957. The semaines sociales continued to meet annually until 1960. After that, it met twice more, in 1962 and 1964.

3 Justification for this approach may also be found in the article by R. Laliberté, 'Dix huit ans de corporatisme militant. L'École social populaire de Montréal, 1933–1950' *Recherches sociographiques* XXI no 1–2 (1980) 55–96.

4 See, for example, Esdras Minville *Le Citoyen canadien-français* (Montreal 1946) and 'L'aspect économique du problème national canadien-français' *Institut social populaire* no 432 (September 1950).

5 Quebec, Royal Commission of Inquiry on Constitutional Problems *Report* (hereafter Tremblay Report) II (Quebec 1956) 8

6 Ibid 6

7 For questions on the extensiveness of the church's involvement, see Gérard Pelletier 'Crise d'autorité ou crise de liberté' *Cité libre* no 2 (June – July) 1–10. Arès presents his views in the following series of articles: 'Le problème de l'anticléricalisme au Canada français' *Relations* no 143 (November 1952) 282–5; 'Anti-cléricalisme et sens de l'Église' ibid no 144 (December 1952) 310–14; 'Le sur-naturel est lui-même charnel' ibid no 145 (January 1953) 3–6; 'Mission de l'Église et ordre temporel' ibid no 146 (February 1953) 33–6.

8 The vehemence of the critique of capitalism varied depending on the spokesman. A particularly harsh critic was Mgr Philippe Desranleau, archbishop of Sherbrooke. For example, see the following statement: 'C'est ce capitalisme qui est la cause de toutes nos misères. Nous devons travailler contre, non pas pour le transformer, il est intransformable; non pas pour le corriger, il est incorrigeable, mais pour le remplacer'; *Le Travail* (September 1949).

9 For Marcel Clément, see his article 'Association du travail et du capital' *Les Semaines sociales du Canada,* 1949. Also see Richard Arès, SJ, 'Capitalisme, syndicalisme et organisation professionnelle' *L'Institut social populaire* no 463 (April 1953).

10 The more liberal position on this issue, favouring the workers, is found in the proceedings of the Sacerdotal Commission on Social Issues. This commission was created by the bishops in Quebec and included mainly chaplains attached to labour unions or Catholic Action groups. See Commission sacerdotale d'études sociales *La Participation des travailleurs à la vie de l'entreprise* (Montreal 1947). In contrast, a very conservative position is found in E. Bouvier, SJ, *Patrons et ouvriers* (Montreal 1951).

11 This is a quotation from a 'course' on the state published in the agricultural newspaper *La Terre de chez nous* 2 March 1949.

12 Jean-Charles Falardeau 'Réflexions sur nos classes sociales' *La Nouvelle Revue canadienne* L no 3 (1951) 3

13 The CTCC later became the Confédération des syndicats nationaux or Confederation of National Trade Unions (CNTU).

14 The UCC evolved into the present-day organization called the Union des producteurs agricoles.

15 The API changed its name in the 1960s to the Centre des dirigeants d'entreprise (CDE) and the CIIQ developed into the present-day Centrale de l'enseignement du Québec (CEQ).

16 Ligue ouvrière canadienne 'Dix ans au service des foyers ouvriers – Manifeste de la L.O.C. à l'occasion de son dixième anniversaire (1939–1949)' *L'École sociale populaire* no 425 (June 1949)

17 This journal has subsequently had several names, most recently being titled *Prêtres et laïcs*.

18 In 1961, there remained about 2,760 locals of Catholic Action in Quebec, embracing about 28,000 militants. Of this number, about two-thirds were students and one-quarter were workers. By 1970, there were only 3,000 militants left; Commission d'étude sur les laïcs et l'Église (Commission Dumont) *L'Église du Québec: un héritage, un projet* (Montreal 1971) 210. The LOC folded in the mid-1960s and was succeeded by the Mouvement des travailleurs chrétiens.

19 See Jean-Charles Falardeau 'The Role and Importance of the Church in French Canada' in Marcel Rioux and Yves Martin *French Canadian Society* Carleton Library (Toronto 1964). Hamelin and Hamelin in a study of the church in the Trois-Rivières area in the early 1950s found that sons of farmers formed the largest block of the clergy. They also noted some evidence that this was beginning to change. See L.-Émond Hamelin and Colette L. Hamelin 'Réflexions sur la structure sociale de l'église trifluvienne' *Ad Usum Sacerdotum* XI no 3 (1955) 70–9.

20 A frank discussion of this failure is found in Wilfrid Gariépy, SJ, 'La paroisse urbaine' *Semaines sociales* (1953) 76–97.

21 Gérard Pelletier 'D'un prolétariat spririituel' *Esprit* XX nos 193–4 (1952) 196

22 See for example the study 'Une paroisse ouvrière de Montréal entreprend de mieux connaître sa communauté humaine' *Prêtres et laïcs* XVIII (October 1968) 382–97.

23 Cited in Louis-P. Audet *Bilan de la réforme scolaire au Québec, 1959–1969* (Montreal 1969) 14

24 For a discussion of the particular traits of the Anglo-Catholic system, see Bernard Lefebvre *L'École sous la mitre* (Montreal 1980).

25 For the argument, see Marcel Marcotte, SJ, 'Les droits de l'État dans l'éducation' *Relations* no 218 (June 1958) 145–8.

26 La Fédération des collèges classiques, Mémoire presented to the Tremblay Commission, 4 June 1954

27 L'Association canadienne des éducateurs de la langue française (Acelf) *L'Éducation patriotique* (Quebec 1957) 6

28 Richard Arès, sJ, *Notre question nationale* III: *Positions patriotiques* (Montreal 1947) 117

29 For this argument, see Charles Bilodeau 'Education in Quebec' *University of Toronto Quarterly* XXVII no 3 (1958) 411

30 See Louis-P. Audet and A. Gauthier *Le Système scolaire au Québec* (Montreal 1969) chap 4 and Lefebvre *L'École, passim.*

31 Lefebvre *L'École* 29

32 This option was chosen by Québécois more often than residents of any other province prior to 1960. See, for example, the figures cited in La Commission royale d'enquête sur l'enseignement (Parent Commission) *Le Rapport* v (Quebec 1966) 17.

33 For a comprehensive discussion of the early history of the colleges, see Claude Galarneau *Les Collèges classiques au Canada français* (Montreal 1978).

34 Ibid 66

35 FCC Mémoire to the Tremblay Commission, 1954

36 Galarneau *Les Collèges classiques* 150

37 For a presentation and discussion of these arguments, see Arthur Tremblay, *Contribution à l'étude des problèmes et des besoins de l'enseignement dans la province de Québec* Annexe 4, Tremblay Report, 1955, 202ff.

38 FCC Mémoire to the Tremblay Commission, 93

39 Lefebvre *L'École* 103

40 Frère Untel *Les Insolences de Frère Untel* (Montreal 1960). Untel, as we shall learn in chapter 6, was a particularly biting critic of the church's administration of education in Quebec. He was a teaching brother who came to prominence after a series of letters published in *Le Devoir* in 1959.

41 Galarneau *Les Collèges classiques* 66

42 Ibid 111

43 For elaboration on this point, see F.-A. Angers *La Sécurité sociale et les problèmes constitutionnels* Annexe 3, Tremblay Report 123–45.

44 Quoted in ibid 138

45 A useful discussion of the history of the social assistance system is found in Gonsalve Poulin *L'Assistance sociale dans la province de Québec, 1608-1951* Annexe 2, Tremblay Report.

3 The Tremblay Commission

1 Quote taken from the order-in-council creating the royal commission, 8 April 1949, and reprinted in the Royal Commission on National Development in the Arts, Letters and Sciences, *Report* (Massey Report) (Ottawa 1951) xi

2 Massey Report 4

3 La Chambre de Commerce du District de Montréal (CCM), Brief presented to the Massey Commission, 1949, 26

4 'Éditorial: Le Rapport de la Commission Massey' *Relations* no 127 (July 1951) 169–70

5 Figures reported in Massey Report 141. The commission did not examine separately the universities in English and French Canada. The lower relative proportion of francophones qualifying as veterans might have lessened the crisis for French-language universities.

6 Ibid 6

7 Ibid

8 Ibid 8

9 For this argument, see chapter 12 in ibid, 132–6.

10 I use the word 'mainly' here consciously because there were some individuals supporting the proposals. See for example the article 'L'aide fédérale aux universités,' in the progressive clerical journal *Ad Usum Sacerdotum* VII no 2 (1951). Also see the article 'Le Rapport Massey' by Jean-Pierre Houle in *La Nouvelle Revue canadienne* I no 5 (1951) 1–8.

11 Richard Arès, SJ, 'Avant et après le Rapport de la Commission Massey' *L'Institut social populaire* no 488 (November 1951)

12 'Considérations en marge du Mémoire de la Chambre de Commerce du District de Montréal soumis à la Commission Massey en relation avec l'aide financière que le gouvernement a l'intention d'apporter aux universités canadiennes' Procès-Verbaux du Conseil d'Administration, 1951, CCM Documents

13 Angers was named to the Commission générale in 1955.

14 A useful discussion of the origins of this crisis is found in Donald V. Smiley *Constitutional Adaptation and Canadian Federalism since 1945*, Documents of the Royal Commission in Bilingualism and Biculturalism, No. 4 (Ottawa 1970).

15 F.-A. Angers 'La Chambre de Commerce et les Relations fédérales-provinciales' *Relations* no 115 (July 1950) 190–3; 'Comment la centralisation progresse' *L'Action nationale* XL no 3 (1952) 191–206

16 Angers 'L'Ontario a signé!' ibid no 2 (1952) 159

17 These demands are contained in the CCPQ document 'Relations fédérales-provinciales en matière d'impôts: Opinion officielle de la chambre' CCM Documents, 1952–3.

18 For his initial reluctance see René Durocher et Michèle Jean 'Duplessis et la Commission royale d'enquête sur les problèmes constitutionnels' *La Revue d'histoire de l'Amérique français* XXV no 3 (1971) 341.

19 Ibid 348

20 Act to institute a Royal Commission of Inquiry on Constitutional Problems, *Statutes of Quebec* 1–2 Elizabeth II, chap 4, 1953

21 Biculturalism was central to the charge of the Royal Commission on Bilingualism

and Biculturalism of the 1960s. 'Dualism' figured prominently in the report of
the Task Force on Canadian Unity in the late 1970s. 'D'égal à égal' was a
pivotal concept used by the Parti québécois in its white paper, *Quebec-Canada:
A New Deal*, on sovereignty-association in the 1980 referendum.

22 Durocher and Jean 'Duplessis' 342
23 A fifth volume (titled volume IV) was a compendium of statistics.
24 Durocher and Jean 'Duplessis' 342
25 See, in particular, E. Minville *Le Citoyen canadien-frànàis* (Montreal 1946);
    'L'Aspect économique du problème national canadien français' *L'Institut social
    populaire* no 432 (September 1950). Minville's writings are being collected and
    edited by the publisher Fides. The first volume is *L'Économie du Québec et la
    science économique* (Montreal 1979).
26 Durocher and Jean 'Duplessis' 351
27 Arès's major work on nationalism has been published in five volumes in two
    periods. The first three volumes appeared under the title *Notre Question nationale*
    – volume I, *Les faits*, appeared in 1943, volume II, *Positions de principes,* in
    1945, and volume III, *Positions patriotiques et nationales,* in 1947, all published
    by Les Éditions de l'Action nationale in Montreal. The remaining two volumes
    appeared thrity years later. *Nos Grandes Options politiques et constitutionnelles*
    appeared in 1972, and *L'Église et les projets d'avenir du peuple canadien
    français,* in 1974, both published by Les Éditions Bellarmin in Montreal.
28 Durocher and Jean 'Duplessis' 342
29 Ibid 341
30 Royal Commission of Inquiry on Constitutional Problems (RCICP) *Report* II
    (Quebec 1956) 15
31 Ibid 16
32 Ibid 21
33 Ibid I (Quebec 1956) 36ff
34 Ibid 38
35 Ibid 40
36 Ibid II 36
37 The commissioners speak of a possible federal government with institutions that
    always take account of Canada's duality, where English and French are on an
    equal footing, where French can be used by all francophones no matter where
    they live in Canada, where all publications are bilingual, where competent
    French Canadians are an important component of the public service, etc. How-
    ever, they do not appear to have believed such changes very likely and proceed
    accordingly. See ibid 76–8.
38 Ibid 71
39 Ibid III (Quebec 1956) book I 323
40 Ibid III book II 230

41   RCICP, Annexe 5, F.-A. Angers *Le Problème fiscal et les relations fédérales-provinciales*, and Annexe 11, *La Centralisation et les relations fédérales-provinciales*. Angers wrote a third report that also was used extensively in another area, Annexe 3, *La Sécurité sociale et les problèmes constitutionnels*.
42   See for example his article 'La Chambre de Commerce et les relations fédérales-provinciales.'
43   Angers 'Le Canada français face à l'A.A.B.N.' in *L'État du Québec* (St-Hyacinthe 1962) 101
44   RCICP *Report* III book II 234
45   Claude Morin 'La famille a droit à la justice distributive et à la sécurité sociale' *Semaines sociales du Canada* (1959) 166–89
46   See RCICP *Report* II part IV chap 7, 225–50.
47   This was the class most directly affected by the new industrial institutions of 'British origin' selected for study by the commission. These were also the people furthest away from the control of the traditional institutions of French Canada, as we have seen in chapter 2.
48   RCICP *Report* II 72
49   Guy Rocher *Le Québec en mutation* (Montreal 1973) 20
50   RCICP *Report* II 74
51   Frank R. Scott 'The Constitutional Background of Taxation Agreements' *McGill Law Journal* 2 No 1 (1955) 1–10
52   RCICP *Report* III book II 29
53   Ibid 32
54   Ibid 40
55   The SCER was founded in 1946 under church auspices to promote increased settlement in rural areas. It, in turn, helped found the Société d'études rurales in 1951 to explore the directives of the church on rural life. The SCER appeared to follow an earlier body, the Société nationale de colonisation, founded in 1920 by the Société Saint-Jean-Baptiste de Montréal (SSJBM). Members of the SER were Albert Rioux, former head of the Union Catholique des cultivateurs (UCC) and a Duplessis cabinet minister; Mgr Paul-Émile Gosselin, secretary of the Conseil de la vie française; Mgr Félix-A. Savard; Arès; Dominique Beaudin, writer for *L'Action nationale* and former editor of the UCC paper *La Terre de Chez Nous;* Marcel Clément; C.-E. Couture; and Georges-Noël Fortin.

4 Economic policy: A road to independence?

1   See, for example, Jean-Marc Léger 'Pour sortir du mensonge' *L'Action nationale* XLIV nos 3–4 (1954) 376.
2   See the editorial 'Une mise au point' in ibid XL no 2 (1952) 85–7, which was a response to an article by Léger, 'Le rendez-vous des illusions' in ibid XL no 1 (1952) 47–54.

3   Gilles Bourque and Anne Legaré *Le Québec: la question nationale* (Paris 1979) chap 7

4   Everett C. Hughes and Margaret L. McDonald 'French and English in the Economic Structure of Montreal' *Canadian Journal of Economics and Political Science* VII (November 1941) 493–505; Roger Vézina 'La position des Canadiens-français dans l'industrie et le commerce' *Culture* XV (September 1954) 291–9; André Raynauld *La Propriété des entreprises au Québec* (Montreal 1974) 46

5   See, in particular, J. Melançon 'Retard de croissance de l'entreprise canadienne-française' *L'Actualité économique* 31 (January–March 1956) 503–22.

6   *Le Bulletin de la SSJBM* VII no 4 (1958) 2; Pierre Laporte 'Soyons riches, ou nous périrons' *L'Action nationale* XLVI no 1 (1956) 33

7   See *Le Bulletin* VII no 6 (1958) 1.

8   Ibid V no 1 (1956) 5

9   SSJBM *Canada français et Union canadienne* (Montreal 1954) 110

10 Jean-Louis Roy *Les Programmes électoraux au Québec* II (Montreal 1971) 369

11 Further discussion of Corpex and similar efforts may be found in Dorval Brunelle *La Désillusion tranquille* (Montreal 1978).

12 For an early elaboration of this proposal, see CCPQ, Brief presented to the provincial government, October 1959.

13 Brunelle *La Désillusion* 105

14 The Fédération des travailleurs du Québec was founded in 1957 as a result of a merger between the Fédération du travail de Québec (AFL) and the Fédération des unions industrielles du Québec (CIO).

15 These figures were adapted from Dominion Bureau of Statistics (DBS), *Iron Ore* Catalogue 26–005, 1957–61.

16 B. Brouillette 'Le minérai de fer au Canada' *L'Actualité économique* XXXVI no 1 (1961) 68–104

17 For the Eaton proposal, see Conrad Black *Duplessis* (Toronto 1977); Mgr N.-A. Labrie 'Les matières premières de la Côte-Nord doivent rester à la Côte-Nord pour le bénéfice de notre province' *École sociale populaire* no 422 (1949).

18 *La Réforme* 13 April 1955 3

19 F.-A. Angers 'Le problème économique au Canada français' *L'Action nationale* XLIX no 3 (1959) 173

20 *Relations* Éditorial: 'Du rôle de l'état' (December 1959) 311

21 Commission sacerdotale d'études sociales *La Participation des travailleurs à la vie de l'entreprise* (Montreal 1947)

22 Ibid 13

23 On this letter and related issues, see S.H. Barnes 'Quebec Catholicism and Social Change' *Review of Politics* XXIII (1961) 52–76; 'The Evolution of Christian Trade Unionism in Quebec' *Industrial and Labour Relations Review* XII (1959) 568–81.

24   CTCC, Congrès annuel *Procès-Verbal 1957* Resolution #29; *Proces-Verbal 1958* Resolution #45

25   CTCC *Procès-Verbal 1958*. For a discussion of the implementation of this principle, see Louis-Marie Tremblay *Le Syndicalisme québécois* (Montreal 1972) 58ff.

26   For an indication of the conservative argument, see F.-A. Angers 'Les évènements' *L'Action nationale* L no 1 (1960) 74–7; Alfred Charpentier 'Un enseignement méconnu' *Relations* no 225 (1959) 232–4; *Le Devoir* 12 August 1959 for a report on the brief of Les Anciens Aumôniers.

27   Paul-Émile Léger 'Lettre pastorale: Nos responsabilités chrétiennes en face du chômage' *Relations industrielles* XIV no 1 (1959)

28   CCPQ, Mémoire soumis au Ministère de l'Industrie et du Commerce et au Ministère des Richesses naturelles, 23 May 1961

29   Reported in *La Réforme* 10 June 1961

30   René Paré 'La Société générale de financement' *L'Action nationale* LI no 4 (1961) 303–10

31   Pope John XXIII *Mater et Magistra* in *The Encyclicals and Other Messages of John XXIII* (Washington, DC, 1964) 265

32   Ibid 312

33   These difficulties are described in Jacques Parizeau 'De certaines manoeuvres d'un syndicat financier en vue de conserver son empire au Québec' *Le Devoir* 2 February 1970; Richard Brunelle et Pierre Papineau 'Le Gouvernement du Capital' *Socialisme québécois* no 23 (1972) 106ff.

34   CCPQ *Politiques d'action 1975* (Montreal 1975) 161

35   Québec 'Loi concernant les sociétés de développement de l'entreprise québécoise et modifiant la Loi sur les impôts '*Lois du Québec,* 1976, chap 33 sec 12

36   The most important of these papers was Ministère de l'industrie et du commerce 'Une politique économique québécoise; Document de travail' 28 January 1974. Also see Québec, Développement économique *Bâtir le Québec: Énoncé de politique économique* (Québec 1979).

37   Quebec, Executive Council *A Quebec Policy on Foreign Investment: Report of the Interdepartmental Task Force on Foreign Investment* (Quebec 1973)

38   MIC 'Une politique économique' 33

39   Québec *Bâtir* 4

40   On this continuity, see also Brunelle '"Bâtir le Québec": continuité et apologie' *Le Devoir* 22 October 1979.

41   See Le Parti québécois *Programme 1971* (Montreal 1971) 7; *Programme 1973,* (Montreal 1973) 11; *Programme 1975* (Montreal 1975) 12.

42   Québec *Bâtir* 72

43   'Sobey devient le plus gros actionnaire de Provigo' *Le Devoir* 24 August 1979

44   See also Reed Scowen 'La politicisation de la Caisse de dépôts et de placements' *Le Devoir* 29 July 1980.

45 Françoy Roberge 'Banque royale et Domtar déménagent 100 emplois à Toronto' ibid 9 May 1979

46 Pierre Fournier *Les Sociétés d'État et les objectifs économiques du Québec: une évaluation préliminaire* (Quebec 1979) 39

47 Wendie Kerr 'Quebec Risk Capital Firm Started' *Globe and Mail* (Toronto) 17 January 1981

48 M. Nadeau 'La Nord-Américanisation de l'entreprise québécoise' *Le Devoir* 22 January 1981

49 Ministère de l'industrie et du commerce *Rapport annuel* 1965–6

50 The two new programs were, respectively, the Regional Industrial Development Assistance Act and the Financial Assistance Programme for High Technology Industries.

51 Fournier *Les Sociétés d'État* 66

52 CRIQ *Le Rapport annuel* 1977–8

53 Paul Morisset 'Quebec améliore ses "outils" pour promouvoir les ventes à l'étranger' *Le Devoir* 19 August 1980

54 See Black *Duplessis*.

55 Mgr N.-A. Labrie 'Les matières premières'

56 CCPQ *Mémoire* 23 May 1961

57 Fournier *Les Sociétés d'État* 80

58 For the RIN, see its program, printed in *L'Indépendance* III no 9 (1965) 7.

59 Michel Nadeau 'Québec suivra Sidbec le plus près' *Le Devoir* 29 November 1979

60 'Les activités manufacturières de Sidbec ont atteint la rentabilité' ibid 29 April 1980

61 Figures drawn from Table 1 in Canada, Statistics Canada, *Iron and Steel Industry,* Catalogue 41.203, various years. In terms of furnace capacity, Quebec possessed 4.98 per cent of the Canadian total in 1969 and 11.91 per cent in 1978 (ibid Table 16).

62 Canada, Statistics Canada *Iron Ore* Catalogue 26-005

63 Fournier *Les Sociétés d'État* 87

64 Normand Alexandre *Vers Une Politique québécoise de l'amiante* Ministère des Richesses naturelles, 12 February 1975, mimeo.

65 Ibid

66 Le Parti québécois, *Programme 1975* 16

67 Alexandre *Vers une politique* 136

68 Ibid 139

69 Groupe de travail sur l'amiante, Transformation de l'amiante, Brief presented to La Commission permanente des richesses naturelles, Projet de loi #70, Loi constituant la Société nationale de l'amiante, 21 June 1977

70 Marcel Pépin 'Une société bâtie pour l'homme' in CSN, Congrès *Procès-Verbal 1966* (Montreal 1966)

71   CSN *Procès-Verbal 1970* (Montreal 1970) 13

72   CSN *Procès-Verbal 1966* (Montreal 1966) 35

73   For an example of the tempered stance of the FTQ toward reform, see the editorial 'Trade Unionism and Revolution' in *Le Monde ouvrier* March 1967.

74   'Le MTC, une expérience de deux ans' *Prêtres et laïcs,* XVIII no 3 (1968) 152

75   In the period 1 November 1970 to 14 May 1971, the Department of Labour and Manpower reported 15,240 layoffs in 180 plants in Quebec: figures cited in 'The State Is Our Exploiter: FTQ Manifesto' trans Claude Hénault in Daniel Drache ed *Quebec – Only the Beginning: The Manifestoes of the Common Front* (Toronto 1972) 187.

76   See CSN, Congrès *Procès-Verbal 1972* (Montreal 1972) Report on the Address of the General President

77   FTQ *L'État, rouage de notre exploitation* (Montreal 1971), and CEQ *Phase One* (Montreal 1970)

78   For a full description of developments at the FUIQ, see Michel Grant 'L'Action politique syndicale et la FUIQ' MA Thesis, Faculté des Sciences sociales, Université de Montréal, 1968.

79   The largest losses to the CSD came from the following federations: Bâtiment et bois (8117); Mines, métallurgie et produits chimiques (11755); and Textile, vêtement, chaussure (13490). See the table in CSN *Procès-Verbal 1974* (Montreal 1974) 79.

80   According to CSD figures, the regional representation at its founding congress was as follows: Saguenay–Lac St-Jean 18, Quebec 78, Victoriaville and Trois-Rivières 76, Sherbrooke 45, Montreal 58, Granby and St-Hyacinthe 37, and Ottawa-Hull 9; CSD *Procès-Verbal du Congrès de fondation* (Montreal 1972) 32.

81   CSN *Procès-Verbal 1974* 81

82   Fournier *The Quebec Establishment* (Montreal 1975) 84–8

83   *Le Devoir* 1 May 1972

84   Le Parti québécois *Programme 1973* (Montreal 1973) 10

85   For the church militants, see the document issued in 1974 and reprinted under the heading 'Rencontre des militants chrétiens du monde ouvrier '*Prêtres et laïcs,* XXXV no 1 (1975) 55.

86   Carol Jobin *Les Enjeux économiques de la nationalisation de l'électricité* (Montreal 1978) 45

87   *Faits et tendances* XIII no 7 (1962) 1–3

88   For a discussion of a telegram sent by the Quebec Division of the CMA to the cabinet in the fall of 1962 voicing its opposition, see *Industrial Canada* LXIII (1962) 102.

89   Jobin *Les Enjeux* passim

90   Jobin draws heavily on the theory of state monopoly capitalism developed by

the Parti communiste français. The theory is criticized strongly by Nicos
Poulantzas, among others. See his *Classes in Contemporary Capitalism* trans
David Fernbach (London 1978) section I.

91 See the review of Jobin's work by André Blais and Philippe Faucher *Canadian
Journal of Political Science* XII No. 4 (1979) 809–16.

92 For a description of these processes, see Gérald Fortin *La Fin d'un règne*
(Montreal 1971) 17–56 and Camille G. Legendre 'Organizational Technology,
Structure and Environment: The Pulp and Paper Logging Industry of Quebec'
unpublished Ph D thesis, Michigan State University, 1977.

93 Brief to the Provincial Government, October 1971; Brief to the Parliamentary
Committee on Lands and Forests, August 1972

94 Brief to the Minister of Lands and Forests, November 1971, 1

95 Ministère des terres et des forêts *Exposé sur la politique forestière* 2 vols
(Quebec 1972)

96 Ibid I 72–3

97 Ibid 73

98 L'Assemblée nationale du Québec, Commission permanente des richesses
naturelles et des terres et forêts, Études des perspectives d'avenir de l'industrie
des pâtes et papiers *Mémoire*

99 See for example the brief submitted to ibid by International Paper.

100 'Un complexe forestier de $100 millions à Maniwaki' *Le Devoir* 3 March 1981

101 Arnaud Sales *La Bourgeoisie industrielle au Québec* (Montreal 1979)

102 Ibid 131

103 Ibid 183

104 Québec, L'Office de planification et de développement du Québec *Analyse
structurelle à moyen terme de l'économie du Québec* (Quebec 1977) 238

105 Carmine Nappi *The Structure of Quebec's Exports* Accent Quebec Series, C.D.
Howe Research Institute (Montreal 1978) 25

106 Ibid 38–9

107 William Leiss *The Limits to Satisfaction: An Essay on the Problem of Needs and
Commodities* (Toronto 1976)

5 Political control of cultural development

1 The church in Quebec was deeply involved in the discussions surrounding the
Vatican Council, and its own predisposition was to withdraw from non-
apostolic activities. This tendency is analysed by Neil Nevitte in 'Religion and
the "New Nationalisms": The Case of Quebec' Ph D thesis, Duke University,
1978.

2 The white paper has since been published in part in Jean-Paul L'Allier *Pour
l'évolution de la politique culturelle* Document de travail (Quebec 1976) 16–33.

3 Ibid

4   Québec, Le ministre d'État au Développement culturel *A Cultural Development Policy for Quebec* 2 vols (Quebec 1978)
5   Ibid i 11
6   Ibid 43
7   Ibid 46
8   Ibid 47
9   Ibid 59
10   For a description of these, see the excellent work by Jean-Louis Roy, *La Marche des Québécois: le temps des ruptures 1945–1960* (Montreal 1976) part i.
11   These measures are described in Donald Smiley *Constitutional Adaptation and Canadian Federalism since 1945*, Documents of the Royal Commission on Bilingualism and Biculturalism, No. 4 (Ottawa 1970) 9–23.
12   For example, this demand was made by the Fédération des Sociétés Saint-Jean-Baptiste du Québec (FSSJBQ) in a resolution passed at its 1964 convention and transmitted to the provincial government. It was also made by the Société Saint-Jean-Baptiste de Montréal (SSJBM) in its brief *L'Éducation nationale* (Montreal 1962) presented to the Royal Commission on Education. It also was a demand consistently made by the Rassemblement pour l'indépendance nationale (RIN).
13   Canada, Tax Structure Committee *Report* (Ottawa 1966) 13–14
14   Ibid 49
15   Canada, Constitutional Conference, First Meeting *Proceedings* (Ottawa 1968) 76.
16   CSN, Congrès *Proces-Verbal 1968* Resolution #43 and brief to the federal cabinet, 1970; FTQ, resolution presented to its 1967 convention
17   Canada *Income Security and Social Services* (Ottawa 1969)
18   Tax Structure Committee *Report* 21. This proposal was not carried out, however, as all the provinces except Quebec were opposed. For further discussion, see George E. Carter *Canadian Conditional Grants since World War II* (Toronto 1971) 93ff.
19   *Income Security* 70–104
20   Richard Simeon *Federal-Provincial Diplomacy* (Toronto 1973) 115 and chap 5. A concession along these lines was made in the unsuccessful Victoria Charter, the document of constitutional reform proposed in 1971.
21   Simon McInnes 'Federal-Provincial Negotiation: Family Allowances 1970–1976' PhD thesis, Carleton University, 1978, 554
22   George E. Carter 'Financing Health and Post Secondary Education: A New and Complex Fiscal Arrangement' *Canadian Tax Journal* XXV No. 5 (1978) 534–50
23   Quebec *Cultural Development* i 48
24   SSJBM *Le Canada français et l'union canadienne* (Montreal 1954) chap 5
25   For a description of the events surrounding the production of this work, see Georges-Émile Lapalme *Le Vent de l'oubli* (Ottawa 1970) 240ff.

26 His letter of resignation is reproduced in L'Allier *Pour l'évolution* 14.
27 Ibid 60
28 Victor Lévy-Beaulieu '3) Le noeud: le Conseil de la culture du Québec' *Le Devoir* 3 July 1976
29 Lévy-Beaulieu '4) Des voeux pieux à la dure réalité et aux coupables omissions' ibid 10 July 1976
30 Lise Bissonnette 'Un nationalisme en perte de culture' ibid 30 September 1980
31 François Hertel 'Les évolutions de la mentalité canadienne-française' *Cité libre* no 10 (1954)
32 See for example Jean-Marc Léger 'C'est l'heure d'affirmer la fraternité française' *L'Action nationale* XXXVII no 2 (1951) 87–92; 'Échec à la langue française dans notre enseignement' ibid XLVII no 1 (1957) 32.
33 *Le Devoir* 21 April 1960
34 For an account of the relationships developing at this time, see Jean-Pierre Teinturier 'La coopération France-Québec' *Commerce* LXX no 8 (1968) 44–8.
35 CTCC, Brief presented to the federal Cabinet, 16 December 1955
36 Speech reported in *France-Quebce* January 1970
37 Constitutional Conference, First Meeting *Proceedings* 30
38 Canada *Federalism and International Relations* (Ottawa 1968); Canada *Federalism and International Conferences on Education* (Ottawa 1969)
39 *Federalism and International Conferences* 50–2. These proposals originated in a series of letters exchanged between Pearson and Johnson.
40 Quebec, Commission of Inquiry on the Position of the French Language and on Language Rights in Quebec *Report* (hereafter Gendron Report) III (Quebec 1971) 170
41 For a brief discussion of the statements of Pius XII on immigration, see Jean-Baptiste Lanctôt 'Le problème des migrations' *Semaines sociales du Canada* 31e Session, Mont Laurier, 1954, 199–225.
42 *La Semaine religieuse de Quebec* LXII (1951) 10 May 1951
43 See for example 'Éditorial' *L'Action nationale,* XXXV no 1 (1950) 4; 'Éditorial' *Relations* no 106 (1949); Union catholique des cultivateurs *La Terre de Chez Nous* 7 February 1951, 3; CCDM Brief to the Tremblay Commission, Tremblay Report V (1955).
44 Gendron Report III 465–6
45 Noted in ibid 203. Even French-language immigrants had difficulty. They were not accepted in the Catholic school system, and the Protestant school system opened its first French-language school only in 1958. In 1970, there were only four schools of this kind.
46 Ibid 280ff
47 Hubert Charbonneau, Jacques Henripin, et Jacques Legaré 'La situation démographique des francophones au Québec et à Montreal d'ici l'an 2000' *Le Devoir*

4 November 1969. These figures were their pessimistic estimates. Their optimistic estimates were 79.2 per cent francophones in Quebec and 60.0 per cent in Montreal.

48   Jean-Marc Léger 'Le Canada français face à l'immigration' *L'Institut social populaire* no 482 (1956)

49   See, for example, SSJBM *L'Information nationale* July 1966; CSN, Congrès *Proces-Verbal 1966* Resolution #37.

50   Gendron Report III 109ff

51   Fernand Larouche 'L'immigrant dans une ville minière. Une étude de l'interaction' *Recherches sociographiques* XIV no 2 (1973) 203–28

52   See for example its brief submitted to the Board of Broadcast Governors in 1959, in *Le Bulletin de la SSJBM* VIII no 5 (1959) 5.

53   Alliance Laurentienne *La Laurentie* (September 1958) 25; LAN 'Éditorial' *L'Action nationale* XLVI no 4 (1956) 318. The RIN adopted this position at its convention in October 1962. See André d'Allemagne *Le RIN et les débuts du mouvement indépendantiste québécois* (Montreal 1974) 82.

54   Le Parti québécois *La Solution: Le programme du Parti québécois* (Montreal 1970) 90

55   Ibid

56   See for example the brief submitted to the Gendron Commission by the Association canadienne de radio et de télévision française (October 1970) 19, and CCPQ *Politiques d'action 1976* (Montreal 1976) 130.

57   Jean-Paul L'Allier, Ministre des Communications *Pour une politique québécoise des communications: Document de travail* (Quebec 1971)

58   Ibid 5

59   Ibid A16

60   Quebec, Department of Communications *Quebec: Master Craftsman of Its Own Communications Policy* (Quebec 1973)

61   Ibid 84ff

62   Ibid 87

63   Canada, Minister of Communications *Proposals for a Communications Policy for Canada* (Ottawa 1975) 21, and *Communications: Some Federal Proposals* (Ottawa 1975) 11

64   Canada *Communication* 13

65   Gérard Pelletier 'Déclaration' *Le Devoir* 17 July 1975. For further discussion of this dispute, see the editorial by Claude Ryan, 'Bouder ou s'accommoder?' *Le Devoir* 17 July 1975, and the reply by Pelletier in *Le Devoir* 2 August 1975.

66   See the discussion in R. Brian Woodrow, Kenneth Woodside, Henry Wiseman, and John B. Black *Conflict over Communications Policy: A Study of Federal-Provincial Relations and Public Policy* (Montreal 1980)

67   Murray Edelman *The Symbolic Uses of Politics* (Chicago 1964); Claus Offe

'Class Rule and the Political System. On the Selectiveness of Political Institutions' *German Political Studies* I (1974) 31–57.

6 Educational reform

1 *L'Education au Québec face aux problèmes contemporains: Documents relatifs à la Conférence provinciale sur l'éducation* (Saint-Hyacinthe, Quebec, 1958) 17

2 Ibid 20

3 See for example the papers they gave at the 1956 session of the Institut canadien des affaires publiques: Arthur Tremblay 'La démocratisation de l'enseignement' in *L'Education: Rapport de la 3e Conférence annuelle de l'ICAP, 26 au 30 septembre 1956* (Montreal 1956), and J.-C. Falardeau 'Conditions et conséquences d'une démocratisation de notre enseignement' in ibid.

4 Jean-Louis Roy *La Marche des Québécois: le temps des ruptures 1945–60* (Montreal 1976) 273

5 Ibid 253

6 CCPQ, Mémoire annuel soumis au Premier Duplessis, February 1958, 33

7 For the SSJBM, see *Le Bulletin de la SSJBM* IX no 4 (1960) 4, and for the CEE, ibid IX no 1 (1960) 8.

8 L'Alliance laurentienne, Brief submitted to the Royal Commission of Inquiry on Education (Parent Commission), 1 November 1961

9 For example, see the speech given by Paul Gérin-Lajoie on the occasion of the fiftieth anniversary of the École des hautes études commerciales (*La Réforme* 2 November 1960) and see the report on a speech by Premier Lesage (ibid 17 June 1961).

10 Roy *La Marche* 267

11 These groups included both the CCPQ and the CTCC.

12 Tremblay was at that time associate director of the École de Pédagogie et Orientation at Laval. Later he was to resign from the commission in order to become the province's first deputy minister of education. Other members were Paul Larocque, a businessman from Montreal; David Munroe, the director of the Institute of Education at McGill; Sister Marie-Laurent de Rome, a professor of philosophy at the Collège Basile-Moreau; Jeanne Lapointe, professor in the Faculty of Arts at Laval; and John McIlhone, associate director of studies for the Montreal Catholic School Commission. Louis-Phillippe Audet was the secretary.

13 'Éditorial' *Relations* no 248 (August 1961) 201

14 Pierre Charbonneau 'Lettre ouverte à Gérard Pelletier' *Cité libre* no 32 (1960) 23–6. The article was prompted by an earlier one by Pelletier, 'Feu l'unanimité' ibid No 30 (1960) 8–11.

15 Other members of the executive committee were Judith Jasmin, Dr Jacques MacKay, Pierre Leboeuf, Gilles Rochette, Jean-Marie Bédard, Jacques Godbout,

Jacques Guay, and Jean Le Moyne. The advisory committee included Solange Chaput-Rolland, Pierre de Bellefeuille, Robert Élie, and Marcel Rioux.

16 See for example 'Sur la liberté de l'esprit' *L'Esprit* xx (August–September 1952) 178–89.

17 Mouvement laïque de la langue française *L'École laïque* (Montreal 1961). Also see MLF *Justice et paix scolaire* (Montreal 1962).

18 Maurice Blain 'Situation de la laïcité' in *L'École laïque* 41–59

19 'Editorial' *Relations* no 246 (June 1961) 146

20 FCC *Notre Réforme scolaire* I: *Les Cadres généraux*, II: *L'Enseignement classique*; brief submitted to the Parent Commission, June 1962

21 It was both fitting and ironic that Gérin-Lajoie should become the engineer of educational reform – fitting because he had been involved in the area since the Tremblay Commission hearings, when he had helped prepare the briefs of both the FCC and the Fédération des Commissions scolaires catholiques du Québec; ironic because the former group was to become a prime adversary as the reforms proceeded.

22 For a brief description of the Charte, see *La Réforme* 3 June 1961.

23 Royal Commission of Inquiry on Education (Parent Commission) *Report* part I (Quebec 1963)

24 Ibid 88

25 See the Labour Day message of the Canadian bishops in 1963, 'Indispensable Collaboration between Public Authorities and Intermediate Organizations' *Relations industrielles* xix no 1 (1964) 124–9, and Gérard Dion 'Corps intermédiaires: groupe de pression ou organisme administratif' ibid xix no 4 (1964) 463–77.

26 Ibid 96

27 'La confessionalité est un aspect important du système scolaire et le gouvernement, dans le projet de loi actuel, a pris un soin infini pour l'assurer. D'autre part, il faut maintenir en même temps, le caractère représentatif des organismes, la démocratie des structures, l'efficacité du ministère, l'unification du régime scolaire et éviter de perpétuer une ségrégation qui crée deux sortes de Québécois'; Paul Gérin-Lajoie *Pourquoi le Bill 60?* (Montreal 1963) 102.

28 Léon Dion *Le Bill 60 et la société québécoise* (Montreal 1967)

29 The preamble contained several other provisions. For a full presentation of the changes in the bill from its initial version to its final version, see Québec, Ministère de la Jeunesse *Bill 60: Communiqués et notes explicatives sur la loi instituant le ministère de l'Education et le Conseil supérieur de l'éducation* 1964 (typewritten).

30 Dion *Le Bill 60* 148

31 Cited in ibid 58

32 This was the view of Paul Gérin-Lajoie. See *Pourquoi le Bill 60?* 83.
33 CCQP, Brief submitted to the Parent Commission, September 1962
34 CMA (Quebec Division), Brief submitted to the Parent Commission, 13 July 1962
35 F.-A. Angers, 'Nos éducateurs ont-ils perdu le nord?' *L'Action nationale* LII no 1 (1962) 11–21
36 SSJBM 'L'Éducation nationale: Mémoire soumis à la Commission Parent' ibid LI nos 9–10 (1962)
37 'Éditorial: La Fédération des collèges classiques du Québec' *Relations* no 151 (1953)
38 Parent Commission *Report* II 4
39 Ibid 20
40 Ibid 30
41 'Training for technical and professional careers is what is most urgently required of public education to satisfy the aspirations of our youth and the needs of our province'; ibid 59.
42 This had also been a recommendation of the Parent Commission; ibid 257.
43 Compare the following figures for library loans: Alberta (Calgary) 104,239, Carleton 103,442, UBC 649,410, Saskatchewan 199,251, Toronto 549,116, McGill 337,978, Laval 36,959, Montreal 63,000, Sherbrooke 13,500; cited in *Relations* no 300 (October 1965) 297.
44 Parent Commission *Report* IV chap 1
45 MSA *Ce Pays qu'on peut bâtir* (Montreal 1968) 12
46 This appears to be the perception of a group of metal workers in Montreal studied by J. Dofny and H. David. See their article, 'Aspirations des travailleurs de la métallurgie à Montréal' *Cahiers internationaux de sociologie* XIX no 40 (1966) 125.
47 SSJBM 'Éducation nationale' passim
48 Lionel Groulx 'Le Rapport Parent' *Revue d'histoire de l'Amérique française* XX no 3 (1966) 458–66
49 Jacques Poisson 'La dynamique de l'assimilation dans le Rapport Parent' *Maintenant* no 125 (April 1973) 26
50 Richard Arès, SJ, 'Le Rapport Parent: I – Approbations, réserves, et inquiétudes' *Relations* No 290 (February 1965) 35–6
51 Arès 'L'École et la nation' *L'Action nationale* LIX no 4 (1969) 315–48
52 'Le Rapport Parent' *Parti pris* II no 7 (1965) 2–8
53 CEQ, Phase I in Daniel Drache ed *Quebec: Only the Beginning: Manifestoes of the Common Front* (Toronto 1972)
54 Fernand Dumont and Guy Rocher 'L'expérience des CEGEPs: urgence d'un bilan' *Maintenant* no 127 (January 1973) 173
55 Quebec *A Cultural Development Policy for Quebec* II (Queebc 1978) 380

56   Québec, Ministère de l'Éducation du Québec (MEQ) *L'Enseignement primaire et secondaire au Québec: Livre vert* (Quebec 1977); Québec, MEQ *L'École québécoise: Énoncé de politique et plan d'action* (Quebec 1979)

57   MEQ *L'École québécoise*

58   Parent Commission *Report* IV 27

59   Ibid 28

60   Ibid 103

61   Ibid chap 5 and 6

62   The councils were given powers to regulate the use of the school facilities and the conduct of students in the schools.

63   The concept of a pluralist school developed by the parents is outlined in Jocelyne Durand, Guy Durand, Lucie Proulx, and Jean-Pierre Proulx *La Déconfessionalisation de l'école ou le cas de Notre-Dame-des-Neiges* (Montreal 1980) 100–15.

64   Two groups in particular supported the parents: the Association québécoise pour l'application du droit à l'exemption de l'enseignement religieux (AQADER) and the Regroupement scolaire de l'Île de Montréal. Also see the statement by the Conseil supérieur de l'éducation 'L'École Notre-Dame-des-Neiges: Un virage lucide' *Le Devoir* 31 May 1979, and that by the Commission des droits de la personne, 'Liberté de religion et confessionalité scolaire' ibid 21 December 1979.

65   A useful article along these lines is that by Michel Krauss, 'N-D.-des-Neiges et le Québec' *Le Devoir* 20 December 1979.

66   Mgr Paul Grégoire 'Promotion de l'école catholique' *Le Devoir* 26 May 1980

67   Jacques Cousineau, SJ, 'Pourquoi des écoles catholiques publiques' ibid 1 May 1980. He writes: 'Il y a encore des gens en 1980 pour trouver étrange que Québec ne soit pas une province comme les autres, avec ses écoles publiques confessionnelles, c'est à dire catholiques ou protestantes. Ces gens voudraient sans doute que Québec soit comme le reste du Canada.'

68   Marcel Pépin *Le Système scolaire en question: Document de travail* (Montreal 1974)

69   The following is the class representation found by Escande (the figures in parentheses represent the percentage of the whole population as compiled from the 1961 census): 9.3 per cent (6.91) were from the upper class, 54.2 per cent (27.78) from the middle class, 29.9 per cent (46.14) from the working class, and 2.6 per cent (16.45) from the farming class; Claude Escande *Les Classes sociales au CEGEP* (Montreal 1973) 78.

70   The following is the class representation (with the 1962 Université de Montréal percentage in parentheses): upper class 22 per cent (22), middle class 38 per cent (35), lower class 40 per cent (38); Louis-Bernard Robitaille 'L'UQAM n'a pas réalisé sa "vocation populaire"' *Le Devoir* 21 December 1971.

71 CEQ *École et luttes de classes au Québec* (Quebec 1974) 23–35
72 CCPQ, Brief presented to the *Conseil supérieur de l'éducation* and reprinted in
    Faits et Tendances XVII no 3 (1966) 7; SSJBM *L'Information nationale* V no 8
    (1966) 5; Secrétaire de l'Épiscopat du Québec 'Les institutions privées et la
    réforme scolaire' *L'Église candienne* II no 1 (1969) 6–7; Parent Commission
    Rapport III chap 7; Union nationale, in J.-L. Roy ed *Les Programmes éléctoraux
    du Québec* (Montreal 1971) 412; Parti libéral in Roy ed *Programmes* 431
73 For a discussion of the details of the bill, see CEQ *La Situation de l'enseignement
    privée au Québec* (Quebec 1975) 11ff.
74 CEQ, resolution presented at its special convention in 1970 and reprinted in ibid
    153; Parti québécois *Programme 1975* (Montreal 1975) 23
75 Antoine Baby, Pierre W. Belanger, and Rolland Ouellet 'Les orientations des
    étudiants du cours collégial' in *L'Étudiant québécois, Défis et dilemmes: Rapports
    de recherches* (Quebec 1973) 59
76 CEQ *L'Enseignement privé* 60
77 The following were the important organizations of this kind: the Association des
    institutions de niveaux pré-scolaire et élémentaire du Québec, the Association
    des institutions d'enseignement secondaire, and the Association des collèges du
    Québec. For further discussion, see CEQ *L'Enseignement privé* 104ff.
78 For a sample statement by the CCPQ, see its newsletter, *L'Action* II no 6 (1975)2.

7 Language policy and cultural development
I would like to thank Richard Y. Bourhis and Esther E. Enns for their
comments on earlier drafts of this chapter.

1 Uriel Weinreich *Languages in Contact: Findings and Problems* (The Hague
   1964) 99
2 This process is described in ibid.
3 See Dell Hymes 'Linguistic Aspects of Comparative Political Research' in
   R.E. Holt and John E. Turner ed *The Methodology of Comparative Research*
   (New York 1970) 295ff.
4 Many of Whorf's more influential essays are found in *Language, Thought and
   Reality* (Cambridge 1956).
5 Whorf 'Language, Mind and Reality' in ibid 252
6 This is not to say that the white paper follows a strictly Whorfian line. The
   analysis is fairly complex, but the logic of the argument often leads to a Whorfian
   position; for example: 'In other words, even if English, Italian, and Greek can
   and should be freely spoken in Quebec, everyone should at least be able to
   communicate by means of one common language. But the logical consequences
   must be accepted. A language is not simply syntax or a string of words. It is an
   expression of the more meaningful aspects of community life'; Quebec *A Cultural Development Policy for Quebec* (Quebec 1978) 43.

7   Hymes 'The Ethnography of Speaking' in Joshua Fishman ed *Readings in the Sociology of Language* (The Hague 1972) 131

8   Hymes 'On Linguistic Competence' in J.B. Pride and Janet Holmes ed *Sociolinguistics* (Baltimore 1972) 269–93

9   In this connection, see Howard Giles, Richard Bourhis, Peter Trudgill, and Alan Lewis 'The Imposed Norm Hypothesis: A Validation' *Quarterly Journal of Speech* LX No. 4 (1974) 405–10.

10   For a selected bibliography and critical review of Bernstein's work, see Norbert Dittman *Sociolinguistics: A Critical Survey of Theory and Application* (London 1976).

11   For a favourable review of this work, see ibid chap 4.

12   See Hymes 'The Ethnography of Speaking' and 'Models of the Interaction of Language and Social Life,' in J.J. Gumperz and Hymes ed *Directions in Sociolinguistics: The Ethnography of Communication* (New York 1972).

13   Hymes 'Linguistic Aspects of Comparative Political Research'

14   For a useful expansion of this review of Whorf's hypothesis, see B. Weinstein *The Civic Tongue: Political Consequences of Language Choices* (New York and London 1983) chap 2.

15   The concepts of formal and informal language are drawn from R. Bourhis 'Language Policies and Language Attitude: le monde de la francophonie' in E.B. Ryan and H. Giles ed *Attitudes toward Language Variation* (London 1982) 34–62.

16   J.J. Gumperz 'The Speech Community' *International Encyclopedia of the Social Sciences* IX–X (1968) 381

17   See William Coleman and David Easton 'The Concept of Support for the Political Community Reconsidered' in S.K. Sharma ed *Dynamics of Development* (New Delhi 1978).

18   Weinstein *The Civic Tongue* 42–5

19   Gumperz 'The Speech Community' 382–3

20   Paul L. Garvin and Madeleine Mathiot 'The Urbanization of the Guarani Language: A Problem in Language and Culture' in J. Fishman ed *Readings in the Sociology of Language* (The Hague 1972) 365–74

21   Bohuslav Havránek 'The Functional Differentiation of the Standard Language' in *A Prague School Reader on Esthetics, Literary Structure, and Style* trans Paul L. Garvin (Washington, DC, 1964) 3–16

22   Jan Mukarovský 'Standard Language and Poetic Language' in ibid 18. Much of the poetry emerging from the *Parti pris* group in Quebec in the 1960s was written in joual, against the background of standard French. The poetry drew much of its impact from this contrast.

23   Garvin and Mathiot 'Urbanization' 368–74

24   For evidence on the perception of the status of French, see R. Bourhis 'The

Impact of Bill 101 on Cross-Cultural Communication in Montreal' R. Bourhis
ed *Conflict and Language Planning in Quebec* (Clevedon, England, 1984).

25 Weinstein *The Civic Tongue* 44

26 I gleaned these data from survey of the computer output from the study in the
offices of the CNTU in Montreal. The results of the survey have never been
published.

27 The results of the survey are reported in the business publication *Les Affaires,*
Montreal, 29 March 1971, 13–4.

28 Figures in support of this statement can be found in a report on a survey by the
Centre des dirigeants d'entreprise (CDE) of francophone-owned firms. The report
is contained in the brief of the CDE to the Gendron Commission.

29 See Everett C. Hughes and Margaret L. McDonald 'French and English in the
Economic Structure of Montreal' *Canadian Journal of Economics and Political
Science* VIII No. 4 (1941) 493–505; Roger Vézina 'La position des Canadiens-
français dans l'industrie et le commerce' *Culture* XV no 3 (1954) 291–9; André
Raynauld *La Propriété des entreprises au Québec* (Montreal 1974).

30 Serge Carlos *L'Utilisation du français dans le monde du travail au Québec*
Étude E3, Gendron Commission (Quebec 1973)

31 Commission of Inquiry on the Position of the French Language and on Language
Rights in Quebec *Report* I (Quebec 1972) 37

32 Ibid 44

33 Ibid 91

34 Ibid

35 Ibid 77

36 See Guy Girard, Jean-Claude Otis, et Normand Proulx *Le Stock de ressources
humaines hautement qualifiées du Québec et la production des universités québécoises* Étude no 2, 'La production des universités québécoises et la formation
universitaire au Quebec: 1975' (Montreal 1978).

37 William Coleman 'The Class Bases of Language Policy in Quebec, 1949–1975'
Studies in Political Economy No. 3 (spring 1980) 106–9

38 Many of these changes are discussed in William Coleman 'From Bill 22 to Bill
101: The Politics of Language under the Parti québécois' *Canadian Journal of
Political Science* XIV No. 3 (1981) 459–86

39 Professionals working for a single employer and not interacting with the public
could be issued a permit without having to pass the examination; Quebec,
Charte de la langue française in *Les Lois du Québec 1977* chap 5 article 40.

40 'Moral persons' refers to corporate entities such as business enterprises, private
associations, and the like.

41 See ibid articles 144, 145.

42 This point is discussed further in Coleman 'From Bill 22' 479.

43 See OLF *Rapport annuel 1979–80* (Montreal 1980).

44   Claude-Armand Sheppard *The Law of Languages in Canada* Studies of the RCBB No. 10 (Ottawa 1971) 111–18

45   Ibid 119ff

46   Ibid; all of part 4 is relevant.

47   CVF 'Le bilinguisme des édifices fédéraux à Ottawa' Annexe IV in CVF *Bilinguisme et biculturalisme au Canada* (Quebec 1965) 144–6

48   Alexandre Dugré, SJ, 'À 30% du population, 30% des positions' *Relations* no 127 (July 1951) 189

49   SSJBM *Le Bulletin de la SSJBM* III no 9 (1955) 2

50   Reported in *La Terre de Chez Nous* 30 May 1951

51   Royal Commission on Bilingualism and Biculturalism *Report* I (Ottawa 1967) xxxix–xlvii

52   Ibid 8–17

53   Official Languages Act *Report* Commissioner of Official Languages, 1971, 106

54   Commissioner of Official Languages *Sixth Annual Report 1976* (Ottawa 1977) 33

55   These differences are analysed in W. Coleman 'A Comparative Study of Language Policy in Quebec: A Political Economy Approach,' in M.M. Atkinson and M.A. Chandler ed *The Politics of Canadian Public Policy* (Toronto 1983) 21–42.

56   See Ministère des Affaires culturelles, *Rapport annuel 1966–67* (Quebec 1967).

57   L'Action socialiste pour l'indépendance du Québec 'Manifeste' *La Revue socialiste* I (1959) 33

58   This was a demand contained in the briefs to the Gendron Commission by the Royal Bank of Canada, Molson's Brewery, the Canadian Manufacturers' Association (Quebec Division), the Centre des dirigeants d'entreprise, the Protestant School Board of Greater Montreal, and the Provincial Association of Protestant Teachers.

59   PSBGM Brief to the Gendron Commission 8

60   See, for example, F.-A. Angers 'Une situation intolérable pour le Québec; celle des enfants néo-canadiens à Montréal' *L'Action nationale* LIII no 4 (1963) 376.

61   Coleman 'The Class Bases' 108

62   Jeremy Boissevain *The Italians of Montreal*, Studies of the RCBB, No. 7 (Ottawa 1970) 38

63   Statement by an Italian immigrant reported in ibid

64   A brief description of this dispute can be found in Paul Cappon *Conflit entre les Néo Canadiens et les francophones de Montréal* (Quebec 1974) 9ff.

65   In a study of the Italian community in Montreal, a clear distinction in the motivation for learning each language is found. Thirty-one per cent interviewed said that they studied English because it facilitated moving to other parts of Canada, and 24 per cent said that it made finding a job easier. Of respondents who sent their children to French schools, the main reason cited was that the

French schools were nearer (32 per cent); noted in Boissevain *The Italians of Montreal* 34.

66   Boissevain (ibid 42) gives the following figures for marriages contracted by Italians in Quebec. In 1951, 94 per cent of marriages contracted by Italian-born people were to people of Italian birth or descent, 3 per cent were to French Canadians, 1 per cent to English Canadians, and 2 per cent to others; for the same group the figures in 1962 were 87 per cent to Italians, 9 per cent to French Canadians, 1 per cent to English Canadians, and 3 per cent to others. For Canadian-born Italians the figures were (1951) 41 per cent to Italians, 40 per cent to French Canadians, 14 per cent to English Canadians, 5 per cent to others; (1962) 24 per cent to Italians, 52 per cent to French Canadians, 18 per cent to English Canadians, and 6 per cent to others. Respondents were asked which ethnic group the last non-Italian friends to visit their home were; 78 per cent responded: French, 16 per cent: English, and 6 per cent: other.

67   Ibid 48

68   Ibid 57

69   Jacques Hamel in his study of the FSSJBQ/MNQ states that Bill 63 was a turning point as far as support for the authorities was concerned; 'La Culture politique du MNQ' MA thesis, Université Laval, 1973, 121. The AQPF suggested that the day Bill 63 was passed, 28 November, should become a national day for Quebec, with people wearing signs of mourning and making donations to organizations defending the cause of French Quebec.

70   The fact that francophones could attend English schools was challenged by parents in Ste-Foy. Chief Justice Jules Deschênes of the Quebec Superior Court heard the case and ruled against the parents. For excerpts from his decision, see *Le Devoir* 30 December 1975.

71   Parti québécois *Programme 1975* (Montreal 1975) 26

72   See the following briefs to the parliamentary committee studying Bill 22: Conseil du Patronat 4, Montreal Board of Trade 3, CCPQ 9, Alcan 7.

73   These recommendations are discussed in their respective briefs to the commission on Bill 22.

74   The commission felt that the numbers of children involved hardly warranted coercion and that the introduction of French as the language of work would be a far better inducement to integration. Further, it felt that a number of measures adopted in the late 1960s and early 1970s needed to be given a chance to prove themselves before more drastic measures were taken. It pointed to the creation of the COFI, new classes for immigrants, various nurseries and summer camps, and other programs of the Department of Immigration as examples. See its *Report* III 271. Dion's arguments are discussed in ibid 272.

75   Claude St-Germain *La Situation linguistique dans les écoles primaires et secondaires du Québec de 1971–72 à 1978–79* (Montreal 1979)

76   See Camille Laurin, Ministre d'État au Développement culturel 'Quelques scéna-

rios concernant l'avenir linguistique de la région métropolitaine de Montréal' unpublished 25 July 1977.

77   Régie de la langue française *Rapport annuel 1976* (Quebec 1977) 341. Also see D. Taylor and L. Simard 'Language Planning and Intergroup Relations: Anglophone and Francophone Attitudes toward Bill 101' in Bourhis ed *Conflict and Language Planning in Quebec.*

78   OLF *Rapport annuel 1978–79* (Quebec 1979) 10–11

79   Pierre Bouchard and Sylvie Beauchamp-Achim *Le Français, langue des commerces et des services publics: Le point de vue de la clientèle* Dossiers du Conseil de la langue française no 5 (Quebec 1980) 56

80   OLF *Rapport annuel 1978–79* 10–11

81   This point is discussed at greater length in Coleman 'The Class Bases' 110–11.

8 The movement for political independence

1   Alliance laurentienne 'Justification sommaire de la déclaration' *Laurentie* no 103 (March 1958) 222

2   Alliance laurentienne 'Introduction' ibid no 101 (1957) 1

3   ASIQ 'Manifeste' *La Revue socialiste* I (1959) 25

4   In a study done of militants of the RIN, Pelletier found that only 19.1 per cent were regular churchgoers, and 60.5 per cent stated they engaed in no religious practices. The militants were mainly young professionals, semi-professionals, and students; Réjean Pelletier *Les Militants du R.I.N.* (Ottawa 1974) 16.

5   Jacques-Yvan Morin 'The Need for a New Canadian Federation' *Canadian Forum* No. 521 (June 1964) 664–6; 'In Defence of a Modest Proposal' ibid No. 529 (February 1965) 256–8; 'Quel est le minimum de changements constitutionnels nécessaires à l'épanouissement de la nation?' in En Collaboration *Le Devenir politique du Québec* (Quebec 1965) 26–35. For the SSJBM, see *Le Fédéralisme, Acte de l'Amérique du Nord britannique et les Canadiens-français* (Montreal 1964).

6   For Lévesque, see *Le Devoir* 11 May 1964.

7   Richard Hamilton and Maurice Pinard 'The Bases of Parti Québécois Support in Recent Quebec Elections' *Canadian Journal of Political Science* IX No. 1 (1976) 16

8   Ibid

9   Figures were reported in Véra Murray, *Le Parti québécois: de la fondation à la prise du pouvoir* (Montreal 1976) 33–4.

10   Ibid passim

11   Jane Jacobs *The Question of Separatism: Quebec and the Struggle over Sovereignty* (New York 1980) 21

Chronology

1875		Abolition of the Department of Education
1908		Creation of the first collège classique for girls
1912		Creation of the École sociale populaire
1921		First meeting of the Semaines sociales du Canada
		Founding convention of the Confédération des travailleurs catholiques du Canada (CTCC)
1924		Founding of the Union catholique des cultivateurs
1931		Publication of the encyclical *Quadragesimo Anno* by Pius XI
1939		Founding of the Ligue ouvrière catholique
1941		First issue of the Jesuit journal *Relations*
1946		Establishment of the Department of Social Welfare and Youth with Paul Sauvé as minister
1947	*April*	La Chambre de Commerce du District de Montréal submits to the federal government its brief on the crisis in fiscal relations between governments.
	September	Ontario and Quebec do not sign Tax Rental Agreements.
1949	*February*	Start of the strike by asbestos miners affiliated to the CTCC at Asbestos, Quebec
	April	Appointment of the Royal Commission on National Development in the Arts, Letters and Sciences (Massey Commission)
1950	*February*	First issue of *Cité libre* published
	April	Publication by the Quebec bishops of the pastoral letter *Le Problème ouvrier en regard de la doctrine sociale de l'Église*
1951	*May*	Submission of the report of the Massey Commission

	June	Federal government introduces a new system of grants for universities.
1952	*October*	Publication of special issue of the French journal *L'Esprit* on French Canada
	October	Only Quebec refuses to sign a Tax Rental Agreement with the federal government.
1953	*February*	Appointment of the Royal Commission of Inquiry on Constitutional Problems (Tremblay Commission)
	June	Formation of the Conseil d'expansion économique
	November	Beginning of public hearings of the Tremblay Commission
1954	*February*	Premier Duplessis levies a personal income tax on Quebec residents amounting to 15 per cent of the federal tax.
1955	*February*	Secondary-school status given to écoles primaires supérieures
1956	*February*	Submission to the premier of the Report of the Tremblay Commission
	September	Founding of the group Le Rassemblement
1957	*January*	Founding of the Alliance laurentienne by Raymond Barbeau
1958	*February*	Provincial Conference on Education
	May	Jean Lesage replaces Georges-Émile Lapalme as leader of the Parti libéral du Québec.
1959	*April*	Founding of the Action socialiste pour l'indépendance du Québec
	September	Death of Maurice Duplessis. Paul Sauvé becomes premier.
	October	Frère Untel writes his first letter to André Laurendeau, editor-in-chief of *Le Devoir*.
1960	*January*	Death of Paul Sauvé. Antonio Barette becomes premier.
	June	Parti libéral du Québec wins the provincial election; Jean Lesage becomes premier.
	September	The Confédération des travailleurs catholiques du Canada deconfessionalizes and renames itself the Confédération des syndicats nationaux (CSN).
	September	Founding of the Rassemblement pour l'indépendance nationale
1961	*February*	Formation of the Conseil d'orientation économique du Quebec
	February	Appointment of the Royal Commission of Inquiry on Education (Parent Commission)
	February	René Lévesque becomes minister for the newly organized Department of Natural Resources.
	March	Jean Marchand becomes general president of the CSN.

April		Founding of the Mouvement laïque de la langue française
May		John XXIII releases the encyclical *Mater et Magistra*.
October		Premier Lesage opens the Maison du Québec in Paris.
November		Creation of the Department of Cultural Affairs (and the first Office de la langue française) with Georges-Émile Lapalme as minister
November		Paul Gérin-Lajoie announces the Grande Charte de l'Éducation.
1962	*January*	Editorial by André Laurendeau in *Le Devoir* calling for a royal commission on bilingualism and biculturalism
	June	Establishment of the Société générale de financement
	November	Parti libéral re-elected in an election called on the issue of nationalizing a number of large hydro-electric power companies
1963	*January*	Announcement of the government's intention to proceed with the nationalization of the hydro-electric power companies
	April	First volume of the Parent Commission is released, calling for a significant secularization of education in Quebec under a department of education.
	May	Provincial government establishes the Special Parliamentary Committee on the constitution.
	June	First version of Bill 60 on educational reform is introduced to the legislature and withdrawn after pressure from the bishops.
1964	*January*	Revised version of Bill 60 is passed by the legislature.
	September	Lapalme resigns, in protest against inattention to culture, as Minister of cultural affairs and is replaced by Pierre Laporte.
	October	Release of second part of the Parent Report, treating pedagogical structures
	November	Passage of legislation creating as a mixed corporation the Sidérurgie du Québec (Sidbec)
1965	*February*	Quebec signs an agreement with France for exchanges in the fields of education and culture.
	March	A directorate of immigration is set up within the Department of Cultural Affairs.
	March	Passage of the Established Programs (Interim Arrangements) Act by the House of Commons
	June	Creation of the Caisse de dépôts et de placements du Québec

	June	Marcel Pépin succeeds Jean Marchand as general president of the CSN.
	July	Creation of the Société québécoise d'exploration minière
	November	Unpublished white paper on culture is prepared in the Department of Cultural Affairs.
1966	*March*	Passage of order-in-council leading to the creation of the Collèges d'enseignement général et professionnel (CEGEPs)
	March	Release of the final section of the Parent Report, which focused upon the issue of confessionality
	June	Daniel Johnson and the Union nationale defeat the Parti libéral in a provincial election.
1967	*April*	Department of Federal-Provincial Relations is reorganized as the Department of Intergovernmental Affairs.
	May	Death of Lionel Groulx, the 'father of French-Canadian nationalism'
	July	Controversial visit of Charles de Gaulle, president of France, to Quebec
	September	Beginnings of disputes over language of instruction in St-Léonard
	October	Publication of volume I of the Report of the Royal Commission on Bilingualism and Biculturalism
	October	Founding of the Mouvement Souveraineté-Association by René Lévesque following his departure from the Parti libéral
	November	First national assises of the États généraux du Canada français
1968	*February*	Government of Quebec activates Radio-Québec established by Duplessis in the 1940s.
	July	Sidbec is converted from a mixed enterprise to a public enterprise and purchases the assets of Dosco.
	September	Daniel Johnson dies. Jean-Jacques Bertrand succeeds him as premier.
	October	Founding of the Parti québécois. René Lévesque is chosen as its first president.
		Dissolution of the Rassemblement pour l'indépendance nationale. Members are called upon to join the Parti québécois.
	November	Creation of a separate Department of Immigration
	December	Appointment of the Commission of Inquiry on the Position of the French Language and on Language Rights in Quebec (Gendron Commission)

	December	Founding of the Université du Québec
1969	*January*	Permanent secretariat established for the Conseil du Patronat du Quebec
	February	Creation of the General Council of Industry
	June	Passage of the federal Official Languages Act
	October	Introduction of Bill 63 giving parents the right to choose the language of instruction of their children. Mass protests result.
	December	Creation of the Centre de recherche industrielle du Québec
1970	*April*	Robert Bourassa leads the Parti libéral back to power. The Parti québécois captures 23 per cent of the popular vote, electing six members.
	October	Kidnapping of James Cross and Pierre Laporte by the Front de libération du Québec. Laporte is killed following proclamation of the War Measures Act.
1971	*October*	Publication by the CSN of the document *Ne comptons que sur nos propres moyens*
1972	*April*	Strike by the Common Front of public-sector unions. Union leaders are arrested and jailed.
	May	Founding of the Centrale des syndicats démocratiques
	December	Publication of the report of the Gendron Commission
	December	The SGF is converted from a mixed to a public corporation.
1973	*February*	Publication of white paper *Le Québec maître d'oeuvre de la politique des communications sur son territoire* by Jean-Paul L'Allier, minister of communications
	October	Parti libéral wins the provincial election. The Parti québécois increases its share of the popular vote to 30 per cent and becomes the Official Opposition.
1974	*June*	Passage of the Official Language Act (Bill 22)
	September	Report of the Interdepartmental Task Force on Foreign Investment (Tetley Report)
1975	*September*	Significant protests by non-francophones against Bill 22
	October	Agreement signed with the federal government giving Quebec increased powers over immigration
1976	*May*	Publication of green paper *Pour l'évolution de la politique culturelle* by Jean-Paul L'Allier, minister of cultural affairs
	June	Intensification of the dispute over the language to be used in the air over Quebec
	November	Majority Parti québécois government is elected to power.

1977	*April*	Dr Camille Laurin introduces his white paper on language. The Charte de la langue française is introduced in the legislature.
	May	Agreement signed with the federal government increasing further Quebec's jurisdiction over immigration
	June	Creation of the Société de développement coopératif
	August	Passage by the Legislature of the Charte de la langue française (Bill 101)
1978	*April*	Claude Ryan is selected to succeed Bourassa as leader of the Parti libéral.
	June	Publication by Dr Camille Laurin of white paper *A Cultural Development Policy for Quebec*
1979	*May*	The Conseil supérieur de l'éducation agrees to request by the École Notre-Dame-des-Neiges to have its confessional status revoked.
	June	Formation of the Banque nationale du Canada following a merger of the Banque canadienne nationale and the Banque provinciale du Canada
	September	Publication by Bernard Landry, minister of state for economic development, of the report *Bâtir le Québec*
	November	Publication of PQ white paper on sovereignty-association
	December	Montreal Catholic School Commission overturns the decision by the Conseil supérieur de l'éducation on the École Notre-Dame-des-Neiges.
1980	*March*	Debate on the Referendum Question in the National Assembly
	May	Referendum on sovereignty-association is defeated by a margin of 59.56 per cent to 40.44 per cent.

Abbreviations

ACEF L'Association coopérative d'économie familiale
ACELF L'Association canadienne des éducateurs de la langue française
ACJC/AJC L'Association catholique de la jeunesse canadienne française/
L'Association de la jeunesse canadienne française (1951–)
APCM L'Association des professeurs catholiques de Montréal
API L'Association professionnelle des industriels
AQPF L'Association québécoise des professeurs de français
ASIQ L'Action socialiste pour l'indépendance du Québec
ASTEF L'Association pour l'organisation de stages en France
BAEQ Le Bureau d'Aménagement de l'Est du Québec
BNC La Banque nationale du Canada
CBC Canadian Broadcasting Corporation
CCM La Chambre de Commerce du District de Montréal
CCPQ La Chambre de Commerce de la Province du Québec
CCQ La Chambre de Commerce de Québec
CDE Le Centre des dirigeants d'entreprises
CEGEP Le Collège d'enseignement général et professionnel
CFPQ Le Cercle des fermières de la Province du Québec
CIC La Corporation générale des instituteurs et institutrices du Québec
CIQ La Corporation des ingénieurs du Québec
CLC Canadian Labour Congress
CMA(Q) Canadian Manufacturers' Association (Quebec Division)
CNTU/CSN Confederation of National Trade Unions/Confédération des
syndicats nationaux
COEQ Le Conseil d'orientation économique du Québec
COFI Le Centre d'orientation et de formation des immigrants
CPQ Le Conseil du Patronat du Québec

CREE La Commission royale d'enquête sur l'enseignement (Parent Commission)

CRIQ Le Centre de recherche industrielle du Québec

CRPC La Commission royale d'enquête sur les problèmes constitutionnels (Tremblay Commission)

CSD La Centrale des syndicats démocratiques

CSN La Confédération des syndicats nationaux

CTCC La Confédération des travailleurs catholiques du Canada

CVF Le Conseil de la vie française

DBS Dominion Bureau of Statistics

ESP/ISP L'École sociale populaire/L'Institut social populaire

FCC La Fédération des collèges catholiques

FCSCQ La Fédération des commissions scolaires catholiques du Québec

FPTQ La Fédération provinciale des travailleurs du Québec

FQF Le Front du Québec français

FTQ La Fédération du Travail du Québec (1950–7)

FTQ La Fédération des Travailleurs du Québec (1957–   )

FUIQ La Fédération des unions industrielles du Québec

GCI General Council of Industry

ICAP L'Institut canadien des affaires publiques

JEC La Jeunesse étudiante catholique

JOC La Jeunesse ouvrière catholique

LAN La Ligue d'action nationale

LOC La ligue ouvrière catholique

MCSC Montreal Catholic School Commission

MIS Le Mouvement pour l'intégration scolaire

MLLF Le Mouvement laïque de la langue française

MLP Le Mouvement pour la libération populaire

MNP Le Mouvement national des Québécois

MQF Le Mouvement Québec français

MSA Le Mouvement Souveraineté-Association

MTC Le Mouvement des travailleurs chrétiens

NDP New Democratic Party

NFB National Film Board

OLF L'Office de la langue française

PAPT Provincial Association of Protestant Teachers

PLQ Le parti libéral du Québec

PP Parti pris

PSBGM Protestant School Board of Greater Montreal

RCBB Royal Commission on Bilingualism and Biculturalism

RCNDALS Royal Commission on National Development in the Arts, Letters and Sciences (Massey Commission)

REXFOR La Société de récupération et d'exploitation forestières du Québec
RIN Le Rassemblement pour l'indépendance nationale
SAI La Société d'Assistance aux immigrants
SCER La Société canadienne d'établissement rural
SDI La Société de développement industriel
SGF La Société générale de financement
Sidbec La Sidérurgie du Québec
Sna La Société nationale de l'amiante
Soquem La Société québécoise d'exploration minière
Soquip La Société québécoise d'initiatives pétrolières
SSJBM La Société Saint-Jean-Baptiste de Montréal
SSJBQ La Société Saint-Jean-Baptiste de Québec
UCC L'Union catholique des cultivateurs
UN L'Union nationale

Index